The Churches and Abbeys of Ireland

The Churches

BRIAN DE BREFFNY AND GEORGE MOTT

and Abbeys of Ireland

with 268 illustrations, 20 in colour

photographs by George Mott

W · W · NORTON & COMPANY · INC · New York

TITLE PAGE:
St Feidhlimidh's (Felim's) Cathedral, Kilmore, Co. Cavan,
detail of doorway in north wall.

ISBN 0–393–04441–6

Printed and bound in Great Britain

Contents

Foreword

NO JUSTIFICATION need be made for this book, for the panoply of Irish Church architecture deserves to be displayed. We hope that within the limits of the space available we have done this, at least adequately.

We have actually visited all the sites mentioned in this book and in the course of its preparation we covered thousands of miles, by car, by aeroplane (to the Aran Islands), by boat and on foot. We touched the extremities of Ireland, the Giants Causeway, Co. Antrim, Horn Head, Co. Donegal, Belmullet, Co. Mayo, the Dingle Peninsula in Co. Kerry, Cape Clear, Co. Cork, the Hook of Wexford, Howth Head, Dublin, and the Ards of Co. Down, and we went to the islands in the Atlantic Ocean.

Bord Failte Eireann (the Irish Tourist Board) and the Northern Ireland Tourist Board were of invaluable help to us in our travels. Along with our cameras, equipment, Ordnance Survey maps, and notebooks we took a small travelling library: Dr Harbison's precious *Guide to the National Monuments of Ireland*, the *Ancient Monuments of Northern Ireland*, published by HM Stationery Office, Dr Leask's three scholarly volumes on *Irish Churches and Monastic Buildings prior to 1530*, Gwynn and Hadcock's *Medieval Religious Houses of Ireland*, Maurice Craig and the Knight of Glin's useful *Ireland Observed*, Samuel Lewis's *Topographical Dictionary of Ireland*, Father Canice Mooney's articles on Irish Franciscan architecture, and a few others. Sometimes the ghosts of Lord Dunraven and Arthur Champneys with their horses and cumbersome cameras did not seem far away.

The choice of the churches which could be included in this book was not an easy one. Only in several volumes could we have illustrated and annotated all those we saw, studied and photographed. We have endeavoured to include here, nevertheless, the buildings of most importance or interest architecturally, then a personal selection of others chosen for their representational quality, beauty, curiosity or intrinsic historical interest.

The churches of Ireland could not compete in grandeur with those of some other countries of Europe, but they have a quality and interest of their own. Because of Ireland's chequered history in which religious struggles have often been coincident with national, political and social ones, the ecclesiastical architecture has been remarkably affected by contemporary events. Beginning with the centuries of the autocratic Celtic Christian Church with its coenobitic monastic foundations, through those when dual cultures obtained, Gaelic and Anglo-Norman, then Gaelic and Anglo-Irish or Scots-Irish, during the religious struggles when the majority rejected the imposed Reformation and the consequent long night of humiliation when the Penal Laws were enforced, through the years when the Established Church had too many churches and the greater part of the population near to none, prevailing conditions were reflected in the church-building. Then Presbyterian Toleration, Catholic Emancipation, Disestablishment, the Celtic literary and artistic revival and the struggle for Independence in turn left their mark on Ireland's ecclesiastical architectural heritage. To appreciate it knowledge of the historical and social background is necessary, and we have tried to provide this relevantly and objectively.

Not the least of the pleasures in visiting the churches and abbeys of Ireland lies in discovering and rediscovering the ineffable beauty of the Irish countryside, the land, the lakes and the mountains and the islands of the western sea.

Dublin and Rome, 1974

BREFFNY

GEORGE MOTT

CHAPTER I

The Celtic Church

IRELAND REMAINED an isolated and unconquered repository of Celtic culture throughout the first centuries of the Christian era. Escaping invasion by the Roman legions, it never became part of the widespread Roman Empire.

The social order which obtained was a unique one: aristocratic, heroic, complex, conservative and independent. This was a pastoral and agricultural society living off the rich soil. There were no towns. The largest unit in this social order was the clan with its elected monarch. Sometimes the clan owed nominal tribute to an overlord, but otherwise it functioned as a self-governing, self-contained state. At the death or deposition of a monarch his successor was elected within the clan from among the members of the ruling family. The clan comprised a number of septs, each with its own chief; within the sept were the *fine*, family groups descended of a common ancestor, holding property in common and each represented by a chosen leader.

There was no outright individual ownership of land – it was always the joint property of the *fine*, the sept or the clan. The monarch was allotted land for his personal use and maintenance during his reign but did not own it, nor could he alienate it or pass it on to his natural heirs. Similarly clan land was set aside for the maintenance of the levitical families who preserved the laws and pronounced judgment in disputes, and for the bards who commemorated the history and deeds of the clan in epics, and repeated the genealogies.

Land was allotted to the public hospitaller for the purposes of his office which included care of the sick, the aged and travellers. Each clan also had its sorcerers, the Druids, who performed religious rites, usually in open-air ceremonies. Christianity spread through most of western Europe in the wake of the Roman legions, consequently the Church inherited the structure of the Roman civil administration which served as its normal foundation. When Christianity reached Ireland, however, the Church grew and prospered there in its own peculiar way, outside the orbit of Imperial Roman influence.

There were probably already Christian converts in Ireland by the end of the fourth century, for there were sufficient Christians in 431 for Pope Celestine to see fit to appoint a bishop, Palladius, to care for them. However, the general conversion of the Irish, embracing all ranks of society – kings, princes, nobles, learned men, artisans, labourers and slaves – took place in the fifth century. This was achieved peacefully by St Patrick, a devout man who had a deep understanding of the Celtic mind, character and traditions. Patrick was derided by some of his contemporaries within the Church for his lack of learning. His critics knew nothing of the extra-Imperial heroic society where Patrick taught, outside the structure of episcopal sees with diocesan jurisdiction. To them he appeared as an unorthodox itinerant preacher because he travelled about Ireland with a paid retinue of young princes and nobles, distributing gifts to the petty monarchs on his way. Patrick, however, well understood the nature and customs of the society which he was proselytizing; he and his missionaries made no attempt to interfere with the established social order, other than to purge it of Druidism, and replace the heathen priesthood with a Christian one.

Patrick preached the divinity of Christ forcefully and convincingly, and his success was rapid. The enthusiasm he generated is illustrated in the story of his preaching to a prince in Munster prior to baptism. Patrick unintentionally drove his crozier through the prince's foot, but the happy neophyte made no complaint, explaining later that he thought that this was part of the ceremony.[1]

Traces of the old beliefs and superstitions lingered on for centuries. In the eleventh century when the Ulstermen cut down the sacred trees at Tulloghohoge, Co. Tyrone, their behaviour was considered so outrageous that the men of Kinel Owen retaliated by carrying off three thousand cows.[2] The shingles used for St Moling's Church in the seventh century came from a sacred pagan tree, the Eo Rossa, an Irish yew.[3]

The first Christian churches were round huts, similar to the domestic buildings, built of wood or mud. (The pre-Christian Irish had built no temples or other structures that the new religion could use or adapt.)

The earliest authentic account of Patrick's life, in The *Book of Armagh*, written 807-8, contains references to churches built of earth. One was near the well of Clebach: 'et ecclesiam terrenam fecit in eo loco'.[4] But it is clear that wooden churches were preferred where timber was obtainable; the same source recounts that at Tyrawley, Co. Mayo, Patrick built a rectangular church of mud because there was no wood available: 'et fecit ibi ecclesiam terrenam de humo quadratam, quia non prope erat silva'. The writer states specifically that Patrick built rectangular churches in the Barony of Kilmaine, Co. Mayo: 'et posuit in eo ecclesias quadratas'; thus it may be inferred that there were already round church buildings in the vernacular style. Wooden churches continued to be built in Ireland for several centuries. References to them occur in documents such as the *Martyrology of Oengus*, written about the year 800, which mentions a wooden church of the fifth century near Clogher, Co. Tyrone, dedicated to St Derbhfraich.[5] The *Acta Sanctorum* describes the fifth-century church of St Ciaran of Saighir as being of wood.[6] St Columcille's first church at Derry, built in the sixth century, is described in the *Leabhar Breach* as being of timber and wattle.[7] The seventh-century *Book of Mulling* records payment made by St Mullin to the artificer for his church, a brown oratory roofed with shingles of yew wood.[8] The builder was the craftsman-saint Gobban, described in the *Acta Sanctorum* as a famous worker in both wood and stone. The *Annals of Clonmacnois* record that Dermot McKervil, later king, met St Ciaran on the spot where the church of Clonmacnoise was to be built and helped the Saint to construct a house of timber and wattle.[9] The *Martyrology of Donegal* relates that St Mochaoi, the founder-abbot of Nendrum, Co. Down, took 140 young men to cut wattle to make his church.[10] Conchubran's *Life of St Monenna*, written in the twelfth century, states that when the saint founded his monastery in the sixth century it was made of 'smooth planks according to the habit of the Irish who were not accustomed to erect stone walls or have them erected'.[11] St

Bernard of Clairvaux's biography of his contemporary St Malachy, also written in the twelfth century, tells of a miracle which occurred when Malachy was chopping wood for an oratory at Bangor, Co. Down. The oratory, Bernard reported, was finished in a few days and was 'made of smooth planks indeed, but closely and strongly fastened together, an Irish work, not devoid of beauty'.[12] There is also a reference in Bede's *Historia Ecclesiastica Gentis Anglorum*, written early in the eighth century, to the building of the church at Lindisfarne which, he says, was built according to the Irish manner, not of stone, but of hewn oak and covered with reeds: 'more Scotorum, non de lapide sed de robore secto totam composuit atque arundine texit'.[13]

The wooden church was called a *duirtheach* in Irish, literally 'oak-house'. Most of these churches were small, yet the *Annals of Tigernach* describe the church of Rahan, Co. Offaly, in 747 as a 'jointed edifice requiring 1,000 boards',[14] and the wooden church at Revet, Co. Meath, must have been sizeable, for the *Annals of Ulster* report that 260 persons were burned in it in 849.[15]

One of Patrick's converts, Assicus, is described in the *Book of Armagh* as a saint, bishop and goldsmith for Patrick: 'Assicus sanctus episcopus faber aereus [*sic*] erat Patricio'; and it states that he made rectangular patens for Patrick's churches at Armagh, Elphin, Co. Roscommon and Donaghpatrick, Co. Meath.[16] These patens were apparently still in the churches at the time of the account, about 250 years after Patrick's mission (807-8). The *Book of Armagh* also mentions the founding of a church by Patrick in which he erected a stone altar. The first of the canons established by John Comyn, Archbishop of Dublin, at the Provincial Synod in 1186 and confirmed under the seal of Pope Urban III, prohibited priests from celebrating mass on a wooden table (altar) 'according to the usage of Ireland'.[17] This implies that wooden altars were the norm in Early Christian Irish churches.

Patrick ordained 365 bishops and founded a like number of churches, according to another source of his life, Nennius's *Historia Britonum* written in the eleventh century. Not too much weight should be given to these figures, quoted several centuries after Patrick's mission; but Tirechan, writing in the eighth century, asserted that Patrick consecrated no less than 450 bishops, although he specifically named only 42.

The canons attributed to Patrick, Auxilius and Isernius but more probably of the next (sixth) century, define the *paruchia* as being under the control of one bishop, and prohibited priests from saying mass in churches they had built until the bishop of the *paruchia* had consecrated the building. The clerics who lived at home with their wives were also enjoined to wear tunics 'to cover their nakedness and the shame of their bellies', to wear their hair short, and to see that their wives were veiled.[18]

The *paruchia* appears to have been conterminous with the ancient boundaries of the territory of the sept. Because its bishop and clerics were members of that sept, it was as vulnerable as secular property to the depredations of rival, albeit Christian, tribes. Wealth was reckoned principally in cattle, and so in the incessant internecine wars and forays the victors drove off the cattle of the losers. Holy relics seem to have enjoyed immunity, but raiding and despoiling churches was frequent well before the arrival of the Viking raiders. The first recorded Norse raid was not until 795, yet in the two centuries prior to this the annals record many instances of desecration of ecclesiastical property and murder of clerics. The *Annals of Ulster* record the burning of churches at Bangor, Co. Down, in 615 and 755; Connor, Co. Antrim, 616; Armagh, 671 and 689; Tehellan, Co. Monaghan, 671; Kildare, 709, 774 and 778; Clonmacnoise, Co. Offaly, 722, 754 and 757; Coleraine, Co. Derry, 730; Clonfert, Co. Galway, and Kilmore, Co. Cavan, 748; Fore, Co. Westmeath, and Donaghpatrick, Co. Meath, 749; Clonard, Co. Meath, 750 and 788. Kilmore, Co. Roscommon, was burned in 756 by the Ui Cremthainn, who plundered another church in 792. Glendalough, Co. Wicklow, and Ennisboyne were burned in 774; Clonmore and Kildalkey, Co. Meath, 778; Clonburren and Balla, Co. Mayo, 779; Trim, Co. Meath, 783; Derry, 787; Inniskeen, Co. Monaghan, 788, and Aughrim, Co. Galway, 789. In 779 Donnchadh pursued two tribes of Leinstermen and wasted and burned not only their lands but also their churches: 'uastavitque combussit fines eorum ecclesias'.[19]

These ravages, and even more the subsequent Viking raids, combined with the wind and rain to remove practically all remains of the wooden churches. When excavations were made beneath St Mel's Church at Ardagh, Co. Longford, in 1967, traces of a timber building were discovered on the site where St Mel is said to have founded a church in the fifth century. Remains of wooden buildings which preceded stone ones have also been found during excavations at Inishcaltra, Co. Clare, and on White Island in Lough Erne, Co. Fermanagh. On Church Island near Valentia in Co. Kerry traces of a little wooden church were found under a later stone oratory. This proof of the existence of a wooden church in a treeless area is an indication of the preference for this material in Early Christian Ireland.

The conjectural reconstruction of a paleo-Christian Irish wooden church is based mainly on the

Reconstruction of a wooden church. The building is of oak logs, split and hewn into planks for the walls, with whole logs for the supporting beams and around the door. The sides of the roof are a tough thatch of rushes.

appearance of the first stone churches, for these were clearly inspired by structures of timber. The wooden churches were usually rectangular buildings, greater in length than breadth, in a proportion of 3:2, comprising a single chamber with a west doorway and an east window. The saddle-back roofs were steep-pitched, sometimes covered with shingles, sometimes thatched. The roof-ridge was aligned between the east and west gables, and the west gable may have been crowned by a cross or splayed finial.

There is a description of one of the grandest churches in Ireland, St Brigid's at Kildare, in Cogitosus's biography of the Saint,[20] written about 630. Two sarcophagi (of St Conleath and St Brigid) richly embellished with gold, silver, gems and precious stones, stood on either side of the decorated altar. Above them hung gold and silver crowns. Cogitosus does not state specifically whether this great church was built of wood, although he does mention that the dividing walls inside were wooden ones, and that there was painted panelling which suggests a wooden building. The church, Cogitosus wrote, had been enlarged (by 630) to accommodate the great number of faithful. It was not only spacious, it also rose to a menacing height: 'solo spatiosa, et in altum minaci proceritate porrecta'.[21] If the painted panels inside the church were in the style of the decoration of the seventh-century *Book of Durrow* the effect must have been beautiful indeed. The entire east wall was decorated with paintings and covered with linen hangings. According to Cogitosus this important church had many windows and an entrance at each end of the east wall. One was for the bishop and his suite, the other for the abbess and her suite of virgins and faithful widows, whence they entered to reach the altar and take Communion. The laymen entered by an ornamental doorway in the north wall near the west end of the church, while the women of the congregation entered by a plain doorway on the opposite side. The interior was divided by painted panels into three oratories (one of the divisions being in effect a chancel screen), so that the faithful could assemble under one roof, but were divided, as Cogitosus put it, according to their state, rank and sex. This beautiful church was burned in 709, 774 and 778.

A fourteenth- to fifteenth-century source of St Patrick's life contains references to the furnishings of the Patrician churches. In Connaught, this biographer records, Patrick left 'fifty bells, fifty chalices and fifty altar-cloths, each of them in his church'. Elsewhere he writes of the 'smiths making the bells', 'the artisans making the patens and the credence-tables and the altar chalices' and of 'the nuns making the altar-cloths'.[22] There were master-artificers or builders to guide the wrights and the other workers at an early date. Cogitosus's account of Kildare relates that when there was a problem in hanging a new door to the abbess's entrance, the artificers consulted an expert who gave wise counsel: 'praedictus doctor et omnium praevius artifex Hibernensium prudenti locutus est con-silio . . .'.[23] The *Small Primer*, one of the Brehon law tracts, in delineating the grades and their respective honour-prices (*dire*), states that the builder of a strong *duirtheach* was equal in nobility to a chief. The *dire* of an *ollamh*, a wise man who was a master in all building arts, was twenty-one cows; this included six cows for skill in building a *daimhliac* (stone church) and six for a *duirtheach* (wooden church), the stonemasonry of the one and the carpentry of the other being the noblest works in the *ollamh*'s sphere.

It is possible that some of the first Patrician churches were in underground cells. This is implied by the writer of the Rawlinson MS, who, in a rather obscure passage, relates that Patrick told his presbyter of a stone altar at Sliabh Hua under the ground, with four glass chalices at the four angles of the altar, and said to him: 'Beware of breaking the edges of the excavation.'[24] This incident is also mentioned in the earlier biography in the *Book of Armagh*, but only as 'cui indicavit altare mirabile lapideum in Monte Nepotum Ailello'.[25]

The next phase of church-building was in un-mortared dry-stone work, the walls constructed by corbelling horizontal layers of massive stones, wedged where necessary with small cut stones called 'spawls'. The first mention of a stone church is in 789 in the record of the murder of a man in the doorway of a stone oratory at Armagh, reported in the *Annals of Ulster* and the *Annals of the Four Masters*.

The next to be mentioned is the church of St Ciaran at Duleek, Co. Meath, specifically stated in the *Book of Armagh* (written 807–8) to be of stone. Indeed the place-name Duleek derives from *daimhliac*, which indicates the singularity of this stone church at the time. It is reasonable to infer from this and from references to the Irish method of building with wood that the first stone churches in Ireland were built not earlier than the latter part of the eighth century. In Co. Down a stone church of any pretensions was still unusual as late as the first half of the twelfth century.[26]

The advantages of the stone church became apparent after more vulnerable buildings had suffered at the hands of the Viking raiders. Several were built, therefore, in the ninth and tenth centuries. The annals mention events connected with at least fifteen *daimhliacs* between 1020 and 1095. These were at Aghadoe and Ardfert, Co. Kerry; Ardbraccan and Kells, Co. Meath; Durrow, Co. Leix; Lorrha and Emly, Co. Tipperary; Kildare, Co. Kildare; Kil-fenora, Co. Clare; Lismore, Co. Waterford, and Lusk, Co. Dublin.

The *daimhliac* of Duleek, plundered in 1027, may have been incorporated in the present church of St Ciaran, an insignificant medieval building. The others named above have also vanished. At Kells, Co. Meath, there is a small stone oratory, but the report of the *daimhliac* there, completed in 814 and burned in 1060, undoubtedly refers to a larger church, the 'great church' from whose western sacristy the famous *Book of Kells* was stolen in 1007.

Scattered about Ireland are a number of early stone churches. Some are examples of the earliest type, small buildings, often in remote places, which escaped the destruction of the vandals and the encroachments of rebuilding. In Co. Kerry there are curious dry-stone oratories that have the appearance of inverted boats; the most perfectly preserved of these is the oratory of Gallerus in the Dingle Peninsula. Externally the little building measures 23 by 16 feet, but because of the thickness of the walls the internal measurements are only 15 by 8 feet. The maximum height is 16 feet. The doorway, of the type usual in all early Irish stone churches, is flat-headed with inclined jambs, the opening tapering from 2 feet 4 inches in width at the base to 1 foot 9 inches at the lintel. The east gable terminates in a small stone cross, and there is a very small round-headed window in the east wall: no more than a loop on the outside, 1 foot 9 inches in height and $9\frac{1}{2}$ inches wide. The building is of dry-stone work without mortar, but so beautifully laid, with the stones sloping outwards, that it is waterproof.

There are other oratories of this inverted-boat-shape type, for example a ruined one at Bally-moreeagh, also in the Dingle Peninsula, and one on Inishvickillane, the most southern of the Blasket

Boat-shaped oratory, Gallerus, Co. Kerry.

Islands and the nearest parish in Europe to America.

One of the finest early churches in the country is the little building on the sixty-acre St MacDara's Island, four miles off the south-west coast of Co. Galway, most conveniently reached by boat from Carna. The island, of reddish granite strewn with huge stones, has a little grassland towards the centre but is now uninhabited. The church is built of enormous stones, some of them as much as 5 by 2½ by 2 feet. Externally the building is 21 feet 3 inches in length and 16 feet 8 inches in width; internally 14 feet 8 inches by 11 feet 3 inches. The doorway is only 5 feet 2 inches high, with very slightly inclined jambs, the opening being 2 feet 4 inches at the base and 2 feet 2 inches at the lintel, which has a projecting band on the inside of the church, 4 inches deep. The east window is round-headed, the head cut out of one single piece of stone on the outside and another on the inside, very primitively rounded, and with two stones between, in the thickness of the wall. This window is so deeply splayed that it measures 4 feet 7 inches by 2 feet 3 inches inside, but only 2 feet 3 inches by 11 inches outside. There is another window in the south wall, flat-headed and almost square inside. Near the church a wing-shaped stone was found, carved with a human head in the centre.

Cyclopean stonework, the ruins of St Mel's church, Ardagh, Co. Longford.

St Begnet's Church on Dalkey Island, Co. Dublin. The bell-cote is a later addition.

The stone, which is 20 inches high, may have been a finial crowning one of the gables. It and all but one of the crosses on the island are cut out of blue limestone (not found on the island) while the church is entirely of the local granite. The most interesting feature of St MacDara's Church is the antae, which continue right up to the gable and indicate the origins of the design of the building in a wooden church. St MacDara lived in the sixth century; the present church probably replaced an almost identical earlier wooden one. Some stone churches had wooden or thatch roofs, but St MacDara's was of stone, pieces of which have survived. The roof-stones were carefully laid in regular courses, each row projecting slightly over the one below.

On Dalkey Island, just off the coast from Dalkey, Co. Dublin, is an Early Christian stone church which is squarer in shape than most, the external measurements being 27 feet 7 inches by 20 feet 3 inches. The walls are thick: 2 feet 10 inches, and the antae which are 2 feet 7 inches wide project 1 foot 2 inches beyond the walls. This church has the usual flat-headed doorway, with the jambs only very slightly inclined, the width of the opening being only one inch less at the massive lintel. The stones with which the church is built are very rough, apparently surface boulders, and mostly granite. The bell-cote on the

west gable is a later addition, and may have replaced a finial; it was probably added in the medieval period when the island was again occupied. In the early nineteenth century labourers building a Martello tower were lodged in the church; they built a fireplace and broke an opening in the south wall.

On Inchagoill, an island in Lough Corrib, Co. Galway, is a small stone church dedicated to St Patrick. Here, too, a chancel was added later, the original single chamber becoming the nave. The church is built of massive stones, and the original doorway in the west wall is 5 feet 9 inches high, with inclined jambs, the opening being $3\frac{1}{2}$ inches narrower at the lintel.

The best examples of the single-chamber stone churches and oratories of the Early Christian period which have survived without enlargement by the addition of a chancel or incorporation in later buildings, like Temple Benen, Inishmore (pl. I, p. 17), or with later additions, are listed in Appendix I.

Patrick initiated a church with bishops and priests, but some men and women chose to follow a self-imposed discipline as monks and nuns. They did not

Temple MacDuagh, Inishmore, Aran Islands, west front showing antae.

follow a monastic constitution, but organized themselves on a pattern similar to the paleo-Christian coenobitic communities in Syria and Egypt, in groups round a master. Others were anchorites, not attached even to small communities, but wandering about the country.[27] The canons attributed to Patrick, Auxilius and Isernius (but probably written in the sixth century) contain in their final clause, terms of legislation against the 'monachus vagulus' (wandering monk), and prohibited monks and virgins from different places from lodging together in the same hospice.[28]

Early in the sixth century an ascetic movement swept across Ireland. This was heralded by the *Penitential of Vinnian* which imposed such strict rules on laymen and clerics alike that many decided that it was easier to leave the world and attempt to achieve perfect Christian life within a monastic community. Vinnian enjoined married persons to abstain from marital relations not only every Saturday and Sunday, but also for three forty-day periods each year and from the time of conception of a child until after its birth. The married clergy were not to cohabit with their wives at all. Divorce and concubinage, which were prevalent, were forbidden. The penance for a married layman who had intercourse with a female slave was that she should be sold and that he should abstain from all intercourse with his own wife for one year; however, if the slave bore the man a child she was to be separated from him and freed while he was sentenced to a year of strict penance on bread and water. The clergy were ordered not to practise magic or to prepare potions (these obstinate practices had survived from pagan times). The punishment for a cleric who committed murder was ten years' exile, unless he could demonstrate that the victim had been his friend and that he had killed him, not in hatred, but in a sudden burst of anger. In such a case the penance was only six years in exile, three on bread and water and three without meat or wine.[29]

St Enda (died about 530) and St Finnian (died 549) were two great leaders of the spiritual and ascetic awakening. Both gathered round them disciples and postulants, St Enda on Inishmore in the Aran Islands, and St Finnian at Clonard, Co. Meath, where he founded a great school of religious life and learning. Among his students were St Ciaran (born about 516), founder of the great scholastic monastic institution at Clonmacnoise; St Columcille who founded the monasteries of Iona in Scotland, Durrow, Co. Leix, and Derry; and St Brendan the Navigator, founder of the great monastic community at Clonfert, Co. Galway, about 560. St Finnian of Moville (died 579) founded a community at Moville, Co. Donegal. St Fintan (died 603), was renowned for

his extreme austerity; he lived exclusively on a diet of stale barley-bread and muddy water, while the monks of the community he founded at Cloneenagh, Co. Leix, were strict vegetarians who did not even employ animals in their husbandry. St Comgall founded his monastic centre at Bangor, Co. Down, about 557.

The associations of monks who gathered round their teacher lived within a compound surrounded by a roughly circular wall, the cashel. Within this enclosure were the habitations of the monks – usually little beehive-shaped huts called *cloghauns* – the church, some crosses, domestic offices and perhaps also an oratory. The seventh-century *Book of Mulling* has a plan of the monastic enclosures at St Mullins, Co. Carlow, the earliest known plan of such a compound in Ireland. It shows the buildings within a round cashel, with four crosses inside the walls and eight outside.

The monastic foundations varied greatly in size, from the important ones such as Clonmacnoise (which attracted students from all over Ireland), Bangor, Kells or Durrow, to small communities with less than a dozen monks. The larger communities included within the cashel or *vallum* a kitchen, refectory, guest-house, library, school, sacristy, and workshops for the artisan coenobites such as the baker, smith, potter, brazier, brewer and clothier.

St Mochaoi's monastery at Nendrum in Strangford Lough, Co. Down, was built on the site of a pre-Christian settlement, of which three concentric dry-stone cashels survive. Within the innermost cashel the monks built a church, a school-house, and at least four dwelling-huts; the middle cashel they converted into a terrace. Between the middle and innermost cashels were found the remains of workshops of a smith and potter. About 1920 the west doorway of the ruined church was reconstructed, with crosses and sculpted stones found on the site inserted in the rebuilt west wall.

Cashels round monastic enclosures survive at Inchleraun, Co. Longford, Seirkieran, Co. Tipperary, Duvillaun More and Kilmore Erris, Co. Mayo, Inishmurray, Co. Sligo, Church Island and Skellig Michael, Co. Kerry, Lullymore East and Kiltiernan East, Co. Kildare, and Nendrum, Co. Down.

Monks from Irish monastic schools travelled to the Continent, founding monasteries and spreading the learning preserved and developed during the Dark Ages when Europe was overrun by successive barbarian hordes. St Columban (born about 540), from St Comgall's monastery at Bangor, was one of the most influential Irish missionary monks. He founded monastic settlements in France, at Annegray,

Luxeuil and Fontaine, and finally, in 614, what was to become the great abbey of Bobbio in Italy. Irish monks went to Switzerland and Germany too; St Killian was martyred at Würzburg in the seventh century. St Foillan, who died in Belgium in 655, founded the abbey of Fosses near Namur, while his brother St Fursey (died 648), after preaching in England, settled in France and founded a monastery at Lagny-sur-Marne. Salzburg in Austria had an Irish bishop in the eighth century, and there is a persistent, though undocumented, tradition that St Cataldus, the patron of Taranto in the south of Italy, was an Irish monk named Cathal, trained at Lismore, Co. Waterford, in the monastic school of St Carthage.

In Ireland the raiding of churches and monastic communities by rival tribes was a constant annoyance to monks trying to lead a life of scholarship and spirituality, though it was as nothing compared with the horrors they were to suffer at the hands of the Viking raiders. These started at the end of the eighth century and continued for over two hundred years: pillaging, burning, murdering, plundering, and desecrating the sacred relics. In 823 the Norsemen broke open the shrine of St Comgall; in 831 they carried off the shrine of Adamnan; in 845 that of Patrick himself; and in 895 they carried away the holy relic called *Etach Padraic*.

This barbarous example was followed by the Irish, who saw their holiest relics and altars defiled without any immediate divine retribution. By 1136 the men of Breffni were bold enough to carry off St Finnian's sword from the treasury of the monastery of Clonard. The internecine wars continued in the ninth century with renewed ferocity, some Irish chieftains even uniting with the Norse invaders in plundering churches.[30] The first such joint enterprise on record took place in 849, when Cinaedh, King of Connaught, joined the invaders in laying waste the churches and lands of the O'Neills, from the Shannon to the sea. In 951 the monastery of Clonmacnoise was plundered by a joint force of Munstermen and Danes from Limerick. The Irish rulers even pursued their own quarrels on hallowed ground. Early in the ninth century Cellach, King of Leinster, fought a battle actually inside the church of Kildare, and slew many of the community. Many monks of Clonmacnoise and Durrow were slain when Feidhlimidh, King of Cashel, attacked their communities in 832 and burned part of the church door at Clonmacnoise. This was not King Feidhlimidh's first venture of the sort. Ten years before, he had burned Gallen, Co. Offaly, with all the dwellings and the oratory, and also Fore in Co. Westmeath. In 835 he engaged in a battle with the Abbot of Armagh and took the oratory of Kildare by force; in 836 and 838 he seized the abbacies of Cork and Clonfert; in

844 he again plundered Clonmacnoise. Despite this extravagant conduct the King was held in high esteem. He is described in the *Annals of Ulster* as the best of Irishmen, 'Optimus Scotorum', a scribe and an anchorite. In 806 there was a battle between the monasteries of Clonfert and Cork, and another in 816 between the communities of Taghmon and Ferns in Co. Wexford. Frequently abbots and their entire ecclesiastical families were murdered. Clonmacnoise fared particularly badly. The whole enclosure up to the door of the church was burned by an Irish chieftain in 830; the monks hardly had time to restore order before they were attacked by the Danes in 839, and again in 842, when the church was despoiled. At this time the Norse Queen Ota was enthroned on the altar at Clonmacnoise by her husband, and there gave out oracles. In 1132 the Hy Kinsella (a Wexford tribe) attacked the monastery of Kildare, burned a large part of the church, slew many of the community and abducted the Abbess, forcing her into a man's bed.[31]

It is little wonder that monks earnestly seeking a true Christian life sought peace and refuge in lonely and almost inaccessible places, small, barren islands off the western coast, or in lakes.

One of the best-preserved early monastic settlements is on Inishmurray, four miles off the coast of Sligo. The cashel is an unmortared stone wall enclosing an oval area, 175 feet long and 135 feet wide. There were several entrances to the enclosure, which contains the ruins of Early Christian stone buildings: the Men's Church, St Molaise 'house' (which has remnants of its stone roof, and once contained the wooden statue of St Molaise, now in the National Museum, Dublin), the Church of the Fire and the Women's Church. There are also vestiges of a number of *cloghauns*, the dry-stone beehive-shaped stone dwellings of the community.

The island of Skellig Michael off the south-west coast of Ireland rises dramatically from the rough Atlantic breakers like a strange cathedral, towering to peaks 700 feet above the sea. Here stormy petrels, black-billed gulls and puffins breed, and seals frolic about the rocks. Along a ledge 550 feet above the sea a few monks settled in the eighth or early ninth century. On this spectacular site the coenobites built a dry-stone cashel round an area 300 feet long and 100 feet wide. This was a small community, for within the enclosure are only six dwellings, dry-built corbelled stone constructions which could have accommodated at most two persons each. Five of these *cloghauns* were the usual oval beehive-shape outside and one was square, but all have a single rectangular chamber inside. The single square construction has stone pegs on the inside walls (probably for hanging-up book-satchels) and ambries, which suggest that it may have been a school or small library. The church of St Michael close to these dwellings is the only mortared building; its east window has a simple semicircular head. There is also an oratory within the cashel, a dry-stone building which had a curved roof, of the inverted-boat type like the oratory of Gallerus. Above its door is a simple decoration, an inlaid cross of white quartz. Another little oratory, also like an inverted boat, was built outside the cashel on a spur of rock. In the twelfth or thirteenth century the monks left their island (which is inaccessible in rough weather), and settled at Ballinskelligs on the mainland, but the ruins of their little City of God have survived for over a thousand years, an impressive reminder of ascetic life and ardent faith in what was, in their day, the most westerly outpost of Christianity.

Each monastic foundation adopted the constitution devised and instituted by its founder. Some of the coenobitic communities were founded by men like St Finnian of Moville who combined the office of abbot and bishop. Usually, however, the abbot ruled the monastic *paruchia*, and the bishop the episcopal and territorial *paruchia*, while a bishop within a monastic community was under the jurisdiction of the abbot. Monks went out and founded communities in other parts of the country; and because these communities were connected to the mother-foundation, the power of the monastic *paruchiae*, unrestricted by territorial limits, soon eclipsed that of the episcopal ones. By the end of the seventh century the abbot was a more important figure than the bishop, and the monastic *paruchiae* had grown, spread and prospered to such an extent that the ecclesiastical administration was abbatial rather than episcopal. The name of the abbot in Irish was *comarb*, meaning heir, and that is how the successors of the founder were styled. The Abbot of Armagh, for example, was the Comarb of Patrick; the Abbot of Clonmacnoise, the Comarb of Ciaran; the Abbess of Kildare, the Comarb of Brigid. In Ireland, the Pope was called the Comarb of Peter.

Abbatial succession was on the lines of the secular system: the most suitable member of the family was chosen. At Killevy, Co. Armagh, for example, six out of ten successive abbesses belonged to the local ruling family. St Columcille of Iona was succeeded by his own first cousin, and the third to fifth, seventh to ninth and eleventh to thirteenth abbots were of the same family. The right of succession to the abbacy was vested in the founder's kin, as stated in the Brehon Laws: 'The tribe of the patron saint shall succeed to the church as long as there shall be a person fit to be an abbot of the said tribe of the patron saint; even though there should be but a psalm-singer of them, it is he that will obtain the abbacy.'

Skellig Michael, off the coast of Kerry.

This led inevitably to the accession of laymen, often of married laymen. Consequently a spiritual decline set in, hastened by the deleterious effects of the Viking invasions. In some monasteries the offices of abbot and bishop were continuously combined. This appears to have been the case at Armagh, at least until the eighth century. At Kildare the monastery was under the joint jurisdiction of a bishop from the royal family of Leinster and an abbess, the Comarb of Brigid.

Two manuscripts written about 830 by a monk of the community at Tallaght, Co. Dublin, furnish an interesting contemporary account of life in an Irish monastery in the ninth century.[32] The monks at Tallaght followed the rule of their founder Maelruain. He did not allow them to drink beer unless they were going on a long journey, and reminded them, 'the liquor that causes forgetfulness of God shall not be drunk here'. The diet was simple; the monks were warned not to eat herbs cut, blackberries or nuts plucked, kale cooked or bread baked on a Sunday. The only flesh allowed was venison or wild boar, although meat was served to guests, there being hostels for both men and women. Maelruain did not approve of listening to music, but the four Gospels were read aloud at meals. There were also nuns at Tallaght, and the monks were allowed to converse with them, on the slab by the cross in front of the hostel, or in the retreat where they lived. The penance for lust, a sin specifically described as 'frequenting mates and producing children', was seven years' penance on gruel; the same penance applied to those guilty of bloodshed or homicide. There were laymen at Tallaght, too, under the spiritual guidance of the abbot.

By the tenth century many monastic establishments included a bell-house (Irish *cloichtheach*), a tall steeple varying in height from 50 feet to as much as 125 feet, and 40 to 60 feet in circumference at the base. These belfries, detached from the other monastic buildings but usually close to the church, served a double purpose. The bell announced the religious services or warned of the approach of Viking attackers, while the tower provided a refuge where the monks could hide with their valuables. For this reason the doorway was usually at least 6 feet above the ground, and sometimes as much as 15 feet. The *cloichtheachs*, now called 'round towers', were built of stone, the stout walls diminishing in thickness as the tower diminished in girth towards the top. They were generally capped by a conical roof. Inside there were four or more storeys with wooden floors resting on joists. Usually one small window lit each floor except the top one, which had four, to serve as look-out posts. A number of these sturdily built towers survive. Their elegant silhouettes are a conspicuous feature of the Irish countryside today.

Within a monastic compound there were usually crosses, and beautiful examples of these also survive. There are some fine High Crosses at Kells in Co. Meath. The monastery there is remembered for the richly illuminated and decorated *Book of Kells*, the supreme achievement of Irish Celtic art (now in Trinity College, Dublin). The work of monks in the eighth century, it was stolen from the western

High Cross, Drumcliffe, Co. Sligo.

Paleo-Christian cross near the oratory, Gallerus, Co. Kerry.

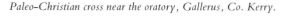

sacristy of the great church at Kells in 1007. The great stone church has vanished, but the Round Tower (where a claimant to the high-kingship was murdered in 1076) still stands.

One of the most perfect surviving High Crosses is the Cross of Muiredach, on the site of the once-great monastic settlement at Monasterboice, Co. Louth. But not all the crosses were within monastic compounds. While most served a didactic purpose, illustrating stories from the Old and New Testaments, some depict secular scenes such as a deer-hunt or a funeral, and some have non-figurative decoration, geometrical patterns or Celtic interlacing, like the elaborately carved eighth-century crosses at Ahenny, Co. Tipperary, or the early one at Carndonagh, Co. Donegal. All testify to the existence of skilled and imaginative sculptors, at least from the eighth century; but strangely, these accomplished craftsmen did not extend their decorative art to the fabric of the churches.

The stone effigies now placed against the wall of the church on White Island, Co. Fermanagh,

I Temple Benen, Inishmore, Aran Islands (p. 12) >

apparently belonged in the earlier church. They were found near to, or built into the walls of, the twelfth-century building, some face down. They may have been considered embarrassing in the twelfth century, for although of Christian subjects, they have a decidedly pagan look.

The Irish Church, with its peculiar institutional development, inclined towards independence, resisting both central and universal authority. Irish monks (some of whom taught at the schools of Charlemagne's court) spread their learning across western Europe, but little cultural influence permeated to Ireland (although such continental writers as Isidore of Seville were quoted in the Irish schools).

The Viking terror which first struck at the end of the eighth century continued with little respite for over two hundred years. The slave-owning, cattle-raiding, independent Irish princes continued to attack one another, as well as defending themselves from the ferocious raids of the Norse invaders, whose fleets sailed up the rivers right into the Irish hinterland. The O'Neills of Ulster, the most powerful of the provincial kings, claimed the high-kingship, although they were not always able to assert their power, and there were long and fierce struggles connected with the succession. In 1001 Brian Boroimhe, the shrewd, vigorous, ambitious monarch of Munster, took hostages from the reigning High-King, Maelseachlainn O'Neill, and thus became High-King of Ireland. Brian was not a constitutional reformer, but he visualized Ireland as a unit. He has been called Ireland's Charlemagne, and indeed, when he went to Armagh in 1005 and confirmed its ecclesiastical supremacy, his secretary made a written record of his wishes in the *Book of Armagh*, and described him as 'Emperor of the Irish' ('Imperator Scotorum').

Some Norse invaders eventually made permanent settlements. The Danes in Dublin set up their own kingdom, embraced Christianity and intermarried with Irish princesses. The invaders built the first towns, such as Dublin, Limerick and Waterford, and it was this development which wrought the first significant social change in Ireland.

During a decade of comparative peace under Brian Boroimhe's high-kingship, communications and churches were repaired. Brian died at the Battle of Clontarf in 1014, when his army defeated the Norse forces and their allies; it was the greatest slaughter that the country had ever experienced, but it finally ended the Viking wars. Yet after Brian's death dynastic struggles for power resumed, and the country was again plunged into discord, anarchy, treachery and turmoil, with the consequent destruction of churches and church property.

Two early Christian figures now on the wall of the ruined church, White Island, Lough Erne, Co. Fermanagh.

< *11 Kilmalkedar, Co. Kerry (p. 32).*

CHAPTER 2

The flowering of Romanesque

IRISH INTERCOURSE with western European countries increased considerably in the eleventh century. Besides the early Irish monastic settlements in the Empire such as Würzburg, new Irish houses were founded at Cologne in 975, at Metz in 992, at Erfurt in 1036 and at Regensburg (Ratisbon) in 1076.

The annals record that during the eleventh century a number of Irish monarchs travelled across Europe, usually on pilgrimages to Rome, although the King of the Deisi went as far as Jerusalem in 1080.[1] In 1026 the King of Cenel Conaill went on a pilgrimage first to Iona and then to Rome;[2] four years later Flaithbhertach O'Neill, King of Ailech, went as a pilgrim to Rome and returned to Ireland;[3] in 1051 Laighnen, King of Gailenga (Morgallion Barony, Co. Meath), made a pilgrimage to Rome accompanied by his wife, and presumably the usual retinue of a petty monarch;[4] one of Brian Boroimhe's sons who had fought at the great Battle of Clontarf, King Donnchadh of Munster, went, when in his late seventies, on a pilgrimage to Rome and died there in 1064;[5] King Donnchadh's half-brother Sitric, the Danish King of Dublin, had been on a pilgrimage to Rome in 1028 with Flannagan O'Kelly, King of Bregha; in 1034 Sitric's son Olaf was killed on his way to Rome, and in 1052 the unfortunate blind King Brian of Leinster died at Cologne.[6]

The eleventh century was one of intensive building activity in the Empire. Cologne boasted several churches of architectural merit, such as St Pantaleon with its remarkable westwork, consecrated in 980; here there was an Irish bishop in the eleventh century. The Irish who travelled through the Empire must have been awed by the size, strangeness and grandeur of churches like Charlemagne's spectacular chapel at Aachen, a sixteen-sided polygon within which an ambulatory ran round an octagonal centre. Those who went to Würzburg saw the cathedral, dedicated to the Irish St Killian martyred there in the seventh

century, and the rotunda of St Mary on the fortress. At Fulda the Irish historian-monk Mael-Brigte (Marianus Scottus) spent ten years as an *inclusus* between 1059 and 1069.[7] There too the Irish monk Anmchad from the monastery at Inishcaltra, Co. Clare, died in 1053 (having been exiled for serving wine to guests without his Abbot's permission),[8] and Irish pilgrims visited the great basilica of St Boniface. Marvellous new cathedrals were in progress in the Rhineland: Speier dates from about 1030 and Mainz from 1081.

Irish travellers whose route crossed England and France saw Westminster Abbey in London, rebuilt by Edward the Confessor, and splendid new churches like St Benigne at Dijon and St Martin at Tours, begun early in the eleventh century.

When the Irish pilgrims finally reached Rome, they must have gazed in wonder before the old basilica of St Peter's, built by Constantine in the fourth century, mounted its staircase and crossed the columned atrium to enter the church, which had a long nave with two aisles on each side, each lit by its own clerestory. They would have knelt in the nave before the great round-headed triumphal arch which gave access to the transept. St Paul's-Outside-the-Walls was another gigantic basilica with a nave and four aisles, its walls brilliantly decorated with mosaics and frescoes.

Whatever the Irish monarchs thought of the superb buildings they saw abroad, whatever tales they recounted at home of the marvels they had seen, they did not, like the Emperor Hadrian in Antiquity, try to emulate in their own states the wonders they had admired in their travels. Nevertheless a change did come to Ireland with the growing awareness of the outside world and its architecture.

Despite internal wars the dawn of the twelfth century ushered in a fairly intensive period of church-building in Ireland. The annals record that Cellach,

Comarb of Patrick and Bishop at Armagh, consecrated many churches during his comarbship, which lasted from 1106 to 1129. He was a pious, spiritual man, endowed with a strong character and sound administrative ability. He had succeeded to the abbacy through family connection, his grandfather and great-uncle having been comarbs before him, but on succession he asked to be ordained to the priesthood. He went about Ireland collecting his tribute in places where his predecessors had failed, made ecclesiastical visitations, and continued the current of reform created by the Synod of Cashel of 1101 by convening the Synod of Rath Bresail in 1110. This was attended by about fifty bishops, three hundred priests and three thousand clerics, as well as Muirchertach O'Brien, King of Munster and High-King, with many nobles.

An attempt was made at this synod to create some order out of the chaos of ecclesiastical administration in Ireland. The number of sees and consequently of bishops was limited to twelve in each half of the country, plus Armagh itself. Dublin, because of its Danish connection, remained under the jurisdiction of Canterbury. Just as there was a high-king in the Irish secular order, the Comarb of Patrick at Armagh was a high-bishop. Brian Boroimhe had confirmed this supremacy, and at the Synod of Rath Bresail, Cellach established it. The southern half of Ireland was placed under the jurisdiction of Cashel. Malchus, Bishop of Waterford, became Archbishop of Cashel, albeit without the pallium.[9] The northern half of the country was under the jurisdiction of Armagh where the primacy was vested. Cellach cleverly consolidated his position still further in 1121 by also becoming Bishop of Dublin, with the agreement of both Irish and Danes.

Decrees regarding respect for churches and sanctity of Church property were made at the Synod of Rath Bresail, but the threat of anathema was not enough to deter the Irish chiefs from their old habit of despoiling churches. Only ten years after the synod, the men of Connaught marched into Desmond and laid waste more than seventy churches. In 1129 the main altar at Clonmacnoise was robbed of its treasures, which included the model of Solomon's Temple bequeathed by the High-King Maelsechnaill, four silver cups given by the Primate Cellach, silver chalices and a gilt cross.[10] The outrageous incident at Kildare when the Abbess was abducted and raped, occurred as late as 1132. Nevertheless, the meeting of the principal clergy of Ireland at Rath Bresail, with exchange and dissemination of new ideas, combined with Cellach's zeal, resulted in administrative improvement, and set off a new spate of church-building. The great stone church at Armagh was re-roofed in 1125, the abbey church of St Peter and St Paul there was built by Imhar O'Hagan, who died in Rome in 1134, and Cormac's Chapel at Cashel was begun in 1127.[11]

Stylistic changes began in a small way, with the addition of decorative mouldings, hood-mouldings and round-headed arches. Part of the east wall of many little stone churches was demolished, and a chancel of finer masonry added, sometimes not even bonded to the old structure. The separation between nave and chancel was marked by a rounded chancel arch, at first plain, like that of Temple MacDuagh on Inishmore, later decorated in the Romanesque tradition.

Temple MacDuagh, Inishmore, Aran Islands, the chancel arch and east end.

Maghera, Co. Derry, lintel.

Banagher, Co. Derry, windows in the ruined church.

One of the earliest surviving attempts by an Irish builder to introduce some adornment of a stone church may be seen at Maghera, Co. Derry. The doorway of the church is square-headed on the outside, with slightly inclined jambs in the early Irish tradition, but on the inside the opening has a semi-circular arch. There is carved decoration on all the exterior stonework of this doorway, including the jambs and facings; the architrave decoration is delicate foliage in low relief. On the massive lintel, 5 feet 6 inches long and 2 feet high, is a sculpted scene of the Crucifixion. The cross is almost a T, barely higher than the Christ who wears a colobium. Beneath the cross kneel Longinus with his spear, and the sponge-bearing soldier. The sculptor has carefully carved in relief the drops of blood which spurt from Christ's wound on to Longinus. A large number of persons are portrayed about the cross: five on the left and six on the right; above are cherubim. The stylistic origins of this type of scene can be traced back to Syria, but by the ninth century it had passed into western Europe.[12] Possibly the sculptor at Maghera took his idea from a ninth-century fresco in the oratory of the basilica of St John and St Paul in Rome, seen by Irish pilgrims. Padre Germano di S. Stanislao, the historian of this basilica, noted the probable derivation of this fresco from the Syrian codex of Rabula in the Biblioteca Laurenziana, Florence, dated 586.[13] Dr Françoise Henry once believed that the Banagher and Maghera doorways, and a similar one at Aghowle, Co. Wicklow, were all of Syrian origin, and executed in the seventh or eighth century.[14] She has since revised this opinion, and assigns the Banagher and Aghowle doorways to the late tenth or early eleventh century, and the Maghera doorway to the eleventh or twelfth.[15]

Dungiven Abbey, Co. Derry, window.

Aghowle, Co. Wicklow. Above, west doorway of the ruined church; right, windows.

However, at Dungiven, Co. Derry, in the south wall of the nave of the ruined abbey church (founded 1100, according to Archdall),[16] there is a window similar both internally and externally to the one at Banagher, four miles away. The similarity between these two windows, and between the Banagher and Maghera doorways, indicates that all three churches were the work of the same architect or the same masons. The scant documentary evidence available points to a building date at the beginning of the twelfth century. The *Annals of Ulster* mention a cemetery at Banagher in 1121, so presumably a church already existed there then. The surviving west doorway and south window of this single-chamber building both show signs of the transition from the simplest Early Christian type to the Romanesque, a transition which seems to have begun under the primacy of Cellach at the beginning of the twelfth century.

The church at Aghowle, Co. Wicklow, appears to be of the same date. The doorway, trabeated in the old Irish manner, has a straight lintel and inclining jambs, but internally, like the doorways at Banagher and Maghera, it has a semicircular arch. The external stonework is granite; the architrave is finely chiselled, its outer face composed of rounded sections, its inner face of squared sections whose inner returns are decorated with moulded bosses. The edges of the jambs are carved with Romanesque-type bead moulding. In the east wall are twin windows which splay inwards. Externally they are most interesting; the archivolts (whose voussoirs show traces of that much-favoured Romanesque moulding, the chevron) are carried by little columns on corbels flanking the windows. Two of the corbels are carved with animal heads. No documentary evidence has been found to help fix the building date of this church, but all the elements appear to be coeval, so that the combination on the windows of Romanesque decorative features and early Irish ones

St Caimin's Church, Inishcaltra, Lough Derg, Co. Clare, detail of chancel arch.

indicates that it belongs to the period when Romanesque forms were first infiltrating into Ireland. They are an advance on the plain round-headed window, like the one at Kilrush, Co. Limerick. The round-headed windows with architraves both inside and out, in the chancel of Temple MacDuagh, Inishmore, are early, simple refinements, but elegant in comparison with the crude slits of the earlier stone churches. The round-headed window in the little church at Toureen Peekaun, Co. Tipperary (which has a flat-headed doorway), has low-relief chevron decoration.

On the island of Inishcaltra in Lough Derg, Co. Clare, where a monastery flourished from the seventh century, there are remains of several churches and an extensive cemetery. The royal family of Munster had close connections with Inishcaltra. One of Brian Boroimhe's brothers was abbot at the end of the eleventh century, and Queen Gormflaeth of Munster, who died in 1059, was buried there. Because of these royal associations, and the importance of the 'Holy Island', it is not surprising to find, in the churches there, decorative elements dating from the early years of architectural improvement.

The church dedicated to the founder, St Caimin, first consisted of a single chamber, the nave, 30 feet 3 inches by 20 feet 3 inches, built of large rough

stones and with projecting antae. This undoubtedly dates from the tenth century, and would have been constructed after the incendiary raid of the Vikings in 922. A chancel, 14 feet 7 inches by 12 feet 6 inches, neatly built of well-squared stones, was added to the east end of the church without being bonded to the east wall. Where the east wall was broken through, a skilfully turned chancel arch was erected, with three orders of voussoirs on the side facing the nave and two on the side facing the chancel, all without any ornament save a grotesque head on the keystone of the side facing the nave. This arch is supported by clustered columns with carved bases on a plinth, and has cushion capitals embellished with a carved grotesque face. Rather similar bulbous capitals appear on the columns of the church doorway at Clonkeen, Co. Limerick, but stylistically the Clonkeen doorway appears to be later than St Caimin's, because the voussoirs of its three orders in the arch and the architrave are completely covered with Romanesque carving, although the jambs are plain.

Clonkeen, Co. Limerick, doorway.

Rahan, Co. Offaly, Church of Ireland parish church, detail of chancel arch.

This is like the west doorway of St Caimin's, which also has more decoration than the chancel arch, and, while it could be coeval with the chancel, might have been added a few years later to replace a flat-headed entrance. The voussoirs of the three orders of the arch above the doorway are decorated, the inner one with chevrons, the middle one with a simple line moulding, and the outer one with elaborate zigzags; the jambs are quite plain. In the full bloom of the Romanesque style in Ireland it became fashionable to cover all the stonework with decoration, carrying the ornamentation right down the jambs.

Reefert Church at Glendalough, Co. Wicklow, probably built about 1100, belongs to the period of transition from Early Christian to Romanesque forms. The nave, 29 feet by 17 feet 6 inches, and the chancel, 14 feet by 8 feet 9 inches, are coeval. While the doorway is of the old flat-headed type, the windows are round-headed, and between the nave and chancel is a plain rounded chancel arch. On the outside of the church the corbels which carried the timber rafters of the roof may be observed. Trinity Church, also at Glendalough, appears to be of about the same date. The west doorway is flat-headed, while the windows are round-headed, and there is a plain semicircular chancel arch.

At Rahan, Co. Offaly, is a curious church which has puzzled architectural historians. Over the cen-

turies it has undergone many changes; the present nave was built in the eighteenth century, but the chancel survives from an early building. Writing in 1845 Petrie (who inclined to antedate early churches) assigned Rahan to the eighth century.[17] Champneys in 1910 disagreed, submitting that the Romanesque decorative motifs at Rahan could not possibly be of such an early date.[18] In 1933 Dr Françoise Henry pointed out the marked resemblance of the columns of the chancel arch at Rahan to columns in the chapel of the Royal Palace of Ani in Armenia, consecrated in 622. She also mentioned the presence of Egyptian and Armenian clerics in Ireland at an early date.[19] The chancel at Rahan originally had a transept, consisting of a small chamber on each side, communicating with it by low round-headed doorways with inclined jambs. Dr Leask, pursuing the idea of Armenian influence, suggested that these rooms may have had their origin in the *diaconicon* and *prothesis* of Near Eastern churches, and he too referred to the Armenian clerics near Rahan,[20] but opted firmly for a building date for Rahan Church not earlier than the twelfth century. This is also Dr Henry's revised opinion.[21]

Claims that mysterious Eastern clerics were present in Ireland are based on a single tenuous reference. The Reverend Charles Plummer's *Irish Litanies* includes one drawn from four texts dating from the twelfth to the eighteenth centuries, the earliest being the twelfth-century *Book of Leinster*. The Litany mentions as Bishops of Cell Achid (Killeigh, Co. Offaly) the 'Cerrui ab Armenia', and also 'Morfesseor do mancharb Egipt n Disuirt Uilaig' (seven monks of Egypt in Disuirt Uilaig, i.e. Dundesert, parish of Killead, Co. Antrim).[22]

It would not be reasonable to place Rahan Church outside the mainstream of Irish stone-church building, and the ensemble of the surviving decorative elements of the chancel point to a date certainly not earlier than the end of the eleventh century, more likely the twelfth century. However, the stylistic affinities of the engaged columns and capitals at Rahan with those at Ani are undeniable,[23] and two theories can be advanced to reconcile this striking resemblance with the time-lapse and distance. The Bagratid dynasty which ruled at Ani collapsed in 1046 when the city passed under Muslim domination. It is unlikely, therefore, that Western Crusaders or pilgrims would have seen it, even if they had strayed from the usual routes. There are two phases of exportation of architectural and artistic forms from Armenia to western Europe. The first was at the end of the eighth century, when Charlemagne attracted to Aix, clerics, artists, scholars and artisans from many countries including Asia Minor. Thus, Byzantine influences and workmanship reached the

Rahan, Co. Offaly. Left, detail of capital of chancel arch; right, window inserted in east gable.

Carolingian Empire, and Irish monks returning from the Irish abbeys in Germany may have imported to Rahan, from a now-vanished Carolingian building, stylistic elements based on an Armenian model. A second wave of Byzantine influence came with refugee monks who fled to the West from the Muslim invaders. A little colony of Basilian monks, for example, settled in the tenth century at Stilo, in southern Italy, and there in the heart of Calabria built a replica of the type of parish church common in Georgia and Armenia in the ninth century. Clerics must also have fled from Ani when the Muslims took it in 1046, and it is possible that refugee monks with their own masons reached Ireland and built on the model of their homeland.

The rooms off the chancel at Rahan were probably used as a sacristy and treasury respectively. They may have carried paired towers, smaller than, but similar to, those of Cormac's Chapel at Cashel. The chancel arch has three orders; only the engaged columns which support it are decorated. Their bases have a stylized foliage design in low relief; the square capitals are also carved in low relief, with human faces at the angles, and palmette motifs below a boldly carved projecting abacus.

The original east window of the chancel has been replaced more than once, while high up in the east gable is a fine round window with good Romanesque moulding and a quatrefoil opening on the inside. Such round windows are very rare in Ireland; there is another at Freshford, Co. Kilkenny. The one at Rahan was probably on the façade of the earlier church, above the gable in the west portal: it seems too elaborate for a lesser function. Its removal to its present position probably took place when alterations were made in the fifteenth century. The blocked-up doorway now beneath it has also been moved from its original position.

Freshford, Co. Kilkenny, Romanesque window inserted in the façade of the Church of Ireland parish church.

About a hundred yards from this church stands another. Its Romanesque doorway, which has lost the flanking pillars, was probably once that of the larger church, inserted in this smaller one at the time of the fifteenth-century changes.

Brian Boroimhe had been crowned King of Munster on the Rock of Cashel in 977. The Rock, a stronghold of the Munster kings since pre-Christian times, remained the capital of Brian's descendants until 1101, when his great-grandson, King Muirchertach, made a gift of it to the Church. The enlightened and intelligent Muirchertach had more international connections than his contemporaries: one of his daughters married Sigurd the Crusader, son of Magnus, King of Norway, and another was the wife of a Cambro-Norman noble, Arnulph de Montgomery. Aware of the need for ecclesiastical reform in Ireland he wrote requesting the Italian-born Archbishop of Canterbury, the Benedictine St Anselm, who also had jurisdiction over the Norse sees in Ireland, to send as the first bishop of Waterford, Malchus (Mael-Iosa O Hanmire), an Irish-born monk, then in England. Anselm agreed and the appointment was made in 1096.

This Malchus, then fifty, had seen the initiation and the first two decades of building of the magnificent Anglo-Norman cathedral-priory of Winchester, where he was a professed monk. King Muirchertach was the most powerful ruler present at the Synod of Rath Bresail. Gilbert, Bishop of Limerick, who presided over the synod, was another of Anselm's protégés. Also a Benedictine, he had been at the abbey of Bec in Normandy under Anselm's abbacy, and at Canterbury. He and Malchus, who wrote to St Anselm as his friend as well as his superior,[24] were the most cosmopolitan and informed clerics at the synod. Through Anselm, who attended the Council of Bari in 1098 and the Lateran Eastern Synod at Rome in 1099, they were abreast of current ecclesiastical thought and developments on the Continent.[25] Malchus lived to be nearly ninety, and for the first four decades of the twelfth century the school over which he presided at Lismore was the most advanced and the most important centre of learning and culture in Ireland.

After King Muirchertach's death the power of the O'Brien dynasty began to dwindle. In 1118 the King of Connaught defeated the Munstermen and split Munster into two kingdoms. The O'Briens were reduced to the kingdom of Thomond while a MacCarthy ruled the other kingdom, Desmond. In 1123 Cormac MacCarthy succeeded as monarch of Desmond, but he was ousted only two years later by his brother, who usurped the throne and banished him. Cormac retired as a pilgrim to Lismore and there spent a year with Malchus.

Malchus's influence on his most famous student, St Malachy, was recognized by that saint's contemporary biographer, St Bernard of Clairvaux,[26] who also recorded that Malchus appointed Malachy to be King Cormac's *magister*[27] during the latter's stay at Lismore. The dethroned King not only studied during this time but also built churches. He gave Malachy land on which to build a monastery, and took an interest in its construction. Unfortunately, Cormac's churches at Lismore have vanished, and the monastery, described by St Bernard as 'Monasterium Ibracense', has not been satisfactorily identified. One suggested locality, Ibrickan Barony, Co. Clare, while not in Cormac's dominions, was in the kingdom of his stepson, Conor, King of Thomond, who helped restore him to power. Another suggested location, Iveragh Barony, Co. Kerry, is near to Cormac's principal place of residence.

In 1127, the usurper having been dethroned and exiled, King Cormac was restored to power. Immediately after his return from Lismore, probably to fulfil a vow made before Malchus and Malachy in case of his restoration, King Cormac initiated the building of a church on the Rock of Cashel. Its unique appearance may well be due to cultural contacts made by Cormac during his time at Lismore.

The architectural ancestry of this building, Cormac's Chapel (Teampuill Cormaic), consecrated in 1134, has been the subject of much controversy. Nineteenth-century writers, fired by nationalism, claimed that Hiberno-Romanesque architecture was an isolated, independent, Irish form. This is untenable, although some still cherish the theory. Later scholars and writers have sought a prototype for Cormac's Chapel, or parts of it, in Normandy, in central and south-western France, in England and in Germany.

Charles MacNeill's monograph on the connections between Regensburg (Ratisbon) in Germany and Cashel, published in 1912,[28] became the basis for a now widely diffused belief that Cormac's Chapel was modelled on a German Romanesque church. It has been frequently asserted that an abbot of Regensburg sent envoys to Cashel 'seven years before Cormac's Chapel was built . . . and through this it was influenced by German Romanesque architecture'.[29]

It has even been asserted that Cormac actually brought masons from the Continent to work on his chapel.[30] However, a careful study of MacNeill's sources show that all that can be claimed with certainty is that there was a traffic of monks, and possibly of artisans, between Germany and Ireland in the first half of the twelfth century. MacNeill cited two documents which mention intercourse between the Irish abbeys in Germany and Cashel.

One is the *Life of Marianus Scottus* written by an Irish monk at Regensburg about 1184–85,[31] fifty years after the consecration of Cormac's Chapel. This states only that Christian, Abbot of Regensburg, returned twice to his native Ireland to collect money for his monastery in Germany, but died in Ireland on his second journey and was buried at Cashel. This Christian only became Abbot of Regensburg in 1133; he obtained a Papal Bull to go to Ireland in 1148 and died between then and 1157. His visits to Ireland are not, therefore, relevant to the style of Cormac's Chapel, built 1127–34.

MacNeill's second source was a version published in 1850[32] of a copy by the seventeenth-century Irish Jesuit historian, Stephen White, of an undated 'early chronicle of Regensburg' which he discovered. According to Wilhelm Wattenbach, writing in 1856,[33] Father White's manuscript was in the Bibliothèque Royale, Brussels (MS 5313), but the whereabouts of the original chronicle is unknown, so that its authenticity cannot be tested; neither is the date or provenance of the original recorded. Analysis of Father White's transcript reveals several discrepancies. A translation of relevants parts of it from Latin is as follows:

Isaac and Gervase who were born in Ireland of noble race and were eminent for piety, learning and eloquence, came to Ireland together with two other Irish-born Irishmen, Conrad the carpenter, and William, and having greeted the King of Ireland, Conor O'Brien, surnamed Slaparsalach, they explained to him the purpose of their journey. They were kindly welcomed and after a few days were honourably sent back to Germany loaded with gold, silver and other precious gifts of various kinds from other Irish princes. This Isaac and Gervase had been sent to Ireland as his representatives by *Dionysius*, the Irishman, Abbot of St Peter's, Regensburg, to ask for assistance and alms from the kings and princes of his native land. The money sent from Ireland purchased for the Abbot a commodious site for a new monastery in the western part of Ratisbon. . . . Neither before nor since was there such a great monastery . . . so perfectly and completely executed . . . because the amount of money sent by the kings and other princes of Ireland was boundless. . . . [King Conor] sent by some powerful and very noble Counts who had crossed themselves and were pilgrims to Jerusalem, immense gifts to Lothair, King of the Romans. . . . Christian, Abbot of the Irish monastery of St James, Regensburg, a noble man of the leading stock of the McCarthy family in Ireland, when the treasures once sent by the King of Ireland to Regensburg were exhausted,

seeing that he got no assistance from mortal men for his brethren, agreed to their request to go to Ireland, his own country, again to seek alms from the most Christian and pious king *Donatus* O'Brien (King Conchor O'Brien, the founder of St Peter's and of the monastery of St James of the Irishmen, being no longer alive) and from other Irish magnates. The said King Donatus and his wife the Queen and the princes of Ireland happily expedited his business and prepared to send him back to Germany with immense treasures, but Christian yielded up his spirit to God in Ireland and is honourably buried before the altar of St Patrick in the cathedral church of Cashel.[34]

St James, the Schottenkirche, of Regensburg was built in 1111, and its high altar was consecrated in 1122. According to the chronicle the funds to purchase the land were raised by Isaac and Gervase and their companions in Ireland, the first mission, which only stayed there 'a few days'. This mission must, therefore, have taken place prior to 1111. This fits with the dates of the abbot 'Dionysius', apparently the Domnus or Domhnall who was abbot at Regensburg from 1098 until his death in 1118. However, the chronicle has it that the envoys went to King Conor O'Brien, 'surnamed Slaparsalach'. This was Conchobar na Cathrach, also known as Conchobar (Conor) Slapar Salach, King of Thomond only, who reigned from 1119 to 1136 and was therefore indeed a contemporary of Emperor Lothair II, who reigned from 1125 to 1137, and to whom it is reported that he sent gifts. These dates cannot be reconciled with those of Abbot Domnus who died in 1118, or with the date of purchase of the site of St James, Regensburg.

The chronicle appears to be equally unreliable concerning the date of Abbot Christian's visit. It is stated that he went to a king 'Donatus O'Brien', but there was no twelfth-century O'Brien monarch named Donatus (Donogh).[35] Abbot Christian died before 1157, so it can be excluded that his benefactor could have been the great church-builder King Domhnall O'Brien, who reigned from 1168 to 1194.

Given that a mission sent by Abbot Domnus preceded the building of Cormac's Chapel, it is unlikely that it had a significant effect on its style in view of the specific statement that the envoys only stayed 'a few days'. Abbot Christian's visit or visits to Ireland were certainly subsequent to the building of Cormac's Chapel and, therefore, cannot be relevant.

A likely source of inspiration of the chapel at Cashel is the church of the Benedictine Abbey of Murbach, consecrated in the same year, 1134.[36] It is situated on the west bank of the Rhine, near Guebwiller in Alsace, and was a famous hostelry for pilgrims and travellers. Its old name was *Vivarius Perigrinorum*, and Irish monks and prelates undoubtedly stopped there *en route* to Bavaria and Rome. Erloff, the Abbot of Murbach immediately prior to the building of the great abbey church, was also Abbot of Fulda from 1114 to 1122,[37] a monastery with long-standing Irish connections. Work began on the abbey church at Murbach in 1122, and while Cormac's Chapel, begun five years later, is tiny compared with Murbach, the striking similarity between the surviving east end of the abbey church and the Irish church seems to indicate that the builder of Cormac's Chapel must have seen Murbach, or a plan of it.

The identity of the designer of Cormac's Chapel may never be known. Liam de Paor opts for Anglo-Norman stylistic origins, basing his argument on the fact that most of the individual decorative elements of Cormac's Chapel can be found in Norman buildings.[38] Taking into consideration the known historical and architectural facts, it can reasonably be advanced that Cormac's Chapel was the work of an Irish Benedictine who had spent some time in England, like Malchus, and possibly some in Normandy, like Gilbert; that he had travelled on the Continent, probably to the Irish houses in Bavaria, and had seen the building of Murbach in progress between 1122 and 1127, when Cormac's Chapel was begun. Malchus's school at Lismore, where King

Cormac's Chapel, Cashel, Co. Tipperary, the east end (above), and (left) Murbach, Alsace, the east end of the Benedictine abbey.

Cormac stayed in 1126, was probably the link between the King and the builder-monk.

The little church at Cashel is a grand one in miniature, a complete Romanesque entity in which the architect successfully amalgamated a number of known Romanesque features, such as paired towers, blind arcading, deeply recessed arched doorways, and the new technique of rib-vaulting, with established Romanesque decorative motifs such as chevrons, pellets and rosettes. He added a vernacular steep-pitched stone roof with steep-pitched gables to match it. These have their origin in the narrow overhanging wooden gables of early timber buildings in Ireland and Scandinavia. Thus he created a unique edifice whose integration and beauty testify to his skill as a designer, and whose excellent construction proves his skill as a builder.

The building is cruciform, having paired towers at the junction of the nave and chancel; a rectangular recess juts out from the east end. From the outside this gives the effect of a three-cell building. The height of the church is out of proportion to its length and breadth, but this was obviously intended by the architect, who accentuated the height by the steep pitch of his roof, and sharply pointed gables. Cormac's Chapel is now dwarfed by the cathedral which was built too close to it in the thirteenth century, replacing an earlier one of 1169. When the church was built its only important neighbour was the Round Tower, but there was probably a low building (perhaps the church mentioned in the annals as existing in the eleventh century) immediately to the west which prevented the architect from making the usual west doorway. It is now so hemmed in by the later structures that its magnificent main entrance, the north porch, is in a cul-de-sac.

The nave is 26 feet 6 inches by 17 feet 9½ inches internally, with outside entrances on its north and south walls; the chancel is 13 feet 6½ inches by 10 feet 10½ inches. The total internal length of the chapel is 46 feet 9 inches. Because of the recess in the east wall of the chancel there is no east window; the recess is lit by small loops in its north and south walls. Originally there were three windows in the west wall, but these were blocked up in the thirteenth century when the cathedral was built. The little church has no aisles, but the architect decorated its north and south walls with two storeys of blind arcading. The nave has a heavy tunnel-vault supported by its massive walls, and further strengthened by plain transverse arch ribs springing from the engaged half-columns of the upper arcade; these columns stand on a shelf which projects above the top of the lower arcade.

The blind arcading continues in the chancel, but here the roof is rib-vaulted. It is now generally agreed that rib-vaulting was first used in Europe in the choir of Durham Cathedral, England, where building commenced in 1093. The rib-vaulting of the Durham choir was completed in 1104 and that of the nave in 1133. The new technique spread rapidly, the architect of Cormac's Chapel was still well in the vanguard in employing it for his building, completed by 1134.

He also had to solve the structural problem of supporting the great weight of the heavy, steeply pitched stone roof. He did this by making a chamber above the tunnel-vault of the nave, so that its walls help to sustain the roof.

It has been often stated that this 'double-roof' was an architectural device already well known in Ireland at the time, and perfected here by the builder of Cormac's Chapel.

The pinpointing of its first appearance in Ireland seems to hinge largely on the correct dating of the building known as 'St Columcille's House' at Kells, Co. Meath. This three-storey stone building was part of the monastic foundation, used as a residence as well as an oratory. Champneys considered its 'double-roof' the ancestor of the one at Cormac's Chapel, but expressed doubts about the antiquity of the building.[39] The usually authoritative Dr Leask rather surprisingly asserted that St Columcille's House is the church of Kells mentioned in the annals as having been completed in 814.[40] Despite the Irish predilection for small churches, this little building, whose internal measurements are only 19 feet by 15 feet 5 inches, can hardly be the one referred to by the annalists as the 'great church of Kells'. The annals record many fires at Kells: the great stone church was burned in 1060, and Kells and its churches in 1095 ('Cennanus cona templait . . . cremate sunt');[41] Kells was again reduced by fire in 1099 and 1111; in 1135 (the year after the consecration of Cormac's Chapel) Kells and many other churches were destroyed by fire ('ab igne dissipatae sunt').[42] It is reasonable to conclude that St Columcille's House was built after this last destruction, possibly for use when the synod was held at Kells in 1152.

It is true that the 'double-roof' of Cormac's Chapel is the more skilful construction; the stone slabs of the outer roof are carried on a regular pointed arch in the upper walls. The arrangement at Kells is cruder, the chamber above the tunnel-vault being divided into compartments by two transverse walls which support the outer roof. But rather than representing the perfection of a vernacular device, Cormac's Chapel may be regarded as the prototype in Ireland, crudely imitated elsewhere by less-skilled masons.

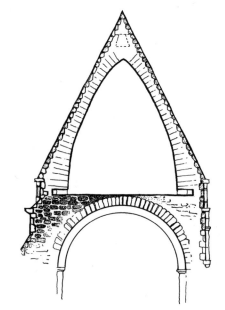

Section of roof of Cormac's Chapel.

St Mochta's Oratory, Louth, Co. Louth.

Section of St Mochta's Oratory, Louth.

Other surviving examples of the 'double-roof' in Ireland, such as St Kevin's Church, Glendalough, Co. Wicklow, St Flannan's Oratory at Killaloe, Co. Clare, and St Mochta's Oratory at Louth, are not earlier than the twelfth century, and there is no reason to believe that any of them antedate Cormac's Chapel. The device continued to be used in Ireland in succeeding centuries; there is a surviving thirteenth-century example in St Doulagh's Church, Co. Dublin.

Cormac's Chapel must have created a great impression when it was built. Being at the centre of Church affairs for the south of Ireland, it was seen by many, who tried to emulate it. Liam de Paor has traced the architectural ancestry of several churches back to it.[43]

Externally, Cormac's Chapel is elaborately embellished. Blind arcading is used profusely, as at Murbach; on the south elevation are three storeys of this arcading, above which is a fourth of engaged half-columns supporting the eaves-course. There is also blind arcading on the towers, which are not identical. The south tower, 10 feet square, is the smaller, housing the belfry and a stair which leads to the chamber above the nave. The north tower, which has a pyramidal stone roof, contained five or possibly six storeys, of which the top three could have been store-rooms as they had no light. This tower has an outside entrance on the ground floor in its east wall, and an elaborate internal doorway in its south wall, communicating with the nave.

The principal of the two entrances to the chapel was the imposing porch on the north side, not the much less elaborate south doorway now in use. The masons increased the thickness of the north wall from 3 to 9 feet to allow for the deep recessing of the magnificent doorway. The opening is rectangular, and thus in the space between the head of the opening and the curve of the arch a tympanum is created. In it is a carving of a small centaur aiming his arrow at a large couchant lion, whose tail with a neatly braided tuft curls up between his legs on to his back. This tympanum and the two inner arch-rings are supported by three orders of jambs; the soffit-arch and the two outermost arch-rings each have their own supporting pillars. The keystone of this ornate arch is a human head; above it is a pedimented gable whose members are carved with running chevrons and rosettes between the vertical bands of moulding. Carved tympana are also found in Norman churches in England and Scotland. One at Ribbesford, Worcestershire, depicts an archer shooting a large fowl; at Stoke-sub-Hamdon, Somerset, a centaur shoots an arrow at a monster.

The interior decorative treatment is lavish; remnants of colour indicate that much of the carving

Cormac's Chapel, Cashel, Co. Tipperary. Above, tympanum of north door; below, north door.

was once painted. The chancel arch is composed of four orders: shallow double colonnettes form the piers of the outermost arch-ring; the piers of the next have human heads carved on their splays; those of the next again are engaged twisted columns, while the innermost piers have engaged columns at the angles. On the voussoirs of the chancel arch are carved naturalistic human heads with high cheek-bones and sharp noses. Another semicircle of human heads is carved over the arch at the east end of the chancel, and the ribs of the chancel vaulting are decorated with human masks. There is a triple-bay blind arcade in the altar recess at the east end of the chancel. Three types of capital are found on the columns of the arcades and arches: the plain cushion capital (a basic Romanesque element found, for example, in the crypt of Canterbury Cathedral, and at Durham, and indeed widely used); the capital carved with human or animal heads; and the scalloped capital with variations.

A ruined church with decorative affinities with Cormac's Chapel overlooks Smerwick Harbour, Co. Kerry, at Kilmalkedar (pl. II, p. 18). It is altogether a more modest project; there is no external decoration save a stone winged finial at the roof-ridge, as in earlier churches, and animal heads at the termination of the antae which, curiously, continue part of the way up the sides of the west gable. The edifice appears originally to have consisted of a single chamber (the present nave, 27 feet 3 inches by 17 feet 3 inches), with a projecting recess at its east end, like the one off Cormac's Chapel. This recess was demolished (traces of it can still be discerned) and replaced by a chancel. The decoration of the north and south walls of the nave is very similar to the upper storey of blind arcading in the nave of Cormac's Chapel. At Kilmalkedar the blind arcading consists of a colonnade of five engaged half-columns with Tuscan bases, cushion capitals and billet-moulded abaci. These columns once supported a barrel-vault, traces of which can be detected. Above this was a steeply pitched stone roof laid in regular horizontal courses of stones, each cut neatly so as to overlap the course below like a tiled roof. The west doorway has slightly inclined jambs, so that the opening is $2\frac{1}{2}$ inches narrower at the top than at the ground. As at Cormac's Chapel there is a tympanum between the flat-headed opening and the arch, but here it is not decorated. The arch-rings are sculpted with chevrons, their zigzags in different planes; the hood-moulding above them has bead decoration, and its imposts are sculpted with beasts' heads.

Another church with elements deriving from Cormac's Chapel is St Cronan's at Roscrea, Co. Tipperary. Only the west façade survives, but this suffices to show its architectural debt. The doorway

Cormac's Chapel, chancel and chancel arch.

St Cronan's Church, Roscrea, Co. Tipperary, façade.

is set in a shallow projecting porch which has a steep gable. The antae formed by the projecting north and south walls are ingeniously treated as pilasters, and have moulding; they are thus integrated with the decorative ensemble of the façade. Between the antae and the doorway on each side are two bays of blind arcading divided by pilasters, with moulded angles, and gabled hood-mouldings over the arches. The whole gives an effect of balance and unity. In the gable above the doorway a standing figure of a cleric is carved, flanked by rosettes; this is reminiscent of the bold projecting vertical moulding flanked by rosettes in the gable of the north porch of Cormac's Chapel.

There is another of these Romanesque doorways in a gabled porch at Freshford, Co. Kilkenny. The original church to which it belonged has long since vanished, and it is now set in the west front of an eighteenth-century church. Like the north doorway of Cormac's Chapel, the Freshford doorway has a human head on the keystone of the arch; the arch-rings rest on pairs of columns with fluted cushion capitals. These rings have a battlement decoration only found at one other place in Ireland – Aghadoe Church, Co. Kerry, built in 1158. In an inscription the builder has left us the name of the founder of the church, 'O'Kerwick' (a Kilkenny family), and also his own name, 'O'Ceannucain'.

A round Romanesque window like the one at Rahan has also been inserted in the eighteenth-century façade.

Aghadoe Church, three miles west of Killarney, was built by Amlaoibh (Auley) O'Donoghue and completed in 1158. The west doorway has at some time been wrongly reassembled. It has slightly inclined jambs, three orders of arch-rings recessed: the innermost plain, the next moulded with chevrons and the outer one with pellets; above these rings is a hood-moulding.

Also in Co. Kerry, at Ardfert, is the church of Temple-na-Hoe. It once consisted of a nave and chancel. The columns at the external corners of the building are unique. Near by is the cathedral, mainly, as it now stands, a thirteenth-century building, but with parts dating from the twelfth century, such as the west wall with its Romanesque doorway and blind arcading which derive from Cormac's Chapel. Here again the cushion capitals, scalloped capitals and billet-moulded abaci may be observed. The doorway of soft reddish sandstone has not weathered well.

St Farranan's Church at Donaghmore, Co. Tipperary, is still another building in the decorative tradition of Cormac's Chapel. It is a nave-and-chancel church, the nave measuring internally 39 feet 6 inches by 23 feet 9 inches, and the chancel

III Killeshin, Co. Leix, detail of doorway (p. 39) >

IV. V Ardmore, Co. Waterford. West front of the cathedral, and detail of arcading (p. 44) >

West door of St Brendan's Cathedral, Ardfert, Co. Kerry.

12 by 8 feet 6 inches; the walls are of uncoursed rubble, 3 feet thick. The fine west doorway has unfortunately been damaged; much of the carving has been destroyed. There was probably once a carving in the tympanum.

Yet another Romanesque church showing stylistic affinities with the decoration at Cormac's Chapel, still farther afield, may be seen at Killeshin, Co. Leix, three miles from Carlow (p. 42). The nave of the present building dates from the twelfth century, probably erected within ten or twenty years after Cormac's Chapel. Three kinds of stone were used for the splendid recessed doorway (pl. III, p. 35) of four orders: fine-grained brownish-purple sandstone, coarse-grained yellowish granite, and a lighter coloured finer-grained granite. The engaged columns which support the arch-rings rise from bulbous bases on square plinths; the capitals have human heads carved at the angles, the first and fourth with curled beards and moustaches, the second and third clean-shaven, their hair intertwined with serpent-like or floriate forms. The pilasters of the first order of the arches of the doorway are also elaborately decorated: on the north side foliage springs from the mouth of a beast (front), and from the heads of small humans who are being devoured by monsters (sides). A mutilated inscription above the lower ledge of the impost mentions a King of Leinster, his name indecipherable; another inscription, on the north shaft of the second order, reads 'Pray for Cellach'.

Christ Church Cathedral, Dublin, has a Romanesque doorway in the south transept, though most of the building is in a later style. Limerick Cathedral has a Romanesque west door which probably belonged to an earlier building. The church on White Island in Lough Erne, Co. Fermanagh, has a simple Romanesque door. A fine Romanesque door is inserted in the south porch of St Thomas, Wicklow.

Often, grand Romanesque doorways have survived where the church to which they originally belonged has fallen into decay. One such was inserted in 1860 into the Church of Ireland Cathedral of St Feidhlimidh at Kilmore, Co. Cavan, as the vestry door (p. 42). It is said to have been brought from the ruined Premonstratensian abbey on Trinity Island in Lough Oughter, three miles away, though O. Davies in his monograph on Co. Cavan churches points out that the evidence that the doorway came from Trinity Island is not absolutely satisfactory.[44] Before being set in its present position it was in the seventeenth-century cathedral of Kilmore. This splendid door, which has four orders of arches and a beaded hood-moulding, has suffered from its moves: some stones have been wrongly placed in re-erecting it. The capitals of the engaged columns of three of the orders are carved with dragon heads. Here, and in

< *VI Nun's Church, Clonmacnoise, Co. Offaly, doorway (pp. 41–2).*

St Mary's Cathedral, Tuam, Co. Galway, Romanesque chancel arch.

Kilteel, Co. Kildare, detail of ruined chancel arch.

the chain pattern of the soffit, Scandinavian influence can be detected. The capitals of the columns of the fourth order are carved with stylized bearded heads, cut off just above the eyebrows; the moustaches and beards merge into interlaced bands issuing from the sidelocks.

Glendalough was an important early religious centre. St Laurence O'Toole was abbot there until he was appointed Archbishop of Dublin in 1163, and several of its ruined churches must date from the period of his abbacy. The most attractive of these is St Saviour's. It is a nave-and-chancel church, the nave measuring 41 feet by 20 feet 3 inches, the chancel 14 feet by 11 feet 6 inches. The decorated Romanesque chancel arch survives, though some of its stones were wrongly set when it was repaired in the last century. The jambs are carved with dragons and a gruesome raven eating a human head; one of the capitals of the piers is carved with a wolf whose tail is intertwined in the hair of a human head.

The quaint-looking little oratory dedicated to St Kevin, the founder of Glendalough, has a miniature Round Tower imposed above the west end as a belfry. This tower, sticking up like a chimney, has earned the building the ridiculous name of 'St Kevin's Kitchen'. The flat-headed west door has a semicircular relieving arch; the chancel arch and chancel collapsed long ago, and only the foundations of the chancel can be discerned. The nave has a barrel-vault with a vaulted chamber above which helped to support the roof (like Cormac's Chapel).

St Flannan's Oratory at Killaloe, Co. Clare, also a twelfth-century construction, likewise has an upper room whose walls help to support the stone roof. It has a fine Romanesque doorway (p. 42).

Killaloe Cathedral, also dedicated to St Flannan, was built about 1185 by Domhnall Mor O'Brien, King of Thomond. There had been an earlier church in which the great King Muirchertach was buried in 1119/20. The beautiful Romanesque doorway, now set in the south wall of the nave, was undoubtedly the main entrance doorway of an earlier church, but it is doubtful that it dates from King Muirchertach's reign; more probably it was built during the reign of his successor, Conor na Cathach. The innermost of its four orders is ornamented with chevrons and lozenges; converging spirals and foliage cover all the enclosed spaces. Only one of its supporting fluted columns survives, carved with lions' heads at the top and lions' paws with human feet below. The next order is carved with animals whose tails are braided into the hair of three human heads, and with entwined serpents on the right-hand pier. These intertwined snakes appear, too, on one of the piers of the third order, and a capital has an amusing procession of griffins each holding the tail of the next. The outermost order has an architrave terminating in serpents' heads.

At Tuam, Co. Galway, the barrel-vaulted chancel of the twelfth-century cathedral survives in the present one, built in the nineteenth century; its Romanesque chancel arch is the most splendid in Ireland. Composed of five orders and a hood-moulding, and each of its five arch-rings is supported by a pair of columns, it spans 16 feet.

A twelfth-century Romanesque chancel arch was partially re-erected at Kilteel, Co. Kildare, about 1935, using the pieces found scattered about the site. It is unique in that it is decorated with figure-sculpture in the tradition of the High Crosses. Samson with a lion, and Adam and Eve appear on the capitals, while the stones of the lower jambs are carved with scenes which include a musician, an acrobat, and a bearded David brandishing Goliath's head on a spear.

The west doorway of the twelfth-century nave-and-chancel church at Ullard, Co. Kilkenny, has undergone alteration. The tympanum has been removed and in its place the innermost arch was added, probably in the sixteenth century. The hood-moulding with pellet decoration and also the deeply cut chevrons in the arch of the Ullard doorway are reminiscent of the doorway of the Nun's Church at Clonmacnoise, Co. Offaly, which according to the *Annals of Clonmacnois* was completed in 1180.

It is not surprising that such an important early monastic site as Clonmacnoise, like Glendalough, should have several old churches. Clonmacnoise was particularly vulnerable to raids because of its situation on the river Shannon. Time and again the Norse raiders and later the Munstermen sailed up the river to devastate and plunder the monastic property. It is related that in the course of one of these depredations the King of Munster violently snatched the head of a king of Meath from its burial-place in the church. According to the annals of the monastery a mouse ran out of the skull and under the mantle of the intruder, who immediately fell sick; then all his hair fell out, and he did not regain health or hair until he had returned the macabre object to its tomb. The Munster raids continued nevertheless.

Close to the marshland along the banks of the Shannon is the twelfth-century nave-and-chancel Teampull Finghin. This edifice has a good Romanesque chancel arch, and at the junction of the nave and chancel, an earlier Round Tower was incorporated into the building on the south side. It is evident that the church and tower are not coeval, for the courses of masonry of the two constructions do not match.

The most striking of the early buildings at Clonmacnoise is the Nun's Church, built a short distance

Teampull Finghin, Clonmacnoise, Co. Offaly.

from the monastic centre and linked to it by a stone-lined causeway. There was a nunnery at Clonmacnoise as early as 1026, but the present church was built or rebuilt after 1172 by Queen Derbhorgaill of Breffny, and finished in 1180. This adulterous Queen,[45] perhaps to make amends for her unfortunate escapade with the King of Leinster (the indirect, far-reaching consequences of which she could hardly have foreseen), spent her widowhood piously. After endowing the nunnery at Clonmacnoise she died on pilgrimage at Mellifont Abbey, to which she had contributed handsomely. The church for the nuns at Clonmacnoise was begun after her husband died in battle in 1172. The Queen, then past middle age, chose the ornate Romanesque style which had been the height of fashion in her prime. Queen Derbhorgaill was connected to the leading dynasties of Ireland; her father was the King of Meath, her mother, Mor, was a daughter of the great King Muirchertach of Munster, while Rory O'Connor the High-King was her nephew, son of her sister, Taillti. Queen Derbhorgaill spent generously for the nuns at Clonmacnoise; the nave measures 19½ feet by 36 feet, the chancel 13 feet 10 inches by 14 feet 3 inches, and the walls are 3 feet thick. The splendid Romanesque west doorway

Four Romanesque doorways: above left, St Feidhlimidh's (Felim's) Cathedral, Kilmore, Co. Cavan; above right, St Flannan's Church, Killaloe, Co. Clare; below left, Monaincha, Co. Tipperary; below right, Killeshin, Co. Leix.

(pl. VI, p. 38) and ornate chancel arch collapsed, but were re-erected in 1865. Missing stones in the arches were sensibly replaced by plain voussoirs. The decorative features of the chancel arch, which has three orders, include boldly cut chevrons, double-chevrons in high relief and fantastic heads. Above the arch is a hood-moulding carved with chevrons enclosing pellets. The hood-moulding of the west doorway is decorated with a serpent, its head to the north, its tail to the south. The first order of this doorway is carved with recessed and beaded chevrons, the second with beasts' heads holding a roll moulding in their mouths; of the third order only one voussoir has survived, and this has foliar decoration on its outer face. The piers are carved with running chevrons which terminate in serpents' heads.

In the ruined cathedral at Annaghdown, Co. Galway, there is a beautifully carved Romanesque window set in the wall of the chancel; it survives from an earlier church built for the Augustinian nuns from Arrouaise in France, to whom the convent (founded by St Brendan in the sixth century for his sister) was granted in 1195.

Sir Benjamin Guinness's generosity and interest preserved the twelfth-century nave-and-chancel Saint's Church on the island of Inchagoill in Lough Corrib, Co. Galway. He paid for the restoration of the building in the last century. The rounded chancel arch and east window are simple and undecorated, but the main west doorway is finely decorated in the Romanesque tradition with heads carved on the capitals and on the outermost arch-ring.

The late twelfth-century church at Dysert O'Dea, Co. Clare, fell into decay; parts of it were built into the present church, probably in the seventeenth century. The exceptional Romanesque west doorway was set in the south wall. It is 6 feet 8 inches

Annaghdown, Co. Galway, detail of carving on a window.

high, and composed of four orders: the outermost carved with twelve strange human heads (one with a long moustache), and a rich ornamentation of flowers, foliage, interlacing and deep-cut chevrons. The right-hand column of this order is octagonal, carved with zig-zags; the left-hand one rounded, its capital carved with a head with interlaced hair. The lancet windows (which were wrongly set in the rebuilding) indicate that the original church was built near the end of the Romanesque period when transitional features like the lancet were used.

Dysert O'Dea, Co. Clare, carving on the west doorway of the ruined church.

The doorway of Clonfert Cathedral, Co. Galway, is considered the crowning achievement of Irish Romanesque work. Liam de Paor traces its architectural ancestry to Cormac's Chapel; its affinities with the north porch of that church and with Roscrea and Killeshin can be discerned. Irish cathedrals were diminutive compared with those in England or on the Continent, and Clonfert is no exception, being only 82 feet in length.

When enlargements and alterations were made to the original church in the fifteenth century, the chancel arch with Tudor decoration was inserted, and the innermost order of the doorway, decorated with a wreath of Tudor leaves, was added. The original doorway is of brown sandstone, while this additional inner arch-ring is of bluish limestone. The five original recessed arch-rings are supported by alternating round and octagonal columns flanked by flat pilasters. The columns stand on square bases, their capitals have square abaci, the edges carved with a running pattern of scroll foliage. Beneath the abaci are rows of little animal heads; an especially fine pair can be observed on the fourth order: one is smiling, the other scowling. The shafts are carved with an amazing riot of motifs, chevrons, circles with pellets, lozenges, chevrons with palmettes, elongated rosettes. The decoration of the arch-rings is equally varied and extravagant. As they recede their soffits are exposed. The first order has a six-petal palmette on each voussoir; the second has dogs' heads holding arris moulding in their mouths, a motif used also at Dysert O'Dea. The decoration of the third order is pateras carved with various rosettes between two rows of moulding. The pateras of the fourth order are arranged in pairs, one on the face of the arch-ring and the other on the soffit. The outermost order has cable moulding curving back and forth in horseshoe-form round circular bosses. A steeply inclined pediment surmounts the arches; it is enclosed by a decorated barge-course carved with pellets and rope moulding. A cone-shaped finial between human heads tops the pediment. Above the arch inside the pediment is a little blind arcade standing on a string-course; each of its six columns is of a different pattern. Under each arch, carved with a floral pattern, is a human head. The remaining space between another string-course and the top is divided into alternating raised and recessed triangular panels. The raised ones are carved with leafwork; in the recessed ones are human heads, four in the bottom row, three in the next, then two and one at the top – all but three bearded.

Clonfert Cathedral was built in 1164, thirty years after the consecration of Cormac's Chapel. In those three decades the Romanesque style had blossomed in three of the four provinces of Ireland. To the imported motifs, Irish masons added Celtic inter-lacing, and also decoration derived from Scandinavian animal-ornament, to make a later Hiberno-Romanesque style.

Giraldus Cambrensis relates that Monaincha Monastery, Co. Tipperary, was a place where no living being of the female sex, either human or animal, might enter without dying immediately. In his time it was granted to Augustinians, and the church appears to date from this revival at the end of the twelfth century. Of the original church, the Romanesque west doorway (p. 42) and chancel arch survive. The bowtell moulding used in the ornamentation is an Early Gothic motif, one of the new decorative motifs to reach Ireland towards the end of the twelfth century.

The *Annals of Innisfallen* record the death in 1203 of Maelettrim O'Duibherathna, the venerable priest of Ardmore, and state that he had 'ordered and finished the church of Ardmore', Co. Waterford.[46] This church, built in the last decades of the twelfth century, combines Romanesque elements with the new pointed arches. It comprises a nave, 72 feet by 24 feet 2 inches, and a chancel, 34 feet 8 inches by 18 feet 3 inches. The entrances to the nave were on the north and south walls, as at Cormac's Chapel; the south door has now been blocked up. As at Cormac's Chapel there is blind arcading on the north and south walls of the nave, but at Ardmore the arches are pointed. The chancel arch, too, is pointed; it has bold moulding and is supported by engaged semicircular pillars on plain bases. The capitals are carved with a variety of foliate designs and fleurs-de-lis. The deeply recessed windows with fluted capitals in the west end of the cathedral are Transitional. The most interesting feature is the arcading on the west front (pl. IV, p. 36). This rests on a string-course and is cut in two places by the tops of two semicircular arches, and in a third place by the spring of another; the niches contain carvings of religious subjects. Besides figures of clerics and bishops there is the popular representation of the devil trying to tamper with the scales in which souls are being weighed, and a delightful Judgment of Solomon. The King is seated on an enormous throne, armed with a long sword; one woman in a long robe holds out the child, another pushes forward with out-stretched arms; to their right a bearded harper plays his little harp (pl. V, p. 37).

Romanesque architecture was not the only foreign element to reach and affect Ireland in the twelfth century. The Cistercians and Augustinians arrived from England and France, and in 1172 the Anglo-Normans invaded the country, bringing social, political and cultural changes.

St Brendan's Cathedral, Clonfert, Co. Galway. Above and below, details of façade and doorway.

CHAPTER 3

The early Cistercian abbeys

BY THE ELEVENTH CENTURY monastic communities like those in Egypt and Syria which still flourished in Ireland had long been superseded on the Continent by monasteries following the Benedictine rule, set down by St Benedict at Monte Cassino in the sixth century. Slowly, however, the Benedictine rule had been weakened, both by the effects of the tumultuous political situation and by certain inherent weaknesses. The monasteries were autonomous and absolutely subordinate to an abbot; as a result the monks were isolated and subject to the qualities of their leader. Monks observed the rule of *stabilitas loci* (remaining all their lives attached to one monastery), so that there was little opportunity for resisting outside interference or manipulation from laymen. Consequently there was a decline in discipline and moral standards. One of the first great reforms to remedy this was brought about by the monastery of Cluny, founded in 910 by William the Pious, Duke of Aquitaine. As the community was directly responsible to Rome, it was not subject to local political interference, and prospered under able and intelligent abbots. The Cluniacs carried out monastic reform effectively in France, the Empire, Italy, Spain and England, with the reformed abbeys establishing close links with Cluny. However, the Cluniacs, a highly aristocratic order, eschewed manual labour and devoted considerable time to ritualistic praying and chanting, and this did not suit all reforming spirits. Other orders developed, motivated by a desire for a return to simplicity and spirituality.

One such order was the Cistercians. In 1098 Robert, the Benedictine Abbot of Molesme, founded a new order in a remote part of Burgundy called Cîteaux (Latin *Cistercium*). Though Robert returned to his monastery, the new community continued, first under Abbot Alberic who died in 1109, and then under Stephen Harding, an English monk who

was abbot until his death in 1134. Stephen, the practical genius of the first years of this new order, laid down its rules and laws. When St Bernard and a group of young Burgundians joined the new movement, this combination of administrative and spiritual genius culminated in a rapid growth of the order all over Europe. By 1150 the Cistercians counted three hundred houses, scattered from Sweden, Sicily and Spain to Croatia, Slovenia and Ireland.

St Bernard of Clairvaux played a dominant role in the history of twelfth-century Europe. His volatile, straightforward character, enormous intelligence and profound spirituality gained the respect of such rulers as William of Poitiers, Roger of Sicily, Conrad of Hohenstaufen and Eleanor of Aquitaine. He was not beyond reprimanding the Pope for too much *actio* in the political and social sphere; his treatise addressed to Eugene III is characteristically outspoken: *Quid fines alienos invaditis? Quid falcem vestram in alienam messem extenditis?* (Why trespass in foreign territory? Why reap in strange pastures?)

The introduction of the Cistercian order to Ireland and the consequent revival of an ailing Christianity there was due to the zeal of St Malachy of Armagh. Malachy was born about 1095. He is described by St Bernard in his biography as 'a barbarian though educated youth, who derived no more injury from his savage lineage than do the fishes of the sea from their native brine'.[1] As a young man he joined the followers of the ascetic Imhar O'Hagan in Armagh, and was promoted to the priesthood at the age of twenty-five.

Despite Cellach's efforts and the Synod of Rath Bresail, the Church was still in a sorry state in Ireland when Malachy was ordained. In the confusion of spiritual and political decay Malachy's qualities could not but be considered outstanding. He was rapidly advanced by his superiors; the Archbishop of Armagh made him co-adjutator in the work of eradicating superstition and introducing ecclesiastical discipline. St Bernard wrote that Irish Christians were either ignorant or negligent of the very salutary use of confession, of the sacrament of confirmation, of the marriage contract. The Irish were partial to divorce; many prominent persons contracted marriages not in accordance with Roman canon law. King Brian Boroimhe, for example, had three, if not four, wives living at one time, and one of these had two other living husbands in Brian's lifetime.

These corrupt practices and perversions of ecclesiastical rule were in part the residue of unexpurgated tribal customs, hereditary abuses, and monastic dominance of judicial affairs. The eight consecutive predecessors of Archbishop Cellach who ordained Malachy were married laymen; the best to be said of them is that they were literate. In St Bernard's words:

> throughout the whole of Ireland there spread that laxity of ecclesiastical discipline, that weakening of corrective authority, that voidance of religion of which I have already spoken; so that everywhere savage barbarism replaced Christian kindness, nay a veritable paganism was propagated in the name of Christ.[2]

In 1124 Malachy was elected Bishop of Connor, and with a band of disciples travelled about Ireland, encountering great resistance, and frequently having to deal 'with not men but beasts. Nowhere had he known such barbarism; nowhere had he found such moral obliquity, such deadly customs, such impiety, such savage laws, such stiffneckedness, such uncleanness of living; men Christian in name, pagan in fact'.[3] During this period St Malachy rebuilt a church (of wood) at Bangor, Co. Down, and installed himself as abbot with ten brethren from Imhar's Abbey at Armagh.

Soon afterwards the Archbishop of Armagh died, having appointed Malachy his successor; but such were the difficulties of disengaging the Comarbship of Patrick from its hereditary traditions that Muirchertach, son of Cellach's great-uncle and predecessor (backed by his family the Clann Sinaich who had monopolized the position for generations), seized the see, and ruled as a tyrant until his death. Muirchertach was succeeded by Cellach's brother Niall (whom St Bernard describes as 'Nigellus Quidam, immo vere nigerrimus'[4] – Nigel, truly the blackest); his behaviour was so discreditable that he was removed by the king, bishops and faithful laity. Malachy, aged thirty-seven, entered Armagh as Primate of Ireland and Metropolitan; as soon as he had restored discipline, he resigned in favour of Gelasius.

In 1139, recognizing that the unsatisfactory ecclesiastical arrangements in Ireland needed intervention from Rome, Malachy set out to consult Pope Innocent II. Passing through England he heard great accounts of the new order of Cistercians, and decided to visit the abbot of the mother-house. So impressed was he by St Bernard that when he reached Rome he asked Innocent II to allow him to pass the remainder of his days at Clairvaux. This request was refused; instead, the Pope appointed Malachy Apostolic Legate for all Ireland. Malachy then requested the pallia for the sees of Armagh and Cashel, but the Pope declared that this dignity must be sought by a general assembly of the laity and clergy of Ireland. On his return journey Malachy again stopped at Clairvaux, leaving four of his companions to be professed Cistercian monks and form the nucleus for a foundation in Ireland.

After Malachy returned to Ireland in 1140 he decided, in the words of his biographer, 'that a stone oratory should be erected at Bangor like those which he had seen constructed in other regions. When he began to lay the foundations the natives wondered, because in that land no such buildings were yet to be found.' St Bernard relates that Malachy's chief detractor accosted him with the words: 'Good sir, why have you thought good to introduce this novelty into our regions? We are Irish [Scoti] not French [Galli]. What is this frivolity? What need was there for a work so superfluous, so proud?'[5] Notwithstanding any local resistance, however, seven Cistercian houses were begun in the 'new style' between 1142 and 1152.

Malachy sent additional recruits to Clairvaux, and Bernard wrote in 1141 advising him to seek and prepare a place in Ireland removed from worldly distractions, like places he had seen in France. Malachy chose a site on the banks of the Boyne, near Drogheda, and was granted the land by Donogh O'Carroll, King of Oriel. The monks who had been left at Clairvaux, joined by French brethren to increase their number, arrived in 1142 to found the monastery. At their head, as abbot, was Christian, a native Irishman. The abbey was called Mellifont (from the Latin Fons Mellis).

The first years at Mellifont were difficult; the French monks quarrelled with the Irish ones. Bernard wrote to Malachy in 1143:

> Concerning our brothers who have returned from that place, it had pleased us well if they had remained, but perhaps those brothers of your country, whose characters are less disciplined and who have lent a less ready ear to advice in these observances, which were new to them, have been in some measure the reason for their return. We

have sent back to you Christian, our very dear son, and yours. We have instructed him more fully, as far as we could, in the things that belong to the order, and henceforth, as we hope, he will be more careful concerning its obligations. Do not be surprised that we have not sent any other brothers with him; for we did not find competent brothers who were ready to assent to our wishes, and it was not our plan to compel the unwilling. Our much beloved brother, Robert, assented on this occasion also to our prayers, as an obedient son. It will be your part to assist him that your house may be set forward, both in buildings and in other necessaries.[6]

Despite the early problems, the success of the new order was astounding. Even before the consecration of Mellifont in 1157,[7] there were daughter-foundations at Bective, Co. Meath; Baltinglass, Co. Wicklow; Boyle, Co. Roscommon; Monasteranenagh, Co. Limerick; Inishlounaght, Co. Tipperary; Kilbeggan, Co. Westmeath, and Abbeydorney, Co. Kerry.

The architect of Mellifont is considered to have been the Robert mentioned in Bernard's letter to Malachy, which implies that Robert assented to go to Ireland because of his special capacity as architect or master-builder.

St Malachy died at Clairvaux in 1148 in the arms of St Bernard. He had been on his way to Rome again to procure the prestigious pallia from Pope Eugene II. These were not granted until the Pope sent his Legate, Cardinal Paparo, to preside over the Synod of Kells in 1152 and grant four pallia to the Irish Church: for Armagh, Cashel, Tuam and Dublin. Thus Dublin finally severed its connection with Canterbury.

The Primate, Gelasius, Archbishop of Armagh, performed the consecration ceremony of the new church at Mellifont in 1157; the founder, Donogh O'Carroll, King of Oriel (who was later murdered and buried in the abbey in 1168), was present with many princes. Muirchertach MacLachlainn, a pretender to the high-kingship, gave 160 cows, 60 ounces of gold and land near Drogheda, while the notorious Queen Derbhorgaill of Breffny gave 60 ounces of gold, a golden chalice and other furnishings.[8]

The kings of Leinster had allied themselves in the past with foreign invaders. In yet another dynastic struggle King Dermot of Leinster (who had abducted Queen Derbhorgaill) was banished from Ireland by the King of Connaught, the then High-King. Dermot crossed to Wales to seek the help of Norman mercenaries in order to regain power. The ambitious and land-hungry Cambro-Norman lords and knights who landed in Ireland with Dermot to

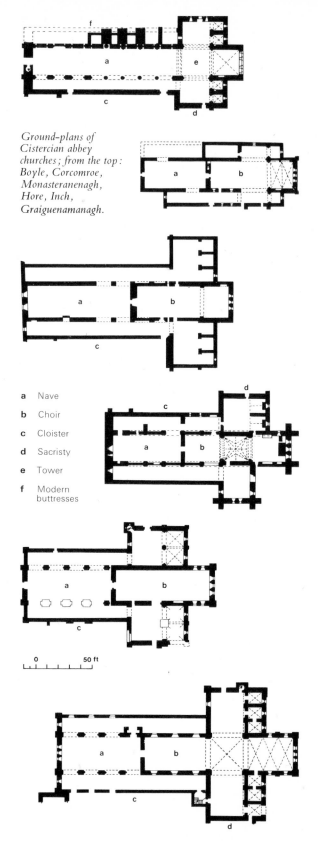

Ground-plans of Cistercian abbey churches; from the top: Boyle, Corcomroe, Monasteranenagh, Hore, Inch, Graiguenamanagh.

a Nave
b Choir
c Cloister
d Sacristy
e Tower
f Modern buttresses

0   50 ft

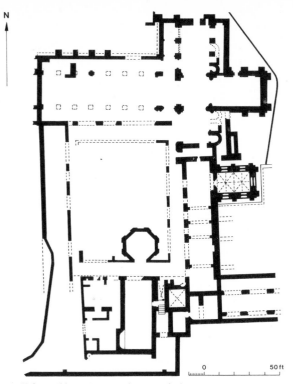

Mellifont Abbey, Co. Louth, ground plan.

Typical Cistercian abbey plan, based on Jerpoint.

a Lay brothers' choir; **b** Monks' choir; **c** Stalls; **d** Screen; **e** Lay night stairs; **f** Processional door; **g** Night stairs; **h** Sacristy; **i** Cellars, etc.; **j** Cloister; **k** Chapter house; **l** Monks' dormitory above; **m** Lay dormitory above; **n** Lay frater; **o** Necessarium; **p** Kitchen; **q** Frater; **r** Pulpit; **s** Drain

make war were the advance guard of an invasion which led to the take-over of Ireland by Henry II, the Norman King of England. In 1170 Dermot married his daughter Eva to Richard de Clare, Earl of Pembroke, better known as Strongbow; when Dermot died the following year at Ferns, Strongbow acted as Over-King of Leinster and kept court at Kildare. Queen Derbhorgaill, whose affair with Dermot had indirectly caused the invasion, had returned to her husband, but he was slain by the Normans in 1172, and she died, a widow, on a pilgrimage, in the abbey of Mellifont in 1193.[9]

The plan of Cistercian abbeys was dictated by the rules of the order; the Cistercians (particularly in their early years) sought to reduce the necessary units to a minimum and, above all, to make the abbey economically self-sufficient. The architect was to strive for utility and simplicity; all unnecessary decoration was to be avoided. 'Leave your body at the door upon entering' was St Bernard's way of putting it.[10]

The Cistercian abbeys of the twelfth century are all remarkably alike in layout. This was due to the practice of following the model of the original community; a chart of Cîteaux's Irish descendants shows the lineage of the houses (p. 50–1). It was usual to choose a virgin site in a remote place with a source of running water for sanitary purposes; a swift-running stream was preferred. It was customary for the highest building, the church, to be built to the north of the cloister, which was the centre of the abbatial complex. This enabled the monks to work or read there, profiting from the sun and sheltered from the wind; the cloister also linked the various buildings. A lavabo was sometimes placed in the cloister, a magnificent octagonal one has survived at Mellifont.

On the east side of the cloister were the chapter-house, parlour, monks' refectory and, above, the monks' dormitory. A particular feature of the Cistercian plan was the placing of refectories at right angles to the cloister-walk instead of along it. On the west side of the cloister were the buildings of the lay-brothers: refectory, cellars (with dormitory above) and garderobes, placed over running water wherever possible. Generally, little remains of the western buildings for they were less soundly con-structed; the lay-brothers were the manual labourers of the community so their lodgings were erected hastily before the other buildings. An outer court contained the guest-quarters, school, granary, brewery, bakery and gatehouse. The only Cistercian monasteries in Ireland where there are remains of these buildings are Dunbrody and Mellifont, which both have vestiges of gatehouses, and Inch, where there are traces of a bakery.

49

Mellifont Abbey, Co. Louth, the lavabo.

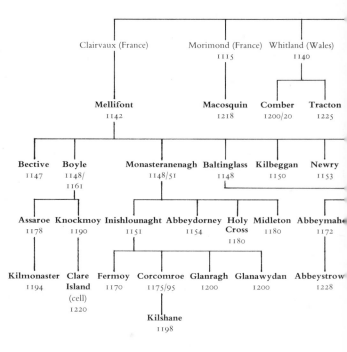

The church was the most important building in the monastic complex; consequently the greatest care and expense was lavished on it. Decoration was theoretically forbidden, and in the earliest abbeys was kept to a minimum. Cistercian churches were cruciform, with transepts and spacious naves with flanking aisles, divided across the middle by a screen to separate the lay-brothers from the monks. There were no aisles in the chancel, but there were two chapels in each arm of the transept. During the day, access to the church was through the cloister area. The monks entered from the east end and the lay-brothers from the west. At night the monks could reach the church directly from the dormitory by way of stairs to the east, while the lay-brothers had a convenient stair from their dormitory to the church at the western extremity of the south aisle. At services monks and lay-brothers occupied wooden stalls built along the sides of the nave, against low walls laid between the pillars which separated the nave from the aisles.

The square-ended chancel, a feature of Burgundian architecture, found easy lodgement in Ireland where rectangular nave-and-chancel churches were the norm. The only appearance of the continental apsidal chapel is in the twelfth-century church of Mellifont, probably introduced by the French builder-monk Robert. Until the revivals of centuries later there are no other examples. Another feature peculiar to Irish Cistercian churches is the placing of the clerestory windows over the pillars of the nave,

rather than over the arches. This may have been done to keep down the height of the walls, though the effect is hardly noticeable.

Little remains of Mellifont; excavations in the late 1950s revealed the outlines of the early church and other buildings. The ground-plan shows the layout. A crypt was discovered under the western end of the church. A more grandiose church was built over the original one about 1225, and the earlier apsidal chapels were eliminated. The lavabo, erected in 1200, is a very beautiful construction for so mundane a purpose, and testifies to the abbey's wealth at that time; although it has the older Romanesque rounded arches, the delicate foliar decoration of the capitals and the effortless handling of the mouldings bespeak the Transitional style. A small part of the cloister, which dates from the original foundation, has been reconstructed. The vaulted chapter-house to the east of the lavabo was built in the fourteenth century.

Baltinglass, Co. Wicklow, was colonized from Mellifont in 1148 by Dermot, King of Leinster.[11] Little remains of the church except the south arcade of the choir and nave. Originally it consisted of a nave with aisles, chancel and transept, probably completed about 1170. The pillars of the south arcade are alternately round and square; the capitals are carved with Irish motifs.

Jerpoint, Co. Kilkenny, settled from Baltinglass,[12] has the most complete remains of a Cistercian community in Ireland. The plan shows the characteristic

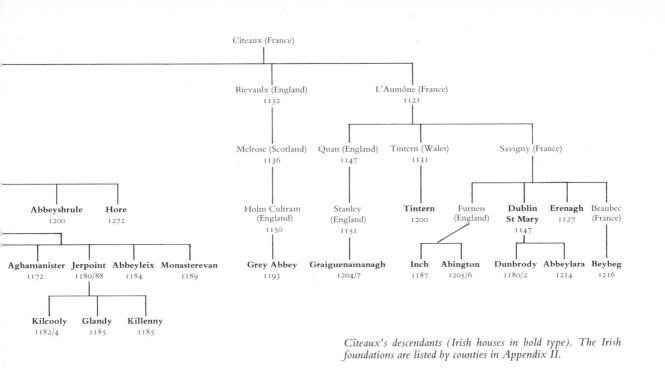

Citeaux (France)

Rievaulx (England) 1132 — L'Aumône (France) 1121

Melrose (Scotland) 1136 — Quan (England) 1147 — Tintern (Wales) 1131 — Savigny (France)

Abbeyshrule 1200 — **Hore** 1272

Holm Cultram (England) 1150 — Stanley (England) 1151 — **Tintern** 1200 — Furness (England) — **Dublin St Mary** 1147 — **Erenagh** 1127 — Beaubec (France)

Aghamanister 1172 — **Jerpoint** 1180/88 — **Abbeyleix** 1184 — **Monasterevan** 1189

Grey Abbey 1193 — **Graiguenamanagh** 1204/7 — **Inch** 1187 — **Abington** 1205/6 — **Dunbrody** 1180/2 — **Abbeylara** 1214 — **Beybeg** 1216

Kilcooly 1182/4 — **Glandy** 1185 — **Killenny** 1185

Cîteaux's descendants (Irish houses in bold type). The Irish foundations are listed by counties in Appendix II.

Jerpoint Abbey, Co. Kilkenny, the west end of the church.

Jerpoint Abbey, above and below, examples of carving on capitals in the nave of the church.

Jerpoint Abbey, decorative stone carving in the nave.

layout of the order. The eastern end of the church dates from about 1160,[13] though the original three-window arrangement was replaced by the present window in the fourteenth century. The rest of the church was built about 1180, and – typical of this period of changing styles – the arches of the nave are pointed in the Gothic style, while the capitals are Romanesque. The pillars of the nave differ considerably from east to west (i.e. from the earliest to the latest). The first two complete pillars (on the north and south) are round with deeply cut square capitals; west of these, on the north side of the nave, there is a square pier followed by a round one; the next-to-last pier is polygonal, while the last one is compound. The remains of the stone screen across the middle of the nave can still be seen, as well as the low walls which lay between the pillars. There is a strong resemblance between Jerpoint and its mother-house Baltinglass, both in the decoration on the capitals of the arcade and the placement of clerestory windows over the pillars, rather than the arches, of the nave. It is likely that the same masons were used successively at the two monasteries.

The decorative carving on the capitals, especially at the east end of the church, is similar to Irish Romanesque work on crosses, and on parts of the doorway at Clonfert, Co. Galway. Some capitals have flat bands of ornaments, others intertwined ribbons, and one, a band of stylized fleurs-de-lis. The outline of the other monastic buildings, except on the western side, can be clearly discerned, and in some cases a good amount of wall is left. The rooms of the eastern range, consisting of sacristy, chapter-house, parlour and day-room, are relatively complete; part of the refectory can still be seen. The cloister is discussed in Chapter 5.

At Boyle, Co. Roscommon, founded in 1161[14] as a daughter of Mellifont, only the impressive remains of the church are to be seen. Though contemporary with Jerpoint, its style is different. Boyle, and Knockmoy, Co. Galway, have similarities with certain Welsh abbeys – the most striking being with Buildwas in Shropshire, near the Welsh border.

Boyle has the conventional cruciform plan, with a nave and aisles, a transept with four chapels and a square chancel. The arch from the transept into the chancel is pointed, and considerably lower than the rounded one from the nave into the transept. The three narrow English lancet windows in the east end date from the early thirteenth century.

There is interesting carving at Boyle: capitals with trumpet-scallops, grotesque beasts, and human figures between trees, can be seen at the west end of the nave. The corbels that support the arch from the nave into the chancel are finely carved with rope-like bands. Trumpet-scallop was a popular

Boyle Abbey, Co. Roscommon, view down the nave >

Boyle Abbey, Co. Roscommon, capitals in the nave.

motif in western England at the end of the twelfth century; it appears that local stonemasons adapted these designs at Boyle, and at other places in Connaught, such as Knockmoy and the Augustinian abbeys of Cong, Inishmaine and Ballintubber.

Unlike those at Jerpoint and Baltinglass, the nave piers of the south arcade of rounded arches at Boyle are all cylindrical. The clerestory windows are placed over the arches in the traditional way. The north arcade of the nave, built at a later date, is in a more advanced style, its piers composed of clustered columns supporting pointed arches. The two arcades are not harmonious. In a time when building was slow, the decision had to be made whether to continue in a manner which had already become obsolescent (retaining the harmony of the entire complex), or to introduce a new style. At Boyle the latter choice was made. The latest part of the church is the western end; its tall lancet window has affinities with three Anglo-Norman churches: Christ Church, Dublin; St Mary's, New Ross, Co. Wexford; and the church of Graiguenamanagh Abbey, Co. Kilkenny. Boyle was predominantly a Gaelic settlement; all its abbots were Irishmen. The imported English architectural features undoubtedly resulted from the employment there of an English master-mason; R. A. Stalley has suggested that the Christ Church master himself worked at Boyle.[15]

The abbey of Knockmoy, Co. Galway, built between 1202 and 1216,[16] had been founded in 1190 for Cistercians from Boyle by King Cathal Crovdearg O'Connor after his ship had sunk in Lough Reagh with the loss of thirty-six of his men.[17] After an eventful reign Cathal died a widower, in the habit of a monk, at Knockmoy in 1224.[18] As a ruler he had been fickle in his alliances. In 1195 he made peace with the Anglo-Normans at Athlone, but four years later burned their castle and plundered their property. He made peace with his neighbour Cathal Carrach O'Connor, then set out to kill him, but his plan was foiled and he was defeated. He then spent many years alternately plotting with the Anglo-Normans to regain his power, plotting against them, or trying to foil their plots against him. In 1210 he met King John. Despite his vicissitudes the annalists wrote of him:

> the battle-prosperous, puissant upholder of the people; the rich excellent maintainer of peace; the meek devout pillar of faith and Christianity; the corrector of the culprits and transgressors; the destroyer of the robbers and evil-doers to whom God gave good honour on earth and the heavenly Kingdom beyond.[19]

and:

> This just and upright King, discreet prince and

VII Clonmacnoise, Co. Offaly, Dean Odo's door (p. 95) >

Knockmoy Abbey, Co. Galway. Above, vaulting in the chancel; below, detail of a pier in the nave.

justly-judging hero, he who of all the Irish nobility that existed in his time had received from God most goodness and greatest virtues for he kept himself with one married wife and from the period of her death until his own, led a single and virtuous life.[20]

Conveniently forgotten was the incident in 1204 when Cathal captured the King of the Glasfhian and blinded him. To relieve the wounded man's agony a woman was brought to provide him with sexual pleasure; he died soon after.[21]

Founding a monastery was a good way for a ruler to atone; it also provided a quiet retreat after an eventful life, and a burial-place for the family. King Cathal's wife was buried in the abbey in 1217, his grandson Tirlogh, King of Connaught, died at Knockmoy in 1266, and Tirlogh's son Brian died in the monastery in 1267. In 1295, Domhnall O'Kelly, King of the Ui-Maine (a powerful Connaught tribe), died in the habit of a grey monk at Knockmoy.

The church has a nave, chancel, and transept with two chapels. It is of considerable size, measuring internally nearly 200 feet in length and 30 feet in width. The nave is simple and austere, but the chancel has rib-vaulting and fine ornamented capitals. The barely visible medieval fresco on the north wall of the chancel is one of the few surviving in Ireland; it was painted about 1400. The nave has pointed arches and interesting carved capitals, probably by

< *VIII Kilconnel Friary, Co. Galway (p. 97).*

< *IX Ross Erilly Friary, Co. Galway (p. 99).*

Corcomroe Abbey, Co. Clare. Below, detail of base of piers of the chancel arch in the church.

the same school of stonemasons who worked at Boyle. The east wing of domestic buildings with the chapter-house is in a fair state of preservation.

Corcomroe, Co. Clare, was founded by the O'Briens between 1175 and 1195 for monks from Inishlounaght.[22] It is situated in about four acres of good land with lush grass, in striking contrast to the ridges of limestone which surround it; hence its original name, Sancta Maria de Petra Fertili (St Mary of the Fertile Rock).

The church, modest in comparison with other Cistercian abbeys, is 135 feet long and 25 feet wide; the transept is 50 feet wide. It was built about 1200 in the standard cruciform shape with only one chapel in each transept arm; the blocked-up pointed arches of the north wall of the nave were surely intended to communicate with an aisle which was never built. On the south side the nave communicates with an aisle-like appendage which does not run its full length and which communicates on the other side with the cloister. The square chancel has a two-bay ribbed vault with fish-bone decoration, and is lit by three narrow lancet windows. The chapels have good carved ornament including flowers and human masks. Little remains of the domestic buildings.

Corcomroe Abbey, detail of carving in the crossing, and below, on capitals.

Corcomroe, tomb of Conor na Siudaine O'Brien in a niche in the north wall of the church.

Monasteranenagh Abbey, Co. Limerick, pillar and capital.

Monasteranenagh, Co. Limerick, was founded between 1148 and 1151 by the O'Briens, who brought monks from Mellifont,[23] but was not built until 1170–94.[24] The lands were confirmed to the monastery by King John, by Letters Patent of 1211.[25] It was dedicated as De Magio, hence its old name, the Abbey of Mage.

The original length of the church, 190 feet, was near to that of the abbey church of Knockmoy; it is 115 feet wide at the crossing. At a later date a wall was laid across the nave to the full height of the church, thus separating the nave and transept. The original foliar capitals, especially at the crossing, owe the freshness of their appearance to having been blocked up for centuries.

In 1172 Henry II, the Norman King of England, invaded Ireland. He wanted to extend his dominions and had coveted Ireland for some time. He had been preceded by the Cambro-Norman mercenaries brought over by King Dermot of Leinster, and wished to establish his authority over them there, lest they set themselves up as independent rulers of the lands they had obtained. Pope Adrian IV (Nicholas Breakspear), an Englishman, had provided Henry with a Bull permitting him to take Ireland in order to rectify the religious administration and morals of the country.

It is questionable whether the Norman invasion mollified the Irish barbarity or further provoked it. The avaricious Normans were certainly more technically advanced, but they plundered and destroyed churches, desecrated altars, stripped priests in churches and carried off women – hardly the behaviour of moral reformers.

King Henry landed with a considerable show of force. Many of the Irish monarchs swore fealty to him, accepting him as if he were their high-king. These monarchs did not take the matter very seriously, accustomed as they were to centuries of shifting alliances.

Cardinal Viviano, the Papal Legate who had arrived in Ireland in 1171, proclaimed the Bull and urged the Irish chiefs to submit to Henry II. The Cardinal favoured the Anglo-Normans by granting them permission, in time of need, to take victuals from churches where the Irish were accustomed to storing them. This custom, based on the principle of sanctuary, provoked the plunder and destruction of many churches, from which the victors might expect to carry off wool, cloth, foodstuffs and objects in precious metals.

The Norman settlers soon established themselves in the eastern counties and then thrust into the hinterland, efficiently building military fortifications as they went. Eventually they penetrated the Gaelic strongholds in the west and intermarried with the Irish, thus slackening their ties with the English Crown. The immediate cultural effect of their arrival at the end of the twelfth century was mainly felt in the east. Many of the Norman knights were as pious as they were greedy; they built churches and founded abbeys with masons and monks brought from England.

Such a man was John de Courcy, who alternated between destroying and plundering churches in the course of his conquests, and endowing and building new ones on the lands he had snatched. In 1183 he brought some Benedictines from Chester in England and built a cathedral friary for them at Downpatrick.[26] This building was destroyed by an earthquake in 1245.[27] He also brought Benedictines from Stoke Courcy in Somerset and Lonlay in France, for whom he founded Black Abbey (St Andrew in Ards) near Inishargy, Co. Down, and Benedictines from St Bees in Cumberland to inhabit the old monastery of Nendrum. He and his wife Affrica, daughter of the King of Man, also endowed two Cistercian abbeys.

In the meantime, de Courcy made incursions into the west, which, when successful, helped to provide funds for his new abbeys in Co. Down. In 1188 he invaded Connaught but was repulsed; the following year he plundered Armagh. In 1196 he defeated the King of the Cenel-Conail and most of Donegal was at his mercy. Two years later he returned to devastate Inishowen, and on his way destroyed the churches of Ardstraw, Co. Tyrone, and Raphoe, Co. Donegal. De Courcy was eventually overcome by another Norman, Hugo de Lacy, who banished him from Ulster in 1203 and took him prisoner after a battle the next year. Subsequently, de Courcy was released when he crossed himself to go on a pilgrimage to the Holy Land.

The Irish, too, made pilgrimages to Jerusalem in the first decades of the thirteenth century. Aedh O'Connor, a son of the King of Connaught, died on the way back to Ireland from Jerusalem in 1224; Ualgharg, King of Breffny, died on his way to the river Jordan in 1231; Maelmuire O'Laghtnan, Archbishop of Tuam, who died in 1249, was a Palmer of the river Jordan.[28]

John and Affrica de Courcy's two Cistercian foundations were Inch, founded 1187, and Grey Abbey, founded 1193, both in the territory he had carved out for himself in Co. Down.[29] The earlier of the two, Inch or Iniscourcy, was erected on the site of the older abbey of Erinagh which he had destroyed.

Inch Abbey, Co. Down, east end of the church.

Grey Abbey, Co. Down, west door of the church.

It was colonized directly from Furness Abbey in Lancashire. Of the church, built about 1200, in the requisite Cistercian cruciform plan with an aisled nave, only the impressive east end remains. The chancel wall has three well-proportioned pointed windows, the middle one being 23 feet high.

The later foundation, Grey Abbey, was also manned from an English Cistercian community: Holme Cultram, Cumberland. There are extensive remains, built between 1200 and 1230, which show features uncommon to the main current of the Irish Cistercians – not surprisingly, considering that English monks were imported part and parcel to build and inhabit the place. The church was without aisles and had a belfry from the outset. The west doorway has three engaged pillars on either side separated by mouldings (one with nailhead ornament), from which springs a pointed arch. It is like west doorways of English cathedrals of the early twelfth century. There are scanty remains of some of the claustral buildings, among them the chapter-house, dormitory and refectory.

In Leinster, Co. Wexford, two other Norman knights built Cistercian abbeys; Hervé de Montmorency founded Dunbrody in 1180/2, and William, the Earl Marshal, founded Tintern Abbey about 1200 to fulfil a vow made during a stormy sea

crossing when he feared for his life;[30] he brought monks from Tintern in Monmouthshire. After the Dissolution, Tintern was granted to the Colclough family who converted it into a residence. Work is in progress to remove the later additions.[31]

Hervé de Montmorency, Strongbow's uncle, and seneschal of all his Irish lands, was a man of great importance in Anglo-Norman Ireland. His wife, the Lady Nesta, was a member of the influential Geraldine family. After a battlesome life Hervé gave away much of his Irish spoils to the Church, became a monk at Canterbury, and returned to Ireland to be the first Abbot of Dunbrody. His wife's cousin, Giraldus Cambrensis, wrote of him: 'Would to God that with his monastic garb his mind had become pious and he had laid aside his malicious temper as well as his military habits.'

Dunbrody was one of the largest of the Cistercian monasteries in Ireland. Even today, the remains are impressive and suggest the dramatic grandeur of the original complex. The church is 195 feet long and 35 feet wide internally; the transept is the widest of any of the Irish Cistercian churches, measuring 130 feet from north to south. The south arcade of the nave collapsed in 1852, but the north side remains; it is 40 feet high and has five pointed arches resting on plain square piers. Some of the arches retain ribbing

Dunbrody Abbey, Co. Wexford, view over the crossing to the night stairs.

on the intrados which spring from corbels with bent foliate tails.

The four trefoil-arch clerestory windows appear to be later than the very austere east end. They are all placed over the piers, and the one before the easternmost window is a double-trefoil arch supported in the middle by a slender pillar with finely shaped mouldings and delicate ornament (*see jacket*). Dr Leask has suggested that this double window may have corresponded to a pulpit placed below it.[32]

The west front of the church with its impressive three-lancet windows was still standing at the end of the eighteenth century.

Nothing but the outline of the large cloister can now be seen; it measured 120 feet square; some of the domestic buildings survive in a ruined state to the east and south. On the east side, just after the transept and sacristy, was the chapter-house, which had a vaulted ceiling of six bays supported by two pillars; following that is the parlour, and then the underbuilding of the dormitory. On the south side are the remains of the refectory and kitchen. In the cloister can be seen the foundations of a circular lavabo, 12 feet in diameter.

William, the first Earl of Pembroke of the Marshal line, who founded the Cistercian abbey of Graiguenamanagh, Co. Kilkenny, had married Isabel, the daughter of Strongbow and Eva, and thus obtained extensive estates in Leinster. He had been a Crusader, had spent considerable time abroad, in Syria and France, but finally came to Ireland to administer his wife's vast inheritance in 1207. He was present at the signing of the Magna Carta in 1216, was a co-executor of King John's will, and Regent of the Realm (which then included England, Ireland, Normandy and other parts of France) during the minority of King Henry III. He died in England in 1219. As well as the Cistercian abbeys of Graiguenamanagh and Tintern, he founded the Augustinian priory at Kilkenny, and the town of New Ross, Co. Wexford, as a base for the administration of Leinster.

William's abbey of Graiguenamanagh was the largest Cistercian establishment in Ireland; its foundation charter is dated 1207.[33] In orthodox Cistercian cruciform shape, with an over-all length of slightly more than 200 feet and a transept measuring 112 feet across, it had three chapels in each arm. This, as Dr Leask has pointed out, was of cathedral size in Ireland. The layout is identical in size and shape to the church of the abbey of Stratas Florida in Cardiganshire, completed in 1201.[34]

Graiguenamanagh was built at a time when the Gothic style introduced from the west of England was being used at Christ Church Cathedral, Dublin. The doorway from the south aisle of the original church of Graiguenamanagh into the cloister is now incorporated into the Catholic church; it is elaborately carved with roll and fillet mouldings and has freestanding columns in the jambs, details which are to be found for the first time in Ireland at Christ Church. It seems probable that the builders of Graiguenamanagh had the help of the English masons who were working on the Dublin cathedral. The east windows appear to be the forerunners of those at St Canice's Cathedral, Kilkenny, which was built immediately after Graiguenamanagh, and is only fifteen miles away. The abbey is now being restored, and when the rubble is removed much of its decoration should appear intact.

Most of the newly arrived Norman knights tackled the organization of their Irish estates with acumen and energy. The settlement of Church affairs on their lands was an essential part of this reorganization. Hugh de Lacy, who was granted the kingdom of Meath, subdivided it among his knights; one of these, Adam de Feipo, was granted the Barony of Skryne with a fee of twenty knights. When he took possession, between 1172 and 1175, there was a monastery of the old order at Skryne, a daughter-

foundation of Iona, dedicated to St Columba. Unable to gain immediate control of the church of St Columba, and rather than take it ruthlessly by force, Adam craftily starved the monks out. He first built himself a castle and next to it a chapel dedicated to St Nicholas. He then had his younger brother Thomas ordained by the Irish Bishop of Clonard, and gave Thomas the new chapel. Next, Adam subdivided his lands among twenty Norman knights and at once organized a strict system of tithes, assigning all of them to the new chapel of St Nicholas. In a letter to the Pope, Adam de Feipo claimed that he was the first Norman in Ireland to give tithes in this manner, and that his brother Thomas was the first Norman to be ordained and instituted to a church in Meath. To secure the situation Adam drew up a charter confirming his grants, and forbidding his heirs to change them in any way whatsoever. Thomas in turn had himself confirmed in his office by Pope Alexander III. After serving as priest in the church at Skryne for a few years, Thomas joined the Cistercian community of St Mary's Abbey, Dublin, of which he eventually became abbot. By this means the right of tithes of the estate at Skryne, the lands of St Nicholas's Chapel (which included St Columba's Church), and the right of presentation to the chapel became vested in St Mary's Abbey.

This transfer did not come about without resistance; both the old monks of St Columba and two or three of Adam de Feipo's knights objected. Adam complained to the Pope that, though the Abbot of St Mary's had been assigned the key of St Columba's by the Irish Bishop of Clonard in the church itself in the presence of all the assembled chapter, within a week two other clerics had been admitted by the Bishop to the tithes of some of Adam's knights.

By 1192, before Adam's death, the old monastic church was securely in the hands of the Abbot of St Mary's, who appointed priests to perform duties there. The chapel of St Nicholas was passed back to the son of Adam de Feipo. Such events are characteristic of what happened to the churches of the old order wherever the Normans were firmly entrenched. The newcomers realized that they would get more co-operation from the Cistercians and new monastic communities with Norman and English affiliations, than from the Irish monasteries of the old order. Thus they put the ecclesiastical affairs of their estates in the hands of the abbeys of their choosing, where they often had close family connections, and the old orders were squeezed out.

CHAPTER 4

The Transitional style and the arrival of Gothic

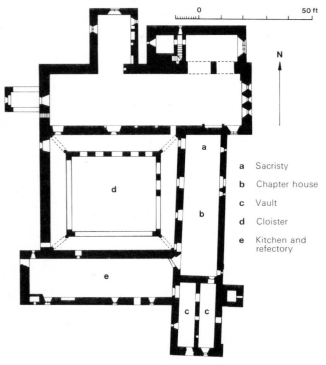

Canon Island Abbey, Co. Clare, ground-plan.

Cong Priory, Co. Mayo, capitals of the slype doorway.

a Sacristy
b Chapter house
c Vault
d Cloister
e Kitchen and refectory

WHEN ST MALACHY visited Arrouaise in France in 1139 he saw that the rule of the Augustinians of that house was eminently suited to most of the old Irish monasteries which he wished to reform. Unlike the exclusive and aristocratic Cistercians, the Augustinians had contact with the people and ministered to their spiritual needs.

Malachy was fortunate in having the support of Turlogh O'Conor, King of Connaught, and other practical-minded laymen and ecclesiastics, who similarly appreciated the necessity of introducing and maintaining a means of canonical instruction. They sought to achieve this by putting monasteries with their dependent churches in the hands of the Augustinian canons.

The King of Connaught founded Augustinian houses at Clonfert, Co. Galway, Clonmacnoise, Co. Offaly, and Clontuskert, Co. Galway. Cong Priory, Co. Mayo, was founded by his son Rory for the Arrouasian house of St Mary the Virgin. In the remains of this great monastery can be seen some finely finished and elaborate decorative carving. The capitals of the slype doorway form a continuous, frieze-like design which incorporates foliage that is related (though indirectly and by way of France) to the classical acanthus. The Transitional appearance of the doors in the cloister range dates them to the first two decades of the thirteenth century.

Unlike the Cistercians, the Augustinians did not adhere to a single plan in building their abbeys. Canon Island, Co. Clare, was founded in 1189 by the indefatigable church-builder Domhnall Mor O'Brien, King of Thomond, who died in 1193/4. This delightful little settlement is on an island in the Shannon. Its church is a plain rectangle 85 feet long and 23 feet wide, with two chapels opening off the north wall. The earlier of the two chapels runs along the main church and is entered by two pointed arches with chamfered piers, typical of transitional styles at this period. The kitchen and refectory lie south of the cloister and are parallel with it – not at right angles as in Cistercian settlements.

Other Augustinian foundations in Thomond ascribed to Domhnall Mor O'Brien are Clare Abbey, Inchicronan, Killone, and Kilshanny Abbey, all in Co. Clare.[1] The present ruins of Clare Abbey are of the fifteenth-century rebuilding. Inchicronan, sometimes inaccessible by land, is a ruin on a narrow lake promontory. The abbey was granted to canons from nearby Clare Abbey in 1189. The church is an aisleless rectangle 66 feet long and 16 feet wide. The east window has foliar decoration on the outside, and is probably of the period of foundation. By 1302 it had become the parish church; later, convent buildings were added, along with a sacristy and south transept. Though the setting of Inchicronan is lovely, the ruins are unimpressive and the modern concrete burial vaults within the church are an unhappy intrusion.

Killone was an Augustinian nunnery; like its neighbours in Thomond it has a pleasant lake-shore position. It is one of the few remaining old Irish foundations for nuns. The east wall of the church has two interesting windows which serve to illustrate a fairly late stage in the Transition: the round arches are antique, the chevron-moulded decoration is Transitional, while the trefoil-headed openings through the windows (which originally led to a roof-walk) are Early Gothic. This window ensemble probably dates from the third decade of the thirteenth century. Building in those parts of Ireland remote from English influence tended toward extreme conservatism; archaic styles and motifs were frequently used.

The abbey of Ballintubber, Co. Mayo, was founded in 1216 by Cathal O'Conor, King of Connaught. The church is aisleless, but with transepts and vaulted chapels and chancel. The repertory is that of the western Irish school of the late twelfth and early thirteenth centuries. The design leans heavily on that of the Cistercian foundations of Knockmoy and Boyle. The round-headed windows in the east end of Ballintubber Church are very like those at Knockmoy, and there are striking similarities between the carved capitals at Boyle and Ballintubber. As R. A. Stalley has demonstrated, the same sculptor appears to have worked in both places.[2] At Ballintubber, however, the more permissive Augustinian rule allowed greater freedom to the carver's fantasy. The church, now in use, has recently been meticulously restored, and gives a fair impression of what a large early thirteenth-century Irish church looked like.

Cong Priory, slype doorway.

Killone, Co. Clare, the east windows.

Ballintubber Abbey, Co. Mayo, crossing and chancel (restored).

Inishmaine, Co. Mayo, carving on east window.

Kilmacduagh, Co. Galway, known as O'Heyne's Church, east windows.

Inishmaine, Co. Mayo, is an Augustinian settlement situated on what was originally an island in Lough Mask, where St Cormac had founded a much earlier monastery. The present ruins date from the early thirteenth century, and the foundation may be attributed to Maelisa O'Conor, the son of Turlogh, King of Connaught. Maelisa is mentioned as the Prior of Inishmaine in the annals and his obituary appears in 1223.[3] In structure the church is small, and of the conservative nave-and-chancel type. The entrance doorway is flat-headed, either preserved from an earlier church or a very late use of this feature. The chancel arch was supported by jambs made up of four slender columns with delicately carved capitals. The hood-moulding of the round-headed east windows terminates in a crude but comical figure of a horseman.

At Kilmacduagh, Co. Galway, the Augustinians had a foundation whose church, named O'Heyne's

Athassel Priory, Co. Tipperary, from the air.

for a local warrior, has elements in common with both Augustinian and Cistercian foundations west of the Shannon. The nave-and-chancel plan is like that of Inishmaine, as are the columned jambs of the chancel arch. The carving on the capitals of these columns is related to that at Monasteranenagh; the bases resemble those at Corcomroe. The east windows resemble those at Inishmaine but are more subtly designed and with superior decoration.

Athassel Priory, Co. Tipperary, was a magnificent Augustinian monastery, built by the Anglo-Norman William de Burgh who came to Ireland in 1177 and died in 1205 after a career of ruthless conquest. His descendants, the Burkes, were continuous patrons of the priory; William's son Walter was buried there in 1208, his grandson Richard in 1326.

An aerial view of the vast ruins gives an idea of the resources of the Anglo-Normans. An outer wall originally surrounded the whole complex, which was entered through a large gatehouse preceded by a bridge over a stream.

The church was built in stages, from 1230 to 1280. It is cruciform and 210 feet long. The choir still stands, lit by five tall lancet windows in each wall. Much of the awesome architectural effect of this building is now lost, as the nave is a complete ruin and the transept arches have been blocked up. The transept appears to have had a tower from the outset. When it was rebuilt in the fifteenth century the nave had already collapsed; the arches were filled in to support it. A beautiful thirteenth-century doorway gives access from the nave to the choir through the screen-wall. The wide recessed arch over the doorway, now blocked up, may have held the great crucifix which provided a dramatic climax to the view up the nave. The fragments of carved capitals found in the ruined nave are of the stiff-leaf design then popular in England.

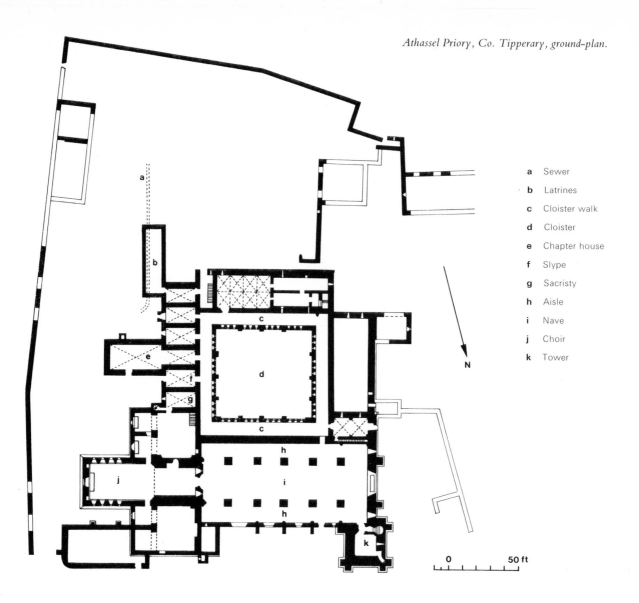

a   Sewer
b   Latrines
c   Cloister walk
d   Cloister
e   Chapter house
f   Slype
g   Sacristy
h   Aisle
i   Nave
j   Choir
k   Tower

0   50 ft

The remains of the domestic buildings are most impressive even in their present ivy-clad state. They are disposed very like those of the Cistercian houses, with a night-stair in the south transept. The refectory lay along the south wall of the cloister, over a vaulted basement. Its grand entrance doorway from the cloister has foliar capitals and chevron mouldings. The enormous dormitory was over the vaulted eastern range, from which emerged the chapter-house. At the southernmost end of the dormitory was a long *necessarium* or latrine.

Of the Benedictine foundations introduced into Ireland during the twelfth and thirteenth centuries the only certain remains are those of the abbey of Fore, Co. Westmeath. A daughter-house of Evreux in France, it was founded by one of the de Lacys at

the end of the twelfth century. The church, built about 1200, is a plain rectangle with a Transitional triple-light east window.

The mendicant orders, Franciscan and Dominican, played a considerable part in the Irish ecclesiastical scene during the thirteenth century. The Franciscans' rule of poverty and their close contact with the people had its effect on their architecture. The churches were simple rectangles, divided into a choir for the brethren and a nave for the laity. Sometimes, as the congregation grew in size, it was necessary to add an aisle to the nave and even a transept, usually on the south side of the church opposite the cloister.

There is evidence that the Franciscans built a church for their community at Kilkenny about

1245 with the help of royal alms.[4] The present remains are of a later period. It is clear that the church was a considerable time in building, suggesting that funds were never plentiful. About the same time, in 1247, royal alms were given to two other Franciscan houses: Castledermot, Co. Kildare, and Waterford.[5] Though both of these churches were considerably altered in later times, what remains of the mid-thirteenth-century buildings suggests the impoverished state of this order. Castledermot has widely spaced single-lancet windows in its north wall and a pair in the west wall; at Waterford, the church (now called the 'French Church') has three simple lancet windows in the east wall.

The Franciscan friary of Claregalway, Co. Galway, was founded about 1240. Like the others, it was considerably altered in later times, but it retains the original widely spaced lancets of the choir.

At Ardfert, Co. Kerry, the Franciscans seem to have fared better. Their church, modelled on the near-by cathedral, is considerably grander than those mentioned previously. It was founded in the 1260s. There remain the impressive five lancets of the east

Athassel Priory. Above, choir; below, door leading into the choir.

Claregalway, Co. Galway, windows in the choir.

69

Ardfert, Co. Kerry, east end of the Franciscan Friary church.

window and the nine trefoiled lancets in the south wall; they are very similar to those in the cathedral.

In the ruined church of the Franciscan friary at Nenagh, Co. Tipperary, there is a row of eleven lancet windows in the north wall of the choir, of about the same date as those of Ardfert; a similar series can be seen in the choir of the thirteenth-century friary church at Strade, Co. Mayo. The scant ruins of the Franciscan friary at Wicklow retain a rather primitive three-light window in the south transept, surrounded by an embrasure on the inside.

The Franciscan friary at Ennis, Co. Clare, was on a much larger scale than most, perhaps because of the royal patronage of Donnchad Cairbreach O'Brien, King of Thomond, who founded it shortly before his death in 1242. The earliest part of the present building is the beautiful five-light east window; this shows stylistic changes which were to find completion in windows such as those at Kilmallock, Co. Limerick, and Kilkenny Friary.

The Dominicans or Friars Preachers are recorded in Ireland as early as 1224, only three years after the death of their founder St Dominic.[6] In 1243, Archbishop MacKeilly founded a priory for them at Cashel, just below the Rock. What remains of the church is of the usual friars' type, a long rectangle without division between choir and nave.

Another early Dominican foundation was at Athenry, Co. Galway, in the 1240s. The church is considerably altered and its most salient features are of a later period. However, the lancet windows in the north wall of the choir are from the original building founded by Milo de Bermingham who was buried there in 1252.

The church of the Dominican friary at Roscommon is mentioned in the *Annals of Loch Cé* as being consecrated in 1257. Its founder, Felim O'Connor, King of Connaught, was buried there in 1265; his tomb-effigy is one of the most remarkable features of the church; it, and the contemporary figure of Prince Conor na Siudaine O'Brien in the church at Corcomroe Abbey, Co. Clare, are the only early Irish royal monumental effigies extant. Several lancet windows remain in the south wall of the nave overlooking the cloister.

The lancet windows of the Dominican friary church at Sligo are well preserved; eight of them, with sandstone trimmings, remain in the south side of the choir. This friary was founded in 1252 by Maurice Fitzgerald, who had been Justiciary of Ireland.

Lorrha, Co. Tipperary, is the site of a Dominican friary with a church built in 1269. This, again, has lancet windows in the choir, with a later variation on this theme: there are six pairs of lancets with a deep single embrasure on the inside for each pair.

The same variation as at Lorrha can be found in the church of the Dominican friary at Rathfran, Co. Mayo, founded in 1274. The use of lancets in a row reaches its most developed form at Kilmallock, Co. Limerick, where the Dominican priory was founded in 1291. The choir, which ends with a great five-lancet window (in a rounded embrasure) has six pairs of lancets which were originally mullioned and had intersected-line tracery.

Little remains to show what the churches were like of the other orders in the thirteenth century. The Carmelites, who appeared about 1260, had as many as twenty-four houses, but nothing remains of them.[7] A branch of the Augustinians called the 'Fratres Cruciferi' or 'Crutched Friars' undertook the work of running hospitals and guest-houses, built along the same lines as the ordinary Augustinian monasteries, but with special facilities for caring for the sick and infirm. Some scant remains of such a foundation can be seen at Newtown Trim, Co. Meath.

Another order which founded monasteries in Ireland during the thirteenth century was that of the Premonstratensians (from Prémontré in France). Of the monastery founded for them at Tuam, near the cathedral (by the Anglo-Norman Burkes of Connaught), little remains except the Transitional east window with three sharply pointed lights. The middle one is decorated with chevron moulding.

Sligo 'abbey', Co. Sligo, windows in the south wall of the choir.

Lorrha, Co. Tipperary, windows in the choir.

Temple Iarlath, Tuam, Co. Galway, east window.

The appearance of these windows suggests a building date about 1230.

Another Premonstratensian foundation was on Trinity Island, in Lough Key, Co. Roscommon; the priory was founded in 1217/18 directly from Prémontré. The abbey was founded sometime later, about 1235.[8] The Premonstratensians set up their houses in a manner similar to the Cistercians, with many affiliated offshoots.

The doomed Knights Templars and their successors the Hospitallers had establishments in Ireland at this time, but hardly a trace of them remains.

The Trinitarian order had one foundation at Adare, Co. Limerick; its remains are incorporated in the present Catholic church.

Cathedrals were built for the dioceses reorganized by the Synod of Kells, 1152. The principal ones were at Dublin, Limerick and Waterford, cities founded by the Norse invaders. The foremost of these, Dublin, was founded in 1038,[9] but little is known of the original aisled building; like Malchus's first cathedral in Waterford it was engulfed by the later building. The Anglo-Normans evidently felt the need for a grander edifice to symbolize their more sophisticated and powerful culture. Under Archbishop Laurence O'Toole the care of the cathedral was entrusted to the Arroasian Canons Regular of St Augustine. Work began just after John Comyn was appointed Archbishop in 1181; he had been a monk at Evesham, so it is not surprising that the plan resembles that of West of England churches such as Tewkesbury, Pershore and Gloucester.

Building at Christ Church was in two distinct stages: first the choir was constructed in Late Romanesque style, then the nave with its Early Gothic design. The cathedral was finished about 1240, but it has undergone considerable alteration. The well-meaning Victorian architect G. E. Street chose to pull down the fourteenth-century choir in an effort to restore the original Romanesque appearance. Fortunately the crypt remains untouched, and from it the plan of Archbishop Comyn's cathedral can be reconstructed. Its most striking feature is the novelty of an ambulatory round the choir; then there is a curious apse-like east end with what look like three chapels leading off it. All this is distinctly English. Unfortunately, little can be discovered of the interior elevation, though the surviving south transept has the typical Transitional double round arches of the triforium with bold chevron decoration, and single round-arch windows in the clerestory.

The capitals at Christ Church show many resemblances to work in the western counties of England; R. A. Stalley recognizes the existence of a definite group of masons from that area.[10] These capitals, both vigorous and imaginative, appear to have been carved in the last decades of the twelfth century; the relief is extremely low in comparison with Romanesque sculpture executed only twenty years or so before.

The building of the choir of Christ Church introduced into Ireland important characteristics of twelfth-century English cathedrals. Among the elements copied, before the full Gothic fashion swept them away, were high-relief chevron design, to be found at Ballintubber, Drumacoo, Cong and Killone, and walls thick enough to allow a passage through them, as at Killone, Co. Clare.

The nave and aisles of Christ Church are among the first appearances of pure Gothic style in Ireland. They were begun about 1212 and finished about 1235. Not only the design, but the actual fabric is West of England: the craftsmen employed probably came from the region of the Bristol Channel or the Severn Valley, and the exact source of the building-stone was Dundry near Bristol. Transportation was not a serious problem, with easy loading at Bristol and unloading at Dublin up the Liffey. Bringing over English stone gave the masons the advantage of working with an accustomed material. Moreover it was just as practical to bring stone by sea from England to Dublin as to venture into the wilder parts of Ireland to quarry it and transport it overland.

In the nave the Early Gothic arrangement has been scaled down. The entire wall-space is divided in half horizontally by a string-course, and into five vertical bays. In the lower half, soaring pointed arches spring from massive piers composed of clustered columns with stiff-leaf capitals, carved with animated heads that peer out from the foliage. The

Christ Church Cathedral, Dublin. Opposite, north wall of nave. Below, capital in the nave arcade.

upper half has a most ingenious design: the clerestory and triforium are incorporated into one large unit encompassed by a pointed arch: slender black marble shafts rise from the level of the string-course joining the triple arches of the triforium with the clerestory above. The over-all effect is serene and poised, and despite its English derivation, strikingly original.

The arrangement in Christ Church has its nearest parallel in the abbey church of Pershore, Worcestershire. The English church, however, lacks the triforium, and the effect is somewhat awkward, with greatly emphasized verticality. The Dublin solution is at once richer and more lyrical.

Leask suggests that the contemporary construction of St Patrick's Cathedral in Dublin inspired a feeling of competition in the Augustinians at Christ Church: 'It is as if the Augustinians – lacking space on the restricted city site for a church on the grand scale of its rival – determined to adorn their buildings in a more sumptuous fashion.'[11]

While few Irish cathedrals are bigger than the parish church of an English market-town, Dublin had two sizeable cathedrals. St Patrick's Cathedral, built on the site of an earlier church outside the city walls, was founded as a collegiate church by Archbishop Comyn. Collegiate churches, an expression of medieval piety, were founded for colleges of secular canons under the jurisdiction of the diocese; the work of these priests was to minister to the laity.

Archbishop Comyn's successor raised St Patrick's to cathedral status. At that time, Christ Church was a monastic establishment; the English Archbishop saw in a secular community, one more manageable, more likely to promote the English interest, and generally more suitable as a metropolitan cathedral.

St Patrick's, the largest ancient Irish cathedral, begun about 1220, appears to have been finished about 1254, the year of its consecration. The Lady Chapel was not completed until 1270. Though roughly contemporary with Christ Church (1181–1240), St Patrick's is different in plan. This may well have been deliberate in view of the competitive spirit mentioned above.

Because St Patrick's was constructed without any significant halts, its style is altogether more homogeneous than that of its rival up the hill. Unfortunately, the building has suffered many vicissitudes over the centuries. Not the least disastrous of these was the Victorian restoration financed by Sir Benjamin Guinness and criticized at the time by serious ecclesiologists. Tourists and worshippers today are reminded of his interest in early Irish architecture by a robust statue of the benevolent brewing magnate outside the south-west porch. More Guinness funds were donated to the cathedral for repairs to the fabric in 1900, by Lord Iveagh.

The north and east walls of the choir, the east wall and east aisle of the south transept, and the three eastern bays of the north aisle of the nave, are much as they were when completed 1220–54.

The nave elevations of the two cathedrals are in strong contrast. The triforium-clerestory arrangement is more orthodox in St Patrick's, where the two stages are kept separate. The design may derive from that of the choir of Worcester Cathedral, completed in 1231.

As building progressed on St Patrick's the design was simplified. This may have been a result of insufficient funds, or of impatience on the part of ecclesiastical authorities to complete the church. In the transept the piers were simplified and the number of arch mouldings reduced; as construction reached the nave, the whole design became even more austere. Because of its simplicity St Patrick's had more influence than the more aesthetically pleasing Christ Church, for it was a convenient prototype; but these two Dublin churches remained unique as entities in Ireland, being more lavish than any other thirteenth-century churches in the country, with ambulatories in the choir, three-stage elevations and stone rib-vaults.

St Patrick's Cathedral, Dublin, north wall of nave.

Waterford old cathedral, the south-east prospect as it appeared in 1739.

The old cathedral of Waterford was regrettably demolished in 1770 by the Bishop, who, alarmed by falling masonry on which he stumbled, allowed the whole fabric to be pulled down. This was the second cathedral on the site, the successor to Malchus's eleventh-century edifice. It was probably built at the end of the twelfth century. In 1212 King John endowed Waterford Cathedral for the support of twelve canons and twelve vicars. In the present Church of Ireland cathedral, which stands on the site, there is a scale model of the medieval building based on old drawings and descriptions. Engravings in Ware's *History of the Bishops of Ireland*, published before the demolition of the old cathedral, show it as a long nave-and-chancel building, without a crossing, but with a tall tower where the north transept would normally be. Clustered round the main building and attached to it were a later parish church and a number of chapels.[12] An old drawing of the interior gives evidence of its derivation from the West of England; the arcade-triforium unit is enclosed in a larger arch. The old cathedral was similar in plan and design to Christ Church, Dublin, though smaller and less elaborate.

The cathedral of St Mary, Limerick, was founded by the church-building King of Thomond, Domh-nall Mor O'Brien. Work on the original building was completed by 1207, the major construction probably having taken place in the period 1180–95.[13] The plan of this twelfth-century building was strongly influenced by the Cistercians. It is cruciform with an aisled nave and a short chancel not much deeper than the transepts. The aisles themselves had arches (a most unusual feature in Ireland), but (unlike the Burgundian churches of the Cistercians) no vaulted bays. Instead, there were simple diaphragm walls which supported the roof over the aisle. The clerestory has rather archaic-looking small rounded windows over both piers and arches.

Later additions of chapels, and the lengthening of the chancel, have all but smothered the original structure, while the Romanesque west door was unhappily 'restored' in the last century.

Not surprisingly, there are similarities between Limerick Cathedral and the Cistercian monastery founded at Corcomroe, Co. Clare, by Domhnall Mor O'Brien. Both churches have sharply pointed nave arcade arches springing from bulky square piers with transitional capitals.

At Killaloe, Co. Clare, the founding of the cathedral has also been ascribed to Domhnall Mor O'Brien. In 1185 the *Annals of the Four Masters* record

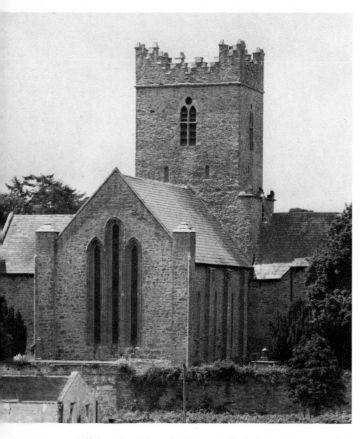

Killaloe, Co. Clare, St Flannan's Cathedral. Above, east end; below, chancel.

the burning and plundering of Killaloe by Cathal Carrach, son of Conchobar Maenmhaighe, in retaliation for the burning of his churches by men from Munster.[14] This earlier building must have been the one founded by Domhnall Mor; the present one is stylistically so far into the Transition as to make its likely date of building 1200–25, long after Domhnall Mor's death.

The doorway of the pre-1185 Romanesque building has been preserved inside the cruciform cathedral, which is aisleless and 20 feet longer than Limerick Cathedral. The three lancet windows in the east end are surprisingly English for a location so far from the Anglo-Norman domain at this time; it is probably relevant that the O'Brien's were on friendly terms with the invaders in the 1190s, and that King John actually stopped at Killaloe in 1197.

The cathedral remains much as it was built, although the transepts have been closed and a glass screen placed across the nave; the vista down the full 150-foot length of the church would be unbroken if not for this addition. Along the chancel, at a point midway up the wall, are carved corbels resembling those at Corcomroe and Inishmaine. The glory of Killaloe is its triple-lancet east window, 36 feet high.

The small cathedral of Kilfenora, Co. Clare, was a simple nave-and-chancel building. The chancel has a very fine east window of Transitional style; generally the building would appear to have been completed about 1200. The three-light window is rounded and framed with moulding. The piers which separate the windows have capitals with carving – one of them representing a group of dwarfed clerics.

A cathedral was built at Kildare in the years following 1223 by Bishop Ralph of Bristol. Of the original building only small portions remain, encased in the present one. The original was cruciform, with transept chapels and a small unaisled nave.

Another aisleless cathedral was that of Cashel, Co. Tipperary, built on the Rock between the Round Tower and Cormac's Chapel. This thirteenth-century cathedral, which superseded one built in the previous century, was an ambitious edifice brought to completion by three successive archbishops: Marianus O'Brien (1224–28), David MacKeilly (1238–52) and David MacCarvill, who died in 1289. It is cruciform, with a very long choir and short nave, like the earlier church of St Mary, New Ross. One of the curious features of the choir is the presence of small windows in the spandrels above the tall Gothic lancets. These appear to have served a purely decorative function.

The cathedral of Ardfert, Co. Kerry, dedicated to St Brendan, now a sadly neglected ruin, was originally a Romanesque building. The larger building that superseded the earlier one was mostly constructed in the thirteenth century; in form it is very like the usual rectangular friars' church. It may owe its origin to the Dominican Bishop of Ardfert, Christian, who held the See from 1252 to 1256. There is a characteristic triple-lancet window in the east end.

The nine lancet windows in the south wall near the east end with trefoiled rear arches form a most attractive arcade. It is easy to see how closely the cathedral was used as a model for the nearby friary.

The cathedral of Downpatrick, Co Down, was a proud Anglo-Norman undertaking, never fully carried out. Already in 1220 the place was in ruins. The thirteenth-century building was the choir of a Benedictine house founded by John de Courcy, who had expelled the Augustinians settled there by St Malachy. Given the size of the choir, it must have been an ambitious project. The present building was constructed on the ruins – a Late Georgian attempt at restoration retaining only traces of the original building.

At Ferns, Co. Wexford, the English bishop, John St John, built an ambitious cathedral during his episcopacy, from 1223 to 1243.[15] The original building had an aisled nave, a transept with a tower and, as at Kilkenny Cathedral which it resembled, a long choir with aisles for half its length.

Cashel, Co. Tipperary, windows in the choir of the ruined cathedral.

Ardfert Cathedral, Co. Kerry, enfilade of windows in the south wall of the chancel, and part of lancets in the east wall.

St Doulagh's Church, Co. Dublin.

Substantial thirteenth-century parish churches, such as those in the Pale, and in the newly founded towns, were comparative rarities in the rest of Ireland, where the people still lived in scattered townlands rather than communities. They continued to use the small primitive churches dotted about the countryside or the churches of the numerous abbeys.

Of the parish churches built, not all were innovations; occasionally, as at St Doulagh's, Co. Dublin, an old-fashioned stone-roofed church with an attached hermit's cell was carefully rebuilt. The old church itself is a vaulted rectangle with an attic whose walls support the steeply pitched stone roof. The tower at the west end of the church contains a number of anchorites' cells built above a ground-floor chamber, said to be the burial-place of the hermit saint, patron of the church. Close by is an octagonal building with a square-headed door on the south side; on each of the other three sides are cross-

shaped windows. It contains a spring, and was probably once used as a baptistery, or it may have been a holy well and shrine.

At Cannistown, Co. Meath, the parish church was most soberly constructed in nave-and-chancel fashion round the chancel arch of an earlier church. The nave has been rebuilt and enlarged, but the chancel, 24 feet long and 15 feet wide, is the original early thirteenth-century construction. The chancel arch has carving on the west side and is plainly chamfered on the east side.

The principal thirteenth-century parish churches are St Mary's, New Ross, Co. Wexford; St Multose, Kinsale, and St Mary's, Youghal, Co. Cork; St Nicholas, Carrickfergus, Co. Antrim (all founded by Anglo-Normans); Killeigh, Co. Offaly; Drumacoo, Co. Galway; Kinlough, Co. Mayo; St Finghin's, Quin, Co. Clare, and Shanagolden, Co. Limerick. Of these, Kinsale, Youghal and Carrickfergus (all with later additions) are in use, as is part of St Mary's, New Ross. The others are ruins.

The grandest of all these churches was at New Ross, where William, the Earl Marshal, and his wife Isabel (daughter of Strongbow and Princess Eva of Leinster), founded a church of cathedral-like proportions about 1210. New Ross had become a thriving port, so it is not extraordinary that such an ambitious parish church should have been built. A cenotaph bearing Isabel's name indicates the interest she took in the place.

The cruciform church was 155 feet long and 136 feet wide across the transepts. The pointed windows of the east choir in particular are fore-runners of Gothic proper. The nave, which was originally aisled, has been adapted and remodelled for use as the Church of Ireland parish church, which occupies all of the ancient building right up to the inner arch of the crossing, so that the transept arms have to be entered separately from outside. The south arm had an aisle with two chapels. The windows have moulded arches with nailhead pattern, ending in carved heads. The earliest parts of the transepts had a dressing in warm pink stone, probably brought from near Bristol. As building proceeded, however, the imported stone was used less and less. Thus the choir has much more of this dressing than the south arm with its chapels.

Another Anglo-Norman port was Kinsale, Co. Cork, whose parish church, dedicated to St Multose, was founded early in the thirteenth century. In size and shape it remains very much as it was: a rectangle divided by a cross-wall into nave and chancel, with north and south aisles and a short north transept arm. An unusual feature for a church of this early date is the tower, contemporary with the original building and, in fact, very much like a Norman keep.

St Mary's Church, Youghal, Co. Cork, windows in south transept.

The parish church of St Mary at Youghal, Co. Cork, was built about the middle of the thirteenth century. Despite restoration and some insertions, there is no essential change in its medieval character. The plan is cruciform, with an aisled nave and a short aisle in the north transept. The aisle arcades have square piers and plain pointed arches; the south arcade has six equal bays, while the north arcade has five and a wider arch to the transept to make up the difference in length. The most notable features of the church, however, are the pointed triple and paired windows of the transept, with hood-mouldings carved with human heads, and the original three-light lancet window of the west end.

Drumacoo Church, Co. Galway, has excellent features in the Transitional style. The doorway in the south wall, of elegant and vigorous design, is related in style to the windows of the Premonstratensian monastery at Tuam. The chevrons on the arch are deeply undercut and have undergone a transformation which makes them hardly distinguishable from their Romanesque counterparts. The capitals, which have a great variety of motifs, seem curiously awkward.

Drumacoo, Co. Galway, doorway of the ruined St Sorney's Church.

The cathedral of St Canice, Kilkenny, illustrates the initial timid approach to Gothic on the part of Irish builders. Hugh de Rous, the first Anglo-Norman Bishop of Ossory (1202–18) began the present structure in 1210, and building continued until 1270.[16]

In plan, the cathedral is cruciform, 224 feet long and 123 feet wide across the transepts, with a central tower. The nave is aisled, and the choir has chapels entered through arcades that run along half its length. In addition to these chapels, there are smaller ones at the extremities of the arms. Thus, the plan bears a certain resemblance to Cistercian abbey churches of a century before. As in other buildings of this date and in this area, much care was taken with the sandstone dressing of windows in the early stages of building, but later on this refinement was abandoned.

The earliest parts of the building are not so confidently Gothic as the latest; the Gothic elements asserted themselves as building progressed from the east end to the west. In the choir there are trios of lancet windows with rounded tops which resemble those at Graiguenamanagh, and may have been copied from them.

The nave is wide and beautifully proportioned, with generously spaced pointed arches supported by composite pillars (quatrefoil in outline) with simple moulded capitals. The clerestory is lit by large quatrefoil windows with moulded surrounds on the outside and deep Transitional embrasures on the inside. The quatrefoil, in fact, is the design motif in the western parts of the building, reaching its apotheosis, as it were, in the fine west doorway.

This doorway appears to have been made by a talented stonemason who worked in and around Kilkenny during the thirteenth century. His work can also be seen in the nave, and in the ruined churches at Gowran and Thomastown, Co. Kilkenny.

St Canice's Cathedral, Kilkenny, view down the nave to the west end from the chancel (left), and the west door (above).

CHAPTER 5

Gothic church-building

THE FOURTEENTH CENTURY in Ireland witnessed a slackening of ecclesiastical building. The reasons are not hard to find in the history of the period. In 1315 the chiefs of Ulster called in Edward Bruce to rule them. He landed in Antrim with six thousand Scots and joined the O'Neills. Marching south, destroying as he went, he defeated the viceroy and was crowned High-King; then he laid siege to Dublin. Eventually he was killed by John de Bermingham and his army was dispersed. The Bruce invasion had perilously weakened the Anglo-Norman rule. Outside the Pale, in the years that followed, Irish chiefs and Norman barons held each other at bay in a series of debilitating skirmishes.

The *coup de grâce*, for any major initiatives in church-building, was given by the Black Death, which reached Ireland in mid-century.

The Gothic style, which had already been introduced into Ireland in the thirteenth century – brought by the Normans and used in their Dublin cathedrals – was not quickly adopted. Throughout the fourteenth century a simple Early Gothic style was the norm. There was never a fully fledged Hiberno-Gothic in the way that there was a Hiberno-Romanesque; at most, certain national peculiarities appear, such as stepped parapets and rather individual window tracery, and some decorative motifs which hark back to earlier Irish models.

Architectural changes can be observed clearly in window designs. The earliest Gothic windows, of the pointed lancet type, provided scant space for decoration. As broader windows were built, what had been the dividing piers between lancets grew more slender, while the stone mullions came to be used as a decorative element in the top of the window, until they separated and became an openwork of stone. Bar tracery progressed, roughly and by various stages, from geometrical intersected-line designs to flowing curvilinear ones.

An early appearance of intersected-line tracery is at Castledermot, Co. Kildare. This Franciscan friary received a generous endowment from the Baron of Upper Ossory in 1302,[1] which enabled the friars to initiate a building scheme, untypical of the order in its magnificence. The choir of the plain church was lengthened and a grand transept added to the north. In this new transept three chapel windows were erected with intersected-line tracery; two of them survive intact.

Intersected-line tracery (or 'switch-line' as it is sometimes known) presented no great challenge to the Irish masons of the early fourteenth century, and became a popular form. Two rather heavy-handed examples may be seen in the south wall of the choir of St Laserian's Cathedral, Old Leighlin, Co. Carlow, still in use as the Church of Ireland cathedral. The large parish church of St Nicholas in the city of Galway has a three-light window of this type in its north transept, built about 1320.

The church of the Augustinian friary at Adare, Co. Limerick (now the Church of Ireland parish church), was handsomely financed by the local potentates,[2] and is one of the best-preserved Irish fourteenth-century churches. Completed in the 1320s,[3] it has a number of small windows with rather clumsy intersected-line tracery, and a large east window with five lights ending in a sombre open-work of lozenges. The plan is that of a typical friary, though the original fourteenth-century building had a narrow south aisle to the nave, rather than the wide one which was added in the following century.

In spite of the innovations in window design, lancets of the type common throughout the thirteenth century were installed well into the century that followed. An excellent demonstration of this lack of enterprise is to be seen in the east window of the choir of the Franciscan abbey in Kilkenny. The impressive composition of seven lancets grouped

81

The Franciscan 'abbey', Kilkenny, east window.

'Black Abbey', Kilkenny, south transept.

together in a single embrasure was built between 1321 and 1323.

The great Franciscan friary in Ennis had a similarly impressive lancet window of five lights within a tripartite composition of great charm and delicacy; it was probably completed shortly before 1306. A contemporary account describes it as being filled with blue glass.[4]

In the Dominican abbey of Kilmallock, Co. Limerick, there is a row of six lancet windows which originally had simple intersected-line tracery – a compromise, perhaps. This group was built about 1300.

The ruins of the Dominican abbey church at Athenry, Co. Galway, contain windows that illustrate almost every stage in the development of tracery, from the mid thirteenth to the mid fifteenth century. The east window was built with an addition to the choir about 1324. It has been reconstructed, and is now a graceless design with four lights ending in rounded cusps and finishing in standard intersected-line tracery. If the reconstruction is accurate, this window represents a clumsy move towards the far more elaborate windows of the north aisle and transept, coeval with the choir extension. The windows in this slightly later part of the church are smaller, but much more skilfully made. The small ones have two lights with intersected-line tracery enclosing elongated, pointed trefoils and quatrefoils. The great window in the north transept was a considerable achievement. The craftsmen employed were highly skilled, possibly a family of masons who spent a good part of their careers working here.

At Jerpoint, Co. Kilkenny, an east window was erected in place of three Romanesque ones (the outline of the two side-windows can still be seen on the outside). This was an ambitious design consisting of three lights with multifoiled heads beneath a large circle with whirling mouchettes. The arch has ball-flower ornament which indicates a date in the first half of the fourteenth century.

There is no documentary evidence to furnish a date for the long south transept of the Dominican 'Black Abbey', Kilkenny, but stylistically its great south window is later than those of about 1324 at Athenry. The window is the largest of its type, with five lights that almost fill the wall. The mullions end in pointed cusps, and within the resultant intersecting lines of the top are skilfully arranged trefoils and quatrefoils, and at the very top, a series of elegant pointed quatrefoils. In the side-wall of the transept are four windows, all of three lights in different designs.

Most building-work during the lean years of this century took the form of improvements, additions or rebuilding. Such was the case at Mellifont, Co.

Louth, where the chapter-house was extended. The extension, to the east of the earlier building, was a complete Gothic room, vaulted, with two bays, the ribs rising from triple wall-shafts. The windows have fully developed curvilinear tracery. At the same time, new piers of clustered columns were erected between the chapels in the transepts.

At Kilmallock, Co. Limerick, the Dominicans added a large aisled transept. This handsome addition has a single cylindrical pillar which divides the two bays with simple pointed arches. The use of ballflower ornament on the capital of this pillar and on the lovely niche near by are noteworthy: this design was rare in Ireland; the only other example of consequence is on the Jerpoint east window. In the spandrels of the niche is some realistic foliage carving – also unusual in Ireland. The charming heads on which the trefoil arch rests are stiff and puppet-like. On the side facing the niche the corbel which carries the arch takes the form of a male bust with hands firmly grasping the moulded top. He is a curious specimen, and, though somewhat defaced, still shows delicately executed buttoned sleeves, carefully combed hair, and hair-band. Perhaps he depicts an Earl of Desmond, gladly shouldering the costs.

At Claregalway, Co. Galway, an aisle with four pointed-arch bays was added to the nave of the friary church. The pillars, as in the Kilmallock transept, are cylindrical, but they have simple moulded capitals.

Some of the building initiative came from the wealthy Anglo-Norman landowners. An instance is the choir added to the Romanesque chancel of St Mary's, Tuam, Co. Galway. The Archbishop,

Kilmallock, Co. Limerick, Dominican Priory church, detail of niche.

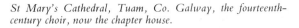

St Mary's Cathedral, Tuam, Co. Galway, the fourteenth-century choir, now the chapter house.

William de Bermingham, who held the office from
1289 to 1312, inaugurated a scheme to rebuild the
cathedral. The choir was finished, but was intended
to be only the first stage of a larger building, for in
that year building funds were solicited for 'the
rebuilding of the church of Tuam begun by the late
Archbishop William and continued by Dean Philip
who petitions for and to complete it'.[5] The choir is
a long rectangle, of very English design, with
buttresses along three sides. The buttresses, which
have weathered offsets with trefoil-headed niches in
the middle section, rise to an arcaded corbel-course
topped by a parapet (a modern restoration). The east
window is five lights wide and resembles English
windows at Exeter Cathedral. The six side-windows
have variations on the design of the large east window,
but scaled down to suit the width of the wall they
occupy. These windows at Tuam are unique, and no
doubt owe their design to the English affiliations of
the Anglo-Norman prelates who built them.

It is more difficult to account for the presence of a
geometrically decorated east window in the abbey
church of Fenagh, Co. Leitrim. The window has
four lights which end in sharply pointed cusps,
surmounted by a circle composed of elaborately
cusped trefoils.

Belfry towers, too, were being added to existing
buildings; few monasteries had them before the
fourteenth century. The Cistercians considered them
a frivolity to be dispensed with (though some early
ones were built nevertheless), and the mendicant
orders at first could simply not afford such expensive
non-essentials.

One of the earliest examples of an added tower is
the 'Magdalene Tower' of the Dominican abbey at
Drogheda, Co. Louth. It is all that now remains of
the priory founded in 1224 by Luke Netterville,
Archbishop of Armagh,[6] and dedicated to St Mary
Magdalene. The Magdalene Tower is divided in half
by a weathered string-course; above this the tower
is slightly narrower. The windows in each storey
are of early fourteenth-century design.

The Franciscan friars in Kilkenny set about building a new tower after they had extended their choir
eastwards in 1321; its construction was under way in
1347. The Black Death struck Kilkenny in 1349, so
it seems likely that the tower was finished before this
dreadful event overtook the community.[7] Smith-
wick's Brewery has grown up around the tower's
graceful form; though this venerable firm respects
the ruins, it would be an improvement if one or the
other could be moved. The corbels inside the tower
are carved with figures bowed in prayer, or cheer-
fully supporting the weight they bear. Each face of
the tower has two-light windows with cusped ogee
heads, quatrefoil centres and transoms.

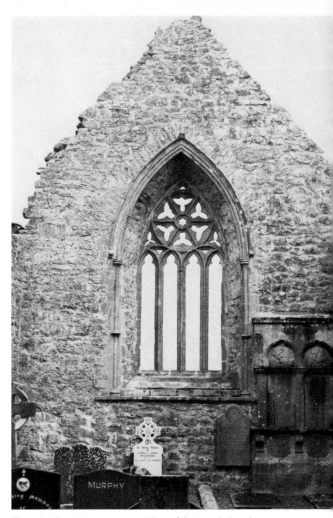

Fenagh, Co. Leitrim, east window of the 'south church'.

In the fourteenth century an unusual, stepped
parapet form was introduced which was to become
popular. An early use was at Kildare Cathedral. The
subject of its origin has been widely discussed; it is
clear that it comes from farther afield than England,
where it does not appear. Similar parapets occur in
south-west France in the Department of Pyrénées-
Orientales, and across the border of Spain in
Catalonia. Dr Leask has suggested that this style was
introduced by pilgrims returning from the shrine of
St James at Compostela.[8]

Whatever their origin, the handsome parapets are
to be seen on many later-medieval buildings, and also
as additions to earlier ones such as the cathedrals of
Ardfert and Cashel, and the parish church of
Gowran, Co. Kilkenny.

After the Black Death in 1348–49 practically no
building was undertaken. A large portion of the

population had been wiped out, and with it a good number of masons and builders. Moreover, abbeys and priories were sacked and destroyed in the course of the numerous conflicts that flared up during the century.

The most important enterprise was St Patrick's Cathedral, Dublin, where in 1372 Archbishop Minot undertook the rebuilding of the four western bays of the north arcade of the nave and the adjoining tower.[9] Work of such scope could only be undertaken at this time by the Anglo-Normans, and even then only in the secure heart of the Pale.

Traditions of stone-carving declined in Ireland during the half-century following the Black Death. The inexpert tomb-effigies of bishops at Kilfenora, Co. Clare, are examples of the rather stiff vernacular style which developed.

The Butlers, Earls of Ormonde, and the Fitzgeralds, Earls of Kildare and Desmond, ruled their vast territories as independent sovereigns, exercising their chiefery over a network of vassals. In Connaught, the Burkes had become completely Irish. Ulster was held by Irish chiefs such as O'Neill and O'Donnell, who, with their clansmen, had regained lands once annexed by the invaders. In the west, the great Irish families like the O'Briens, O'Conors, O'Kellys, O'Sullivans, McCarthys and O'Rorkes were firmly entrenched on their tribal lands, while right on the edge of the Pale the O'Tooles and O'Byrnes held Wicklow. By the middle of the fifteenth century half the country was again in Irish hands, and English authority was considerably diminished.

The English interest might have been held by a strong and efficient central government, but the English monarchs were otherwise engaged. The Scots had no sooner been defeated in 1402 than the rebellious Percys rose in alliance with the Welsh. They were defeated in 1403 and again in 1408. The attention of the Crown was then focused on France where Henry V was victorious at Agincourt in 1415, but the French Wars continued until the English were driven out of all but Calais in 1431. At home there were civil insurrections to be dealt with; in 1450 Jack Cade, an Irishman, with his Kentish followers, succeeded in beheading the Lord Treasurer in London. Attempts at compromise between the rival factions for the English Crown, the Lancastrians and the Yorkists, failed in 1455; civil war broke out and the dynastic struggles that ensued, the Wars of the Roses, continued for the next thirty years until Richard III was defeated at Bosworth in 1485 and Henry Tudor seized the crown. Almost immediately, the new King had further rebellions on his hands: Lambert Simnel's in 1486–87 and Perkin Warbeck's in 1492. The imposter Simnel, a baker's son, had

Tomb-effigies of a prelate (above) and a bishop (below), Kilfenora, Co. Clare.

himself crowned king in Dublin, when he crossed to Ireland during his rebellion.

During this period, the English kings relied more and more on the Irish Earls of Ormonde and Kildare as their deputies. In the course of the fifteenth century, the third, fourth and fifth Earls of Ormonde and the fifth, seventh and eighth Earls of Kildare were at various times entrusted with the royal authority. This resulted in what was virtually a period of aristocratic home rule. Gerald (Garret), the eighth Earl of Kildare, held almost uninterrupted sway for thirty years, and was, in effect, the un-crowned king of Ireland. The loyalty of these powerful earls was often questionable, especially that of the Fitzgeralds of Kildare. The King found it necessary to dismiss his viceroy, Thomas, the seventh Earl, in 1468, and to behead the Earl of Desmond. The Butlers and Fitzgeralds, fortunately for the English, were rivals; they fought in 1402, and never ceased to bicker and forward complaints about each other to the Crown. Dynastic rivalries also divided the Irish. In the north the O'Donnells and the O'Neills were almost incessantly at war with one another, sometimes with allies, sometimes mer-cenaries to swell their forces. The skirmishes between rival clans continued, as well as internal wars between factions within the clan.

Burning and plundering of churches by the Irish had almost, but not entirely, ceased. In the fifteenth century there are reports of the burning of four churches in Co. Westmeath; two of these, Taghmon and Portloman, were also plundered. Four churches were burned in Co. Roscommon, and one in Co. Leitrim. The sacred relics were revered and respected; of these, the most important was the Baculus Iesu, but there were others of note, such as the Crucifix at Raphoe which was credited with shedding blood from its wounds in 1411; it was said to have checked the prevailing epidemic of distemper.

Despite recurrent epidemics of plague, smallpox and a disease which the annalists called 'bed dis-temper', and the political struggles between rival chiefs, the fifteenth century was one of increased prosperity for the Irish. In addition to the wealthy nobles, prosperous new people appeared, such as the *brughaidh-cedah*. These were well-to-do farmers, who wielded considerable influence and authority in rural areas. A wealthy merchant class thrived as well. These people could afford to go as pilgrims to the shrine of St James at Compostela, and many boat-loads left Kinsale destined for Spain. They could also afford to make generous donations to the churches, to endow chapels, and to commission handsome tombs. The Irish nobles lived in a primitive manner compared with their English or continental counter-parts, but not without some trappings of splendour.

Sarcophagus lid now in St Peter's churchyard, Drogheda.

In 1433, Margaret, Queen of Offaly, wife of the Calbhach, O'Conor Faly, gave two huge feasts at which the guests were served both meat and sums of money. Clerks recorded the names of the 2,700 guests, and besides these there were gamesters and poor men. Margaret herself stood outside the great church, clad in cloth-of-gold, surrounded by her dearest friends, clerics and brehons. Her husband remained on horseback to maintain order and see that everyone was served properly. Afterwards, Margaret presented two gold chalices as an offering on the altar.[10]

James Rice, a rich Waterford merchant, was mayor of that city at least eight times between 1467 and 1488. In 1483 he was granted permission to visit the shrine of his patron saint at Compostela; in the same year the chapel he had built on to the cathedral of Waterford was consecrated.[11] In it was placed his free-standing sarcophagus, one of the finest medieval tombs in Ireland. On the top, or *mensa*, James Rice is represented as a decaying corpse with a toad and slimy creatures to heighten the gruesome effect. Round the base of the tomb are saints in niches. Their names are inscribed above their effigies on the chamfered edge.

Another of these macabre *memento mori* tombs is now in the churchyard of St Peter's, Drogheda, Co. Louth. The lid of the sarcophagus was removed from the medieval church when the taste for such things had vanished. The tomb was erected for Edward Golding and his wife, who are represented as skeletons in rippling shrouds, tied at the top and toe. This preoccupation with the stages of bodily decay was a phenomenon of medieval life that cannot be entirely explained, but the Black Death in the previous century no doubt had an influence. Plague, disease or violent death could fall on anyone at any moment, and it was considered prudent to keep this in mind by graphic images. The Church had always preached the transience of mortal things; it appears that this later-medieval society, jaded with images of hell and damnation, was sometimes content only with the tangible effects of physical corruption. There is another of these cadaver tombs at Beaulieu, Co. Louth.

Not all tomb monuments of the time, however, depict their occupants in such a morbid way. It was more usual to be represented in a form which commemorated high repute and achievements.

A very early fifteenth-century tomb (or it may conceivably be late fourteenth century) is that of the O'Cahan chieftain Cooey-na-Gal, who died in 1385. It was erected in the chancel of the priory church at Dungiven, Co. Derry, an establishment associated with the O'Cahan family, who had their stronghold there. The deceased is represented lying full-length on a slab above six trefoil-arched niches containing figures of gallowglasses. The canopy has superb curvilinear tracery.

At Kilconnell, Co. Galway, there are two fine fifteenth-century tomb-niches. The earlier of these has a canopy with bold geometrical tracery and a simple base. The second and later one has flamboyant tracery on the canopy, and six ogee-headed niches with figures of St John, St Louis, the Blessed Virgin, St John the Baptist, St James and St Denis. Both the tracery and the choice of saints suggest French influence; there are other examples of this in Connaught, possibly due to the wine trade through the port of Galway. On this tomb the carved angels in various states of hilarity suggest a less gloomy attitude to life beyond the grave.

At Strade, Co. Mayo, in the north wall of the chancel of the Dominican friary, is another example of a tomb-niche with Flamboyant Gothic tracery. This tomb is one of the most beautiful in the country. The frontal slab is exuberantly carved with eight

Tomb-niche at Strade, Co. Mayo.

ogee-headed niches, similar to, but more accomplished than, those at Kilconnell. The figures sculpted in the panels cannot all be satisfactorily identified. In the left-hand panel are four persons wearing crowns; three of these appear to be the Magi, while the fourth is Christ displaying his wounds. In the right-hand panel is a kneeling figure, probably the deceased (who appears to be dressed in the habit of a monk) and two bishops, flanking St Peter. The window in the north transept has free curvilinear tracery.

At Howth, Co. Dublin, the memory of the fourteenth Baron St Lawrence and his lady is perpetuated by a tomb sculpted about 1470. Lord and Lady St Lawrence lie on the mensa in peaceful repose, surrounded by some of the appurtenances of their class: swords, tasselled cushions and a pet dog. Below are carvings of scriptural figures and saints in ogee-headed niches, and at the western end is a Crucifixion with two angels holding censers and a figure of St Michael the Archangel.

Strade, Co. Mayo, window in the north transept.

This saint was a popular subject for tomb sculpture because he was credited with the responsibility of bearing souls up to heaven. He is thus depicted on a tomb in the Cistercian abbey at Jerpoint, Co. Kilkenny. The Jerpoint figures are the work of masons from a flourishing school not far off at Callan. Their work can be found elsewhere in the region; it is a singularly successful example of an original style resulting from a synthesis of known ones. The Callan workshops, which probably benefited greatly from the patronage of the rich and powerful Butlers of Ormond, flourished through the fifteenth and sixteenth centuries.

The squat figures fitted into niches on the Jerpoint tombs have some characteristics, such as the stylized treatment of the hair, beards and drapery, which can be found in paleo-Christian art in Ireland. The sculptors evidently were inspired or influenced by the old illuminated manuscripts. One possible source, the *Book of Mulling*, was kept in the nearby monastery of St Mullins.

Elsewhere in western Europe the figures in the arcading of altar tombs were 'weepers' or mourners, but in Ireland these were replaced by apostles and saints, or occasionally by a scene from the Passion.

A tomb surround, undoubtedly from the Callan workshops, supports the recumbent effigies of Piers and Margaret Butler in St Canice's Cathedral, Kilkenny. Here the arcades no longer appear. The various stages of the story of the Passion are depicted

Tomb of Piers Fitz Oge Butler in Kilcooly Abbey, Co. Tipperary.

in 'continuous' style, represented within the same framework and without a break. This is a significant development in Irish medieval art, but due to the Reformation and the apocalyptic events which followed the Dissolution of the Monasteries, it went no further.

The standing figures carved between the columns of the cloister at Jerpoint recall contemporary tomb-effigies; they too are almost certainly the work of the Callan masons. Not surprisingly, as Jerpoint Abbey enjoyed Butler patronage, one of the figures is a knight bearing a shield with the Butler arms, and another appears to be his lady. A bishop and a monk are also charmingly carved on the stone membranes which join the columns. The cloister has been re-erected under the direction of the Office of Public Works. The rounded arches of this arcade have been mistaken by some observers for much earlier work; they are probably modelled on the earlier cloister.

The Callan masons were also responsible for some beautiful tombs in the Cistercian abbey of Kilcooly, Co. Tipperary. The tomb of Piers Fitz Oge Butler was carved by Rory O'Tunney, who signed the mensa: 'Roricus O Tuyne scripsit'. It is similar to those elsewhere in the Butler dominions. The knight is shown with his sword at his side; at his feet is a lion (though the sculptor seems to have used a local dog as his model), symbol of fortitude.

Many other sepulchral monuments of the fifteenth and early sixteenth centuries have survived in Ireland, but none of these seems to have been the product of one local school of stonemasons, as at Callan. Some are more sumptuous, such as the O'Crean tomb in the nave of Sligo Abbey. The year, 1506, and the names of the deceased, Cormac O'Crean and his wife Johanna Ennis, are carved on the bevelled edge of the mensa. The decorative carving, though bold and profuse, is decidedly stiff and inexpert when compared with contemporary work in the Kilkenny area. There is a central Crucifixion with a flanking Virgin and St John, along with St Dominic, St Peter, St Catherine, an archbishop and the inevitable St Michael.

Good tombs may also be seen in the cathedral at Cashel, Co. Tipperary, the church of St Nicholas, Galway, Claregalway Friary, Co. Galway, the cathedral of St Mary, Limerick, Askeaton Friary, Co. Limerick, and at the Franciscan and Augustinian friary churches of Adare, Co. Limerick, Lislaughtin Friary, Co. Kerry, Quin Abbey, Co. Clare, in the cathedral of Kilfenora, Co. Clare, and in Dunsany Church, Co. Meath, to name but a few. The friary church at Ennis, Co. Clare, boasts a magnificent tomb built for the MacMahons in 1475; it has an elaborate arched canopy which bears close resemblance

Tomb sculpture in Jerpoint Abbey, Co. Kilkenny.

The Passion depicted on a tomb in St Canice's Cathedral, Kilkenny.

Figures in the cloister at Jerpoint Abbey.

St Nicholas Church, Dunsany, Co. Meath, west end.

to a type of sedilia then in vogue. The carved panels round the base show scenes from the Passion; though in local stone, they are in a style which recalls popular medieval English alabaster reliefs, some of which could easily have found their way to Ennis.

English influence was strongest in the Pale, the comparatively peaceful stronghold of the 'Old English' families loyal to the Crown. Of the churches built in the Pale during the fifteenth century, at least three were built by the Plunkets. These were very similar to one another, but unlike churches of their size elsewhere. The three, at Killeen, Dunsany and Rathmore, all in Co. Meath, were built to serve the churchgoing requirements of a large manor. They are conventional in plan, consisting of a narrow nave and slightly shorter chancel, divided by a stout wall, but they have narrow towers at the west end and a tower-like structure to the north of the eastern end.

These churches, and especially Dunsany, have a fortified air. This is a little difficult to explain, as the Pale was not so vulnerable to attack, and in any case the ample low windows would have given easy entrance to attackers. The three-storey tower at the east end provided a residence for the priest; this is a feature of other contemporary Pale churches.

The church at Killeen was probably the earliest. Sir Christopher Plunket had married Joan Cusack, heiress of Killeen and Dunsany, in 1403; when he died in 1445 their grandson Christopher became Lord of Killeen, their second son Lord of Dunsany, their third son Thomas acquired Rathmore Manor, and the youngest son Rowland eventually inherited Dunsoghly Manor. Sir Christopher had received a grant of money as a reward for aiding Henry VI in 1426.[12] Most probably this was used for the spate of church-building that took place on Plunket property in the second quarter of the fifteenth century.

Killeen Church is mentioned in the will of the first Baron Dunsany, dated 1461. The testator asks to be buried in the chancel of Killeen, and bequeaths valuables to the church of St Nicholas, Dunsany; these included scarlet hangings, an arras, crosiers and chalices of silver and gold, missals, graduals, hymnals and psalters, a chaplet of pearls for the statue of the Blessed Virgin, robes of gold and satin, chasubles, and a legacy to pay priests to pray for his and his wives' souls.

The windows of Killeen Church are its most English feature; well preserved, they are in both the Decorated and Perpendicular Gothic styles then current in England, but due to the usual time-lag making a tardive appearance here.

Dunsany Church was built slightly later, and is a bit larger than Killeen. Comparison of the plans of these churches shows how alike they are. Each has twin towers at the east end, a long, rather narrow nave and the stair that once led to a wooden loft, from which the view of the chancel was excellent.

Rathmore Church was built by Sir Thomas Plunket, who came into possession of that manor when he married the heiress Marion Cruise. His church is very similar to Killeen and Dunsany, but only about one-third their length. It has only one tower at the west end, but has rood-stairs (which continued to the roof), a wall separating nave from chancel, and a sacristy with dwelling-quarters on top to the north of the east end.

St Patrick's Church, Taghmon, Co. Westmeath.

Font of St Nicholas Church, Dunsany.

Dunsany Church preserves one of the finest medieval fonts in Ireland.[13] On it are carved representations of the Crucifixion and the Twelve Apostles, along with many images from the repertory of Christian symbology.

At Newcastle, Co. Dublin, is another simple nave-and-chancel church of the fifteenth century; this one has a fortified tower with three storeys at the west end. The east end originally had a fine tracery window, which was removed and reinserted in the new east wall when the old chancel was abandoned. The nave is now the parish church. The east window, showing definite English influence, is one of the best of its kind in the country. The curvilinear tracery is clearly the work of an accomplished mason, perhaps one brought over from England. The tower's two upper storeys (which served the priest as a residence) are reached by a winding stairway in one corner.

Beyond the borders of the Pale, in the perilous area to the west, the residential tower was a common feature. The churches themselves had a fortified character. When Archbishop Ussher made his visitation of Meath in 1622 he mentioned several of them, describing the tower as 'a little castle at the west end of the church'.[14] This well describes the church at Taghmon, built in the fifteenth century. In 1587 it was owned by the Nugents, one of the important families of the Pale, but it was in ruins by 1622. The tower, built to be impregnable, communicates directly with the church, a simple rectangular hall with a heavy barrel-vault. The windows are a simple, narrow version of English Perpendicular Gothic; one has a grotesque head inserted over it.

The tower itself is four storeys high with vaulted ceilings. The lower part appears to have been used as a store-room, having only two small windows. The second floor probably served as a living-room; it has a fireplace, a chimney, two windows with seats in the embrasures, and a slop-stone. On this floor there is also a small room with a door to the winding stair which gives access to the rest of the tower. Over the living-room was a wooden-floored storey which served as the bedroom and had a garderobe off it. Above this floor was an apartment covered by a pitched wooden roof, completely within, and protected by, the higher battlemented parapets. Kilpatrick Church, now ruinous, resembled Taghmon.

With the Reformation, Taghmon Church passed to the Church of Ireland, but as late as the eighteenth century the minister in charge of the parish still lived in the uncomfortable quarters in the tower. Christopher Dixon, the rascally, eccentric curate who lived there then, was described in Bishop Ellis's Visitation of 1755 as 'a weak man . . . he used to live in the steeple . . . he could not be trusted with money'.[15] Parson Dixon would lower a basket from his eyrie to collect offerings before consenting to come down and perform a ceremony. If he thought the offering inadequate he pocketed it, lowered the basket for more, and refused to budge until he got the sum he wanted. It was bad enough for impecunious couples wanting to be wed or parents anxious to baptize an infant, but worse was the predicament of the Protestant parishioners left with a corpse on their hands.

During the century additions were made to existing churches within the Pale. Some were almost completely rebuilt, such as the thirteenth-century church of St Audoen, the only survivor of the seven parish churches of medieval Dublin. Most of the church is now roofless, though the repaired tower still stands. It was situated in one of the most crowded sections of the city, on a slope between the houses in the Cornmarket and the city wall. The ensemble still conveys something of its medieval appearance.

Fore Abbey, Co. Westmeath, was in the area controlled by the Nugents, but subject to the vicissitudes of border life. Moreover, as it was a Benedictine house founded directly from, and subject to, the French abbey of St Taurin at Evreux, it was in bad odour with the Crown when England was at war

Lusk, Co. Dublin, tower of the fifteenth-century church.

with France. During such periods it was frequently seized as alien property. In the first half of the fourteenth century its buildings were incorporated in the town's fortifications – hence its semi-fortified appearance. At Fore, as at Bective, the monks' quarters were reduced and a new cloister was built. What remains of the cloister arcade bears a strong resemblance to the one at Bective, and may be the work of the same hands.

A large number of belfry towers still stand in the Pale. One of the most striking is at Lusk, Co. Dublin. A large medieval church was built there by the wealthy Archbishop of Dublin. This church has disappeared and a nineteenth-century one now takes its place, but the tower remains; unique in its design, it incorporates three turrets at the corners, the fourth being an ancient Round Tower which does not communicate with the belfry tower.

Outside the Pale, the overwhelming majority of new buildings were monasteries, most of them

Franciscan. Though the Franciscans employed new styles in their buildings, none of them could compare in quality with the additions made to the Cistercian abbeys of Holy Cross and Kilcooly, both in Co. Tipperary.

The illustrious Butlers, Earls of Ormonde, were the patrons of some of the most important medieval buildings. The fifteenth-century earls were cultivated and cosmopolitan men. The rebuilding of Holy Cross may have begun as early as 1400, in the time of James, the third Earl (who built Gowran Castle), but more probably in that of his son James, the fourth Earl, known as the 'White Earl', who succeeded his father in 1405. The White Earl, an educated man for his time, was five times Lord Deputy, and was on good terms with the Plantagenet kings he served. The royal arms, as used by Kings Henry IV, V and VI, appear with those of Butler on a sedilia in the chancel of the church at Holy Cross. King Henry V reigned from 1413 to 1421; the White Earl took the abbey under his protection in 1416. It therefore appears likely, in conjunction with the stylistic evidence of the work, that it was done soon after that date to mark the Butler patronage.

Further work, including restoration, took place at Holy Cross about 1470. This would have been promoted by the White Earl's second son John, the sixth Earl; after an attainder, he was restored to the title by Edward IV, who said of him, 'if good breeding and liberal qualities were lost in the world they might all be found in the Earl of Ormonde'.[16] This John, the sixth Earl, an accomplished linguist, was English ambassador to several European courts. A religious man as well as an intellectual, he died in Jerusalem while on a pilgrimage of devotion in 1478. The standard of building and decoration demanded by these rich, well-travelled and civilized men was the best that Irish masons could produce. Furthermore, Holy Cross was a much-visited place of pilgrimage – its principal relic was a fragment of the True Cross, said to have been presented by Pope Paschal II (though another tradition attributes the donation to a Plantagenet queen). The relic was greatly venerated, and the pilgrims' offerings were a rich source of income in the fifteenth century.

The rebuilding of the abbey church was extensive: a magnificent chancel and transept, with a beautiful east window and graceful ribbed vaulting. The tracery windows of the transept chapels are of the highest quality; the east window, with a bold reticulated pattern, is a most felicitous design.

The sedilia in the chancel, 17 feet high, has three ogee-headed niches with an elaborate canopy topped by a sort of valance. The carving in hard limestone is exquisite. Above the seat-niches are the Plantagenet and the Butler arms.

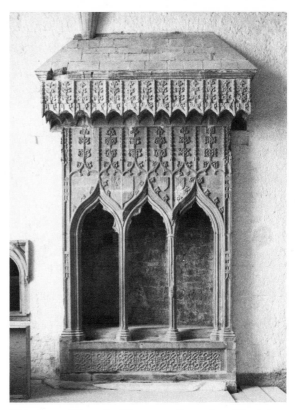

Holy Cross Abbey, Co. Tipperary. Above, the sedilia; below, 'the Monks' Waking Place'.

The purpose of the structure in the transept ('the Monks' Waking Place') is uncertain; probably it was used to house the relic of the True Cross. In such a setting, the relic or reliquary could easily be seen by pilgrims, but was kept out of their reach. The north transept contains a rare fifteenth-century mural of a hunting scene.

In the spaces above the vaulting of the transepts are dwellings for the monks. The rooms over the chapels have fireplaces, and small holes cut to allow a view of the altar. These rooms were reached by a wall-stair in the north transept, or by a stair from the dormitory range in the south transept. There are extensive remains of the claustral buildings at Holy Cross; the doorway of the chapter-house is of curious, almost bizarre, design: an ogee arch within a rounded frame, the whole covered with a pattern resembling Norman billeting.

Kilcooly Abbey, the other Cistercian settlement rebuilt by the Butlers, was almost completely destroyed by armed men in 1444;[17] the subsequent reconstruction is of less extent and humbler nature. During the rebuilding the nave was bereft of its aisles, and a new north transept and tower were added.

At the head of the nave are two elaborately carved stone seats, presumably for the abbot and his deputy. The abbot's seat, on the south side, has an escutcheon with the Butler arms over the ogee-arched canopy.

Kilcooly Abbey, east window.

Kilcooly Abbey, Co. Tipperary, the abbot's seat.

There is interesting carved decoration on the wall leading to the sacristy. One of the subjects is a mermaid holding a looking-glass, closely observed by two admiring fish. Mermaids had long been a subject of interest in Ireland. In 1118 the *Annals of Loch Cé* report that two were caught by fishermen, one in Ossory and the other at Waterford. In the fifteenth century people were just as willing to believe in secular as sacred miracles. The other carvings on this wall represent the Crucifixion, St Christopher, and an abbot or bishop, possibly St Bernard. The design of the handsome east window is an attempt at Flamboyant Gothic tracery.

Unique in Ireland are the misericords in Limerick Cathedral. The black oak choir-stalls, twenty-three in number, were carved for the cathedral about 1480 when the building was renovated and enlarged. They comprise a marvellous collection of grotesque animals and figures, many of them culled from medieval bestiaries, such as a manticore, a fight between a lion and a wyvern, an amphisboena, a wild boar, a lindworm and a griffin.

Other Irish cathedrals were embellished with carvings during renovations and rebuilding in this

century. At Clonmacnoise, Co. Offaly, Dean Odo
O'Malone, who caused the doorway in the north wall
to be reconstructed and decorated with fine sculpture
(pl. VII, p. 55), was eulogized thus by the Four
Masters: 'Dean O'Malone, the most learned man in
all Ireland, died at Clonmacnoise.'[18] The door was
probably executed between 1450 and the Dean's
death in 1461; the masterly craftsmanship is apparent
even though it is damaged. Over the simple arch,
surmounted by a crest of lacy crocketing, are three
figures representing St Dominic, St Patrick and
St Francis. This choice seems symbolic of the monastic
constitution of Ireland: the founders of two important monastic orders of the Middle Ages flank
the founder of Christianity in Ireland.

A similar door exists at Clontuskert Abbey, Co.
Galway, ten miles away. This has an inscription
with the date: 'Mathev: Dei: gra: eps: Clonfertens:
et: Patre oneacdavayn: canonie esti: domine: fi
fecert: Ano: do: mcccclxxi.' (Mathew by the Grace
of God, Bishop of Clonfert, and Patrick O'Naughton,
Canon of this house, caused me to be made Anno
Domini 1471.) The work on this door is bolder and
even more confidently handled. It appears that the
Clonmacnoise masons went on to Clontuskert and
worked with a sureness born of their experience.
The crockets over the arch are large vine leaves
which join in the middle to form an exuberant
pinnacle. The narrow pilasters on either side of the
door end with figures of angels; angels are also
carved between the crockets and the pilaster bases.
The figures represented in the space above the arch,
on either side of the pinnacle, are St Michael the
Archangel (with a sword and the scales for weighing
souls), St John the Baptist, St Catherine, and a bishop.
Surrounding the door are carvings showing a
variety of subjects, including a pelican in its piety,
a mermaid, animals with intertwined heads, and a
dog biting its own tail.

About the same time as the door was erected,
some additions and embellishments were made
within the church itself. The most notable is an
arcaded rood-gallery between the nave and chancel
which has been carefully reconstructed by the Office
of Public Works. The gallery is a beautiful piece of
fifteenth-century work, three bays wide, with simple
pointed arches supported by polygonal columns.

Doors like those at Clonmacnoise and Clontuskert
were popular features of fifteenth-century churches.
Many more examples can be found in the country,
though few are as good as the two named. A simpler
one was built on to the west entrance of the Augustinian church of Ardnaree, Co. Mayo, in the town
of Ballina. Though it has no figure-sculpture, and
some of the decorative elements are missing, the
total effect is undeniably elegant. Another of these

*Lion fighting with a wyvern, detail of a misericord in St Mary's
Cathedral, Limerick.*

*St Michael weighing souls, on the doorway of Clontuskert
'abbey', Co. Galway.*

doorways was added to the church of St Ruadhan at
Lorrha, Co. Tipperary.

A door of this type can also be seen at Dunmore,
Co. Galway, on the west end of the Augustinian
friary church. A memorial plaque identifies the
donor as a member of the de Bermingham family,
Lords of Athenry. Another very small door was

Ardnaree, Co. Sligo (Ballina), doorway of the Augustinian friary church.

erected in the 'upper church' on Devenish Island, Co. Fermanagh. Rosserk Friary Church, Co. Mayo, Limerick Cathedral and Kilmallock Collegiate Church, Co. Limerick, all have good fifteenth-century doorways of this pilastered ogee-arched type.

The last great building phenomenon of pre-Reformation Ireland was that of the Franciscan monasteries. The order had existed in Ireland since the early thirteenth century, and became enormously popular in the fourteenth, particularly in the south and west, where friaries were built near small towns or by the chieftains' castles. Racial and social discrimination within this order had all but disappeared, and the 'mere Irish' were freely admitted, which accounts for the rapid growth of the order.

The Franciscan friars, recruited from the people to minister to the people (whose way of life they shared), managed to establish an intimate relationship, not just with the peasantry, but with the chiefs as well. Buildings were simple and easily adaptable to changing conditions. The lay community contributed parts of the building in many cases; there was none of the grandeur that appeared when a powerful and rich patron was the founder.

In certain respects the friaries differed from the Cistercian prototypes. The church had a section reserved for laymen in the nave, while the clergy and friars used the choir. A belfry tower was usually built over the wall that separated nave and choir, and there was very often an extension with an aisle, built to accommodate growing congregations. The claustral buildings were very extensive, usually well built round a single cloister, sometimes with an additional courtyard. The east range of buildings housed (in its lower storey) a sacristy next to the church, then a chapter-room and a day-room; above this floor, covering the whole area, was the dormitory of the friars with an attached privy. The north range had a large kitchen, refectory, and related rooms such as pantry and buttery. The west range of buildings had no strict arrangement, but as the main entrance was on this side, it usually contained a porter's lodge, vestibule, guest-rooms and administrative offices.

The cloisters were built in such a way that the ambulatories were covered by the upper storey. This made the ground-floor rooms dark and damp. Many of the cloisters survive in quite good condition. In almost all the monasteries built in the fifteenth century, the construction proceeded piecemeal as funds became available.

There is excellent documentation of this process for the Franciscan friary at Adare, Co. Limerick. A Franciscan manuscript in the Bibliothèque Royale, Brussels (No. 3947) specifically names the persons who contributed to the building. The friary was founded in 1464 by Thomas Fitzgerald, seventh Earl of Desmond (the Lord Deputy, later attainted but subsequently pardoned), and Joan, his Countess. The list of donors continues with Cornelius O'Sullivan, who died 16 January 1492. He is described as 'bonus et devotus colonus'; he gave the bell-tower and a gold chalice. The major chapel, dedicated to the Blessed Virgin, was built by Margaret ny Gibbon, wife of Conlaidh O'Daly, a poet. The first of the minor chapels was built by the Lord John, son of the Earl of Desmond; two other minor chapels by a man named Keogh and by Margaret FitzMaurice respectively. Donogh, son of Brian Dubh O'Brien, and Anne, daughter of Donogh O'Brien Ara, built the dormitory. The Knight of Glin and Honora his wife built the infirmary. Domhnall O'Daly and Sabina his wife built one-fourth (one side) of the cloister; another side was built by Rory O'Dea, a Franciscan tertiary, who also gave a silver chalice. Another Franciscan tertiary, Morogh O'Hickey, gave the refectory. The friary was restored in 1875 by the antiquarian Earl of Dunraven.

The large church has a spacious aisled south transept, planned from the beginning. At the east end, along the wall, are the chapels; the tall slender

Adare, Co. Limerick, cloister of the Augustinian friary.

tower, also planned from the outset, separates the long nave and chancel. Though the domestic quarters have suffered damage and decay, the cloister arcade still stands, overgrown with a delicate web of vegetation and surrounded by the neatly mown greens of a golf-course. The friary ruins can be visited on request, without payment of the admission fee to the Adare Demesne and Manor House because it is a national monument.

Near by, in the town of Adare itself, the Augustinians, (whose friary had been founded in the previous century), made some additions and improvements. The arcade of the rebuilt cloister has graceful cusped arches in groups of three, contained in deep embrasures. The Fitzgerald arms are carved on the inner spandrels of the east arcade, so it is likely that this superior work was executed under Geraldine patronage.

The Franciscan house at Kilconnell, Co. Galway, was one of the earliest to be built after the doldrums of the fourteenth century. The earliest work is hesitant; the tower, completed about the middle of the century, and the tomb-niches, already mentioned, are the best features (pl. VIII, p. 56).

Askeaton Friary, Co. Limerick,. is a large Franciscan foundation with impressive remains. It is unique among the new friaries in having the cloister to the south of the church. This was made necessary by the site, which slopes southward and is rocky to the north. The monastery also has another peculiarity: the refectory projects southward from the cloister. Most of the building was done between 1420 and 1440.[19] The refectory wing was probably built later, as was the enormous aisled wing added to the north of the church. The cloister is one of the most accomplished examples of its kind in Ireland. In design it retains elements of the previous century, but it is carried out in hard limestone with a fine rubbed finish. On one of the pillars is carved a crude figure of St Francis; his face has been worn away by kisses – supposedly a cure for toothache. In the south range was a prison for unruly inhabitants. The massive, lofty belfry, shown in a sixteenth-century drawing, has vanished.

The Franciscan friary at Quin, Co. Clare, was built about 1433, after the Pope had granted a licence to a Macnamara prince for the foundation of a friary in 'some convenient place'.[20] The site chosen was the de Clare Castle, which an earlier Macnamara had seized and burned. The massive curtain wall to the south of the four-towered castle was used for the south wall of the nave-and-chancel church; in this wall, windows had to be excavated $9\frac{1}{2}$ feet deep. The east and west ends of the church were built on to the

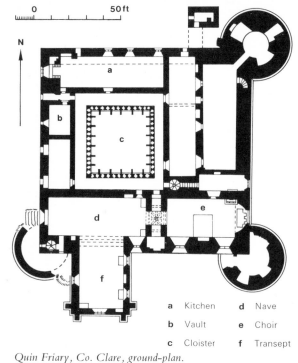

Quin Friary, Co. Clare, ground-plan.

a	Kitchen	**d**	Nave
b	Vault	**e**	Choir
c	Cloister	**f**	Transept

Quin, the Franciscan friary, with the ruined bastion of the castle on whose foundations the friary was built on the right.

corresponding walls of the castle. In the east end, the thick wall had to be considerably altered to accommodate the triple-light window. The church has the usual extension from the nave, and an elegant, very tall tower over the screen separating the nave and chancel.

The claustral buildings are extensive; where possible the strong support of pre-existing walls was employed. The very complete cloister is one of the most interesting in the country. The arcades have slightly pointed arches, disposed in pairs, with buttresses separating them.

Buttressed cloister walls are a singular feature of many Irish monasteries in the fifteenth century. They were necessary structurally to help support the enormous weight of wall above the slender columns, and the thrust of the vaulting concealed behind. At Quin, they also serve the purely aesthetic purpose of enlivening a dull expanse.

The well-preserved friary at Muckross, near Killarney, Co. Kerry, was begun when it was founded in 1448, and continued in various stages over the next fifty years. This time-span is evident in the church, whose windows vary greatly in design, and in the cloister, where the styles of the various arcades differ. Here again the cloister walls are buttressed, but instead of separating the arcades, the buttresses are extensions of the individual piers.

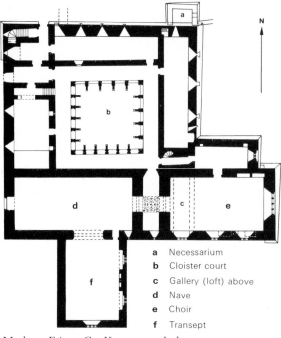

a Necessarium
b Cloister court
c Gallery (loft) above
d Nave
e Choir
f Transept

Muckross Friary, Co. Kerry, ground-plan.

The Papal Brief of 23 April 1468 relates that Domhnall MacCarthy, Prince of Desmond, had founded Muckross 'with the riches given him by God, for the use of the Friars Minor', to be built with 'church, campanile, bell, cemetery, dormitory, refectory, gardens, orchards and other necessary offices', but that the church was not finished because 'the wealth of the said Prince by reason of the strife and insistent wars with which he is vexed by his enemies, is not sufficient'. Fortunately, however, the brief goes on to state, 'the offerings of the faithful are to hand in abundance', so that the work was able to proceed again.[21]

Most friaries received additions as benefactors made further building possible. At Timoleague, Co. Cork, for example, the 67-foot-high tower was added by a Franciscan Bishop of Ross, Edmund Courcy; he also built a dormitory and the library.

Very little remains of Donegal Friary, founded in 1474 by Nuala O'Connor, mother of Hugh Roe O'Donnell, Prince of Tyrconnel.[22] She died before it was finished, and was buried in the specially constructed crypt under the altar. The work was continued by Hugh Roe's wife, who became a Franciscan tertiary; their son Hugh Oge O'Donnell went on a pilgrimage to Rome in 1510 and was received by King Henry VII on his journey home. He eventually took the habit of St Francis and died in the monastery in 1537. Friars from Donegal Friary compiled the *Annals of the Four Masters*

between 1632 and 1636, after the community had been expelled.[23]

At Meelick, Co. Galway, the walls, west doorway and two arches of the south aisle of the fifteenth-century friary church survive. The building has been repaired, and serves now as the Catholic church.

The largest and best preserved of the fifteenth-century Franciscan friaries is that of Ross Erilly, Co. Galway. As seen from the main Cong-Headford road, its extensive remains and tall slender belfry make an impressive silhouette (pl. IX, p. 56). It was a late foundation, probably not earlier than 1498.[24] Its size in a fairly isolated and sparsely populated region bears witness to the popularity of the Franciscans and the upsurge of monastic vocations at this time. Not only is the church large, but it has an unusual double-transept to the north of the nave, larger in area than nave or chancel. This can only indicate that, subsequent to building, and probably only shortly before the Reformation, the friars of Ross Erilly could expect a bumper attendance.

The claustral buildings range over a large area and have a secondary courtyard. The big refectory has a fine reader's niche. Above the refectory was one of the two large dormitories. The fish-tank (an unusual feature) inside the spacious kitchen is fed, rather alarmingly, by the adjacent stream straight from the enormous *necessarium*. The brethren somehow survived this insanitary arrangement, and although frequently expelled after the Dissolution, they were still there in 1641, when the guardian sheltered some of the unfortunate Protestants who escaped from the massacre at Shrule during the rising in that year.

Much smaller than Ross Erilly, the foundation of the Franciscan Tertiaries, beautifully situated on Killala Bay at Rosserk, Co. Mayo, is very well preserved. Founded before 1441,[25] it is the only complete friary of the Third Order Regular to survive.

The Franciscan Third Order Regular had congregations of both sexes, bound by vows of poverty, chastity and obedience, and individual houses were founded in Ireland during the first half of the fifteenth century. While in England there were no regular houses of the Third Order at all, and in Scotland there were only two small ones, in Ireland the order grew apace, eventually numbering over forty houses. It seems that the rule was particularly suited to the Irish. It first took root in Connaught, spreading in the areas where the native Irish population was predominant. The lay members, who banded together into religious communities, strove to live a life of self-sacrifice, while co-operating in the pastoral work of the neighbouring parishes and teaching in the schools. The order soon built up a strong priesthood of its own.

Rosserk Friary, Co. Mayo.

The church at Rosserk has the nave-and-choir arrangement, with a tower over the screen. The transept has two small chapels, with a closet for storing the altar furnishings between them. There is interesting carving in the choir, where a pair of angels and a Round Tower (presumably that of Killala, a few miles away) are sculpted on the elaborate piscina. The claustral buildings are small and compact, and the central courtyard is without an arcaded ambulatory.

Only a mile away from Rosserk is the friary of Moyne, Co. Mayo. This was described in 1460 as being 'letely built [*sic*]'.[26] The usual friary church has a nave 59 feet long and a choir 49 feet long. There is a tall belfry tower over the screen, and a transept divided from the nave by arcading, and widening out towards the south to form an L-shaped area. An unusual chapel, 38 feet long and 16 feet wide, is built out at right angles from the south-eastern end of the choir.

The domestic buildings are very extensive. A convenient stream runs under the kitchen and refectory. The cloister appears to date from the end of the century, and is similar to the one at Ross Erilly. It has arcades of simple but elegant design, and a vaulted ambulatory.

At Ardfert, Co. Kerry, the cloister and the south transept of the church were built in the fifteenth century. The cloister arcade, with arches grouped in threes and joined by a deep embrasure, has the

remnants of its ingenious roof-tiles which formerly channelled the rainwater into the centre of the courtyard, over the top of the ambulatory.

Claregalway Friary, an early Franciscan establishment, was renovated in the fifteenth century, at which time the tower and the east window of the chancel were added (pl. X, p. 121).

Margaret, wife of Owen O'Rorke, founded a friary in 1508 for Franciscans at Creevelea, near Dromahair, Co. Leitrim, the seat of the rulers of Breffny. Monks came from her sister Nuala's friary at Donegal to start the community. Margaret died four years later, in 1512, and at that time only a wooden church had been built. This may be an exception, or it may indicate that temporary wooden churches were still being erected as late as the fifteenth century. The church is mentioned in the report of Margaret's death in the *Annals of Ulster*:

> Margaret daughter of Concubar O'Brien, Queen of Lower Connacht from the Mountain down, first, and wife of O'Rourke after, the unique woman who, of what were in Ireland of her time, was of best fame and hospitality and housekeeping and was richest in gold and silver and every other valuable – died and was buried in a wooden church she built herself for the Friars Minor close by Dromahaire.[27]

The surviving stone church, which has a nave, chancel and south transept, must, therefore, have been built after 1512 – probably the last to be completed before the Reformation. There is a cloister to the north of the church surrounded by domestic buildings, with dormitories on two floors. The tracery of the windows illustrates Irish conservatism: the east window is basically of intersected-line design and the west reticulated, the work of a mason inexperienced in the genre. Despite Margaret's wealth, nothing at the friary is of high quality.

The other mendicant order, the Dominicans, also built and added to a number of monasteries. One, the friary at Burrishoole, Co. Mayo, was built about 1469. Its founder, Richard de Burgo, took the habit of the order and died in his friary, which was recognized by a Papal Bull in 1486.[28] The church consists of a nave and chancel with a south transept. There is a good example of the two-light ogee-headed window, much used in this century, in the north wall of the church.

The Dominican friary at Kilkenny, 'Black Abbey', had a square tower added in the early sixteenth century, the gift of James Larkin and his wife Katherine Whyte, whose names are inscribed on a plaque affixed to the chancel arch. Probably the most handsome square battlemented tower in Ireland, it is also one of the most closely dated, for James Larkin's tomb was erected in St Canice's Cathedral in 1537.

The *Annals of Loch Cé* record the founding of a Dominican friary at Ballindoon, Co. Sligo, in 1507. The murder of Thomas O'Farrell, the founder, is reported in 1527. The building time was short, for the Reformation followed soon after. In 1585 the Prior was found to be in possession of a church, cemetery and half a quire of land; thus the monastery appears never to have had any domestic buildings. Their absence may explain the curious tower-structure in the church, which separates the nave from the chancel. It has six arched openings to the nave, but only two (the central ones) open on the chancel side as well. The lower arches are all the same height. The niches which flank the central passage could have contained altars. The upper storey, reached by a rather perilous stair on the outer wall of the church, has a higher central arch where a crucifix may have been suspended. This stair was an addition; it served to join the gallery with the east end of the chancel. The gallery was lit by tall double-light windows in the north and south walls. The rooms in the tower must have been reached from the gallery and, though the living-quarters these provided were limited, apparently they were used pending the building of a suitable domestic range.

Another unusual feature at Ballindoon is the pair of almost identical windows in the east and west ends, consisting of four cusped lights with intersected-line tracery.

Burrishoole Friary, Co. Mayo, window in the north wall of the church.

Ballindoon Friary, Co. Sligo, the central tower/screen.

Sligo, Co. Sligo, 'abbey' cloister.

The Dominican friary at Portumna, Co. Galway, was founded by the local chieftain, after Cistercians from Dunbrody, who had a chapel there, abandoned the site. Pope Martin V granted a Bull confirming their possessions in 1426.[29] The remains consist of a church with nave and chancel, a south transept with a fine curvilinear tracery window, and remnants of the conventual buildings, including the west and north sides of the cloister arcade.

The Dominican friary in Sligo was severely damaged by fire in 1414. Soon after, it was rebuilt (or at least restored) by a friar, Brian, son of Dermot MacDonogh, chieftain of the area. The work done at this time was probably limited to the church itself; certainly the reticulated east window and the tower are of this period. Later, the domestic quarters were rebuilt, and of these the cloister retains a good section of its ambulatory and arcade. There were buttresses to carry the weight of the upper storeys. The columns of the arcades are carved with a variety of deep-cut, precise, geometrical designs.

The Augustinians also renovated their existing monasteries. Clare Abbey, Co. Clare, had its charter renewed in 1461;[30] about this time the church was repaired, the east window inserted, the tower built, and the domestic ranges erected. The south range has a peculiar two-light transomed window with unusual tracery.

The Augustinian monastery of Murrisk, Co. Mayo, was founded in 1457 on a lovely inlet of Clew Bay.[31] The church has unusual battlemented walls and an old-fashioned intersected-line tracery window. There are remains of domestic buildings, and the base of a tower which had disappeared by 1800.

The church at Drumlane, Co. Cavan, founded in the late thirteenth century, was much altered in the fifteenth, when the heads of abbots or bishops and that of a king were carved outside the door and windows. In 1431 an appeal for alms was made to build a cloister and refectory; much of the present church is from that period.

In Galway city, the prosperous Lynch family carried out major alterations to the parish church of St Nicholas of Myra. The present building retains its original fourteenth-century chancel, but the nave aisles and the transepts were subsequently enlarged. The widening of the south aisle was first undertaken by the notorious mayor Dominick Lynch, who condemned his son to the gallows in 1493, but had to do the hanging himself because no one could be found to carry out what seemed like an over-zealous piece of justice.

Aristocrats of the old faith. Tomb of the eighth Earl of Ormonde and his Countess, in St Canice's Cathedral, Kilkenny.

St Nicholas, Galway, hood-moulding; top of window in south wall

St Mary's, Callan, Co. Kilkenny, south door.

Mayor Lynch's alterations were continued by the terms of his will, dated 1508. Work on the building progressed through the century, but the widening of the south aisle was finished by 1510. Additions later in the century, including the widening of the north aisle, gave the building its distinctive three-gabled west front, unparalleled in Ireland. There are three tracery windows of almost equal size in this end. The central one has reticulated tracery and appears to be the earliest; the one in the south gable is of a complicated curvilinear style; the north window is a later, less successful copy of the south one.

The stepped parapets with quaint carved gargoyles are sixteenth-century features. One of the windows in Mayor Lynch's aisle has a hood-moulding stop in the form of a lion with a luxuriant mane.

St Mary's, Callan, Co. Kilkenny, was built about 1460 with an aisled nave and plain chancel. The south and west doors are elaborately carved, the south one with angels whose gowns turn into intertwined vines.

At Youghal, Co. Cork, the parish church of St Mary underwent rebuilding in 1468. Thomas Fitzgerald, eighth Earl of Desmond, the patron of this work, concentrated on reconstructing and embellishing the chancel, later desecrated by the sixteenth Earl in 1579. It was during this rebuilding that the fine east window was added.

The church at Fethard, Co. Tipperary, was given a handsome battlemented tower near the end of the fifteenth century. The window in the west end, over the door, has curvilinear tracery akin to that of the east window of Kilcooly Abbey.

Church-building in Ireland was brought to a halt by the official proclamation of the Reformation there in 1536, and its consequent sequestrations, despoilings, religious divisions, new alignments and new allegiances.

Piers Butler, eighth Earl of Ormonde, who died in 1539, and his Countess, Lady Margaret Fitzgerald, are commemorated in a beautiful tomb in Kilkenny Cathedral, which soon passed to the reformers. Their effigies, in black marble, show them smiling peacefully towards eternity, aristocrats of the old faith, unaware of the tumult to come.

CHAPTER 6

Reformation, Counter-Reformation and English supremacy

IN 1536 THE PARLIAMENT summoned in Dublin proclaimed the English King, Henry VIII, 'only supreme head on earth of the whole Church of Ireland'. A Royal Commission at once suppressed eight monasteries in Ireland, and fourteen more were dissolved in the following year under the Act of Suppression of Abbeys. A further Act of 1539 officially dissolved the remaining monastic establishments.

The church plate, ornaments and jewels from the abbey treasures were reserved for the Crown. The zealous reformers, however, destroyed many long-revered relics. This immediately incensed the people, and riots ensued. In Dublin, in 1538, the reformers burned the holiest relic in Ireland: the Baculus Iesu, the Staff of Jesus, which had reputedly been in Christ's own hand and was credited with prodigies and miracles in Ireland since St Patrick's time. In the same year the image of the Virgin was destroyed at Trim. The Annalist of Loch Cé wrote that: 'The very miraculous image of Mary which was in the town of Ath-truim, in which all the people of Erinn believed for a long time previously, which healed the blind and deaf and lame, and every other ailment was burnt by Saxons [i.e. English] . . . but there was not in Erinn a holy cross or a figure of Mary, or an illustrious image over which their power reached, that was not burned.'[1]

This destructive zeal, followed in the next century by the vandalism of Cromwell's Puritans, ensured that few pre-Reformation ecclesiastical ornaments or statues survive in Ireland. Those that escaped destruction were hidden. A stone statue of the Virgin and Child, broken into two (unfortunately without the heads), was found in Co. Down. It may originally have been in the church at Ardtole, near Ardglass. Repaired and with the heads restored, probably by a local mason, it has been placed on an outer wall of Dunsfort Catholic Church. A four-teenth-century wooden statue of the Virgin and Child is preserved in the Catholic church of Clonfert, Co. Galway. In the 'Black Abbey' Church of the Dominicans at Kilkenny is a beautiful alabaster carving, said to have been at Kilkenny since the foundation of the monastery in the thirteenth century. Conveniently the date, 1264, has been carved on this representation of the Trinity; God the Father has the Dove on his breast and holds the crucified Christ in his lap. The fourteenth-century ivory figure of the Virgin in the Dominican church, Pope's Quay, Cork, also came from an old Dominican foundation, the friary at Youghal, Co. Cork. In the Carmelite church, Whitefriar Street, Dublin, there is a medieval wooden statue of the Virgin, Our Lady of Dublin; this came from the rich Cistercian abbey of St Mary. The Catholic church at Kilcormac, Co. Offaly, has a wooden *Pietà*, reputedly brought from Spain before the Reformation to the Carmelite foundation there. At the suppression of the monasteries it was moved to a nearby church at Ballyboy; when Cromwell's troops quartered their horses in the church it escaped destruction by being hidden under a rubbish heap. Then for over sixty years it lay hidden in a bog, until it was salvaged by Father Loughlin Lynam, parish priest of Ballyboy, at the beginning of the eighteenth century. Unfortunately this statue has been so overpainted in recent times that it now has the appearance of a common and bright new one cast in plaster. In the Church of Ireland cathedral of St Brigid at Kildare is kept a stone slab with a carving of the Crucifixion. The inscription reads: 'Ecce homo. To them that devoutly say V Pater Noster and V Ave before this image ac grant XXV years and XXV days of Pardon. Medieval wooden figure-carvings which were formerly in the church at Fethard, Co. Tipperary, are now in the National Museum, Dublin.

In 1540 a Commission was set up to survey the dissolved abbey estates in Ireland and estimate the value of their rents and revenues. The Commissioners were empowered to grant leases of the former abbey properties, and the rich abbey lands fell into the hands of fortunate laymen. By 1541 most of the abbeys within the Pale and the districts of English influence had been effectively dissolved. In the Irish districts, where the Crown's authority was only nominal, the law was harder to enforce and the process of dissolution was slower. However, a number of rapacious Catholic Irish chiefs were happy to receive confiscated abbey properties, while allowing the monks to remain about their former houses. Some lay grantees settled on their new estates. The new proprietors of the great Cistercian abbey of Bective, Co. Meath, were content to settle down in the extensive domestic buildings of the monastery, but the family who acquired the Cistercian Tintern Abbey in Co. Wexford made their home in the church itself, converting the chancel into a two-storey residence which extended into the tower. Bishop Knox, who eventually obtained the former Carmelite friary at Rathmullan in Co. Donegal, converted the nave and the south transept of the church into a house for himself, about 1620. He embellished the corners of the east end of the church with Scots-style turrets. The Nugent family, who acquired the former Benedictine abbey at Fore, Co. Westmeath, built on to the domestic buildings against the south side of the church, incorporating some of them into their semi-fortified residence. The seventeenth-century owners of the Franciscan friary at Moyne, Co. Mayo (who allowed the friars to

'Black Abbey' Church, Kilkenny, alabaster carving of the Trinity.

St Brigid's Cathedral, Kildare, Crucifixion carving with inscription granting indulgence.

remain about their old monastery for some years), built themselves a neat two-storey house with mullioned windows adjacent to the old domestic buildings, and beside the stream which ran under the friary latrines. Perhaps those few friars who were permitted to stay on about the church no longer used their old conveniences.

Several years before the Reformation, in 1521, the Lord Deputy, Thomas Howard, Earl of Surrey, had represented to the King the advantages of settling loyal English subjects in Ireland as a method of holding the country. His plan was to subdue the country, region by region, employing a military force of six thousand men. After that, the Lord Deputy advised the King: 'Unless your Grace send inhabitants of your own natural subjects to inhabit such countries as shall be won, all your charges should be but wastefully spent.'[2] Some confiscated abbey lands were, therefore, granted to the English, to encourage settlement in Ireland. This programme of anglicizing the country by importing inhabitants from England gained impetus in the reign of Philip and Mary. Mary, a Catholic monarch, restored the Catholic Archbishop to the Primacy of which he had been deprived in 1551, and instructed her Lord Deputy, Lord Fitzwalter, to do everything possible to favour the Catholic faith in Ireland; in 1557 an act was passed by the parliament at Dublin repealing all the statutes against the Holy See introduced by her father. Nevertheless, Mary was as anxious as her father had been to assert the authority of the Crown in Ireland, and English Catholics were as eager as English Protestants to anglicize Ireland and subdue the Irish. In Mary's reign a plantation of English settlers was arranged. The chief towns of the settlement, Maryborough and Philipstown, and the counties, Kings and Queens (now Offaly and Leix) were named after the Queen and her Spanish husband. The Irish who had held these lands were extirpated and pushed farther west.

Mary I's successor, her half-sister Elizabeth, was a Protestant, and the supremacy of the Crown over the Church was re-established by the Act of Uniformity (1560). This Act was not easily implemented. The Irish clung tenaciously to the old faith. Even in the Pale the attachment to Rome was strong. Father David Wolfe, a Jesuit, reported in 1573 that the citizens of Dublin were almost all Catholic, but were forced to attend the communion and preaching of the heretics. For some years, prominent men politically and ostentatiously attended the Protestant services, while sending their families to mass. If required to take religious oaths as a test of conformity, they did so without troubling their consciences.

Politically, Henry VIII had made Ireland a kingdom by an act of 1542, assuming the additional title of King of Ireland; this was necessary because the English sovereigns' lordship over Ireland had depended on a papal grant. His policy had been to establish the supremacy of the Crown in Ireland by what he described to his Lord Deputy as 'sober ways, politic drifts and amiable persuasions'.[3] The Irish proved less susceptible to persuasion than he expected. One of his gambits was the Policy of Surrender and Regrant, introduced in 1541–42, whereby the Irish chiefs were required to manifest their loyal allegiance by surrendering their clan territories to the Crown. The King immediately regranted the same lands to the chief in person, subject to English law; this meant succession by primogeniture. The important chiefs also received English peerages. The chiefs who were sweetened with such hereditary titles and additional personal power did not all prove to be much more loving or loyal. According to the Brehon Laws the lands were not the chief's personal property which he could alienate. The clansmen were angry at being deprived of their share in the clan lands, and resented losing the right to choose their chief.

Not only the warlike and recalcitrant O'Neills and O'Donnells in Ulster, but also the Geraldine Earls of Kildare and Desmond, were in frequent rebellion. The Irish chiefs plotted endlessly with foreign powers against the English. Even before the Reformation exacerbated the differences between the Irish and the English, the Earl of Desmond had concluded a treaty in 1523 with King Francis I of France, whereby he would wage war on the English as soon as a French army landed in Ireland. In 1534, Conor O'Brien of Thomond, grandiosely styling himself 'Prince of Ireland' and writing regally from 'Our Castle at Clare' submitted himself to the Emperor Charles V, with all his force: 1,600 horse, 2,400 foot-soldiers and 100 castles.[4] In the same year King Henry VIII arrested the Earl of Kildare and imprisoned him in the Tower of London, charged with treasonable activities. The Earl's son, Thomas (known as 'Silken Thomas' because of the fringes on the helmets of his followers), attacked Dublin. Eventually defeated, he surrendered, but his garrison at Maynooth was brutally put to the sword. Thomas himself and five of his uncles were executed at Tyburn in 1537.

Elizabeth, an energetic Queen, realized that it was essential for her to rule Ireland in fact, as well as by title, and bring the whole country under law. Her Irish Kingdom was as rebellious as her father's had been; intrigues proliferated, and her ablest lieutenants were hard put to it to assert her authority. Sometimes a bishop appointed by the Queen was unable to occupy his See. An attempt to settle an English colony in the Ards of Co. Down failed miserably.

Shane O'Neill, the ruler of Ulster, was a powerful and formidable enemy until his death in 1567.

In 1569, Sir James Fitzmaurice, a cousin of the fifteenth Earl of Desmond, hatched a plot which culminated in the Desmond Rebellion. He sent agents to Spain and to the Vatican to arrange that a Habsburg prince, chosen by Elizabeth's brother-in-law and arch-enemy, King Philip II of Spain, should be adopted as their ruler by the Irish. This plan did not materialize, but Fitzmaurice, wanted by the Crown for leading rebellious forays in Munster, fled to Rome in 1575. Once there he persuaded the Pope to sanction a papal expeditionary force which landed in Co. Kerry in 1579. Sir James's proclamation of war called for the Irish to rally against the Queen, in the name of the true faith. 'This war', he declared, 'is undertaken for the defence of the Catholic religion against the heretics. Pope Gregory XIII hath chosen us for general captain in this same war as it appeareth at large by his own letters patent which thing he did so much rather because his predecessor Pope Pius V had before deprived Elizabeth the patroness of the aforesaid heresies of all power and dominion. . . . Therefore now we fight not against the lawful sceptre and honourable throne of England, but against a tyrant which refuseth to hear Christ speaking by his vicar.'[5]

As the majority of the Irish had firmly resisted the Reformation, so far from consolidating the power of the Crown, it provided a banner, the Catholic cause, under which fractious anti-English factions could rally.

The sixteenth Earl of Desmond mounted an unsuccessful rebellion after escaping from Dublin Castle; then he vacillated, lying low, undecided whether to join the new revolt. He finally came out in 1579, attacked Youghal (where he desecrated the parish church) and other towns. The papal force of six hundred Italians and Spaniards, carrying six thousand muskets, landed in Co. Kerry. They were defeated and surrendered, but were brutally slaughtered by the English as an admonition to any other would-be allies of the Irish. Sir James Fitzmaurice died in a minor skirmish; his successor Sir John of Desmond was killed; Askeaton surrendered in 1580, and the short but bloody Desmond Rebellion was over. When the Earl of Desmond was killed three years later, the Geraldine power ended. An act was passed in 1586 to confiscate his estates. They were divided into seignories ranging in size from four thousand to twelve thousand acres, and offered to English adventurers (called 'undertakers'), who were invited to settle their lands with loyal English farmers. These settlers were constantly harassed and attacked by the former occupiers of the land, infuriated by their ejection and eager to avenge such

atrocities of the recent rebellion as those of the English commander, Sir Nicholas Malby. After defeating Sir John of Desmond in an engagement near by, Malby bombarded the abbey of Monasternenagh in pursuit of the Irish who took refuge there. His soldiers then put to the sword the forty terrified old monks, who were clinging to the altar.

The English excused such conduct on the grounds that Catholic clerics were enemies of the state. Dermot O'Hurley, the Catholic Archbishop of Cashel, had been to Rome to plot with Pope Gregory XIII against Queen Elizabeth. He returned to Ireland and was hidden by Catholic nobles, such as the Baron of Slane, but was eventually caught and executed at Dublin in 1584.

Hardly had Munster been reduced to an uneasy quiet than real trouble started in the north. In 1591, Red Hugh O'Donnell escaped from Dublin Castle, reached Donegal, and recaptured his castle and the abbey. He imported three thousand mercenaries from Scotland to bolster his forces, helped the Maguire to retake Enniskillen Castle the following year, and took Sligo in 1595.

Hugh O'Neill, the cunning Earl of Tyrone and the most powerful man in Ulster, played the double role of Queen's Earl and Gael's Chief with consummate skill, until in 1595, with six thousand trained troops at his disposal, he came out against the Crown in open rebellion. The Spanish help he expected did not arrive due to bad weather, but he won an important victory at the Yellow Ford in 1598, completely routing the English forces under Sir George Bagenal. Queen Elizabeth was incensed. She sent her favourite the Earl of Essex to Ireland in 1599, with a huge force. Essex's army was soon reduced to a quarter of its size, fighting the O'Mores and O'Connors in central Ireland and the O'Byrnes and O'Tooles, who conducted a fierce guerrilla-type warfare from the Wicklow Mountains. Essex returned to England in disgrace. The English situation in Ireland was rapidly deteriorating. The MacMahons took Monaghan; the O'Rorkes defeated, captured and beheaded the English Governor of Connaught. The settlement in Munster disintegrated.

The next Lord Deputy, Mountjoy, landed in Ireland in 1600. He was a capable man with two equally capable subordinates, Sir George Carew in Munster and Sir Arthur Chichester in Ulster. A Spanish force of over four thousand men landed at Kinsale in Co. Cork in October 1601. The Ulster chiefs had wanted them to land in the north-west, but the adverse weather forced them to the south coast. The Spanish held Kinsale under siege. The northern Earls, O'Donnell of Tyrconnell and O'Neill of Tyrone were obliged to make the long march south. The other Irish chiefs did not co-ordinate their efforts to help. Brian Oge MacMahon betrayed the battle plans of his own people to the English, and the Irish forces were swiftly defeated by Mountjoy at Kinsale. The Spaniards surrendered and returned to Spain; O'Donnell of Tyrconnell went with them and died there. Tyrone returned north, fending off the attacks of those his soldiers had plundered on the way down. At home in Ulster he suffered continual blows from Sir Arthur Chichester's forces, and finally surrendered to the Crown at Mellifont, Co. Louth, in 1603. In 1607 he and Rory, Earl of Tyrconnell (who had succeeded his brother) sailed from Lough Swilly for the Continent, never to return. With the flight of the Earls, after a series of defeats, the old Gaelic society was doomed.

It is not surprising that during these troubled years under the Tudor monarchs there was practically no church-building, and considerable destruction. The Protestants, few in number, were assigned the old parish churches. In the towns, and in the Pale, they usually managed to hold the churches; but those scattered in other rural areas were rarely able to take possession. It was difficult to tempt English preachers to take Irish livings, as English ones were more lucrative and not constantly fraught with physical danger. Only second-rate preachers accepted the poorer Irish benefices. These men lacked organizing ability, had no Irish, and often hardly any Latin. Many churches left without revenues or incumbent soon fell into decay. Others, used as barracks by troops, suffered damage and destruction.

The first Protestant church to be built as such, in 1579, was at Newry, Co. Down, an English stronghold. The Church of Ireland parish church incorporates this sixteenth-century building, but it has undergone major alterations.

The collegiate church of St Nicholas at Galway, still in use, was one of the few churches in Ireland to be enlarged and improved during the troubled second half of the sixteenth century. In the important mercantile port city the right to appoint the clergy of the collegiate church was vested in the mayor and corporation. Stephen Lynch, a scion of the family which gave the city several mayors, extended the south transept to its present length in 1561. At the same time he raised the roof of the old north transept to match the height of the new one. The triplet windows in the south transept date from that time. In 1583, the then Mayor of Galway, John French, widened the north aisle; that date still appears carved on its central spandrel. In 1590 another Mayor of Galway, James Lynch, installed a wooden belfry (replaced by the present spire in 1683) and presented the church with a chime of bells, one of which survives.

King James VI of Scotland succeeded to the thrones of England and Ireland at Elizabeth's death in 1603; thus one monarch ruled the three countries. In Ireland, Sir Arthur Chichester, who had vanquished O'Neill, succeeded as Lord Deputy in 1605. The epitaph on his elaborate monument in Carrickfergus Parish Church, Co. Antrim, expresses

Chicester monument in the south transept of St Nicholas, Carrickfergus, Co. Antrim.

Kilbrogan Church, Bandon, Co. Cork, detail of tower.

Communion table from Kilbrogan Church, Bandon.

very well the sanguine English viewpoint of the time:

> Sir Arthur Chichester Knight Baron of Belfast . . . after the flight of the Earls of Tiron and Terconnell and other Archtraytors their accomplice having suppressed O'Doughertie . and other northern rebels and setled the plantacon of this province and well and happely governed this Kingdome in florishing estate under James our King the space of 11 yeres and more whilest hee was Ld Deputie and Governor Generall thereof retyred himself into his private government and being mindfull of his mortalitie . . . hath caused this chapell to be repaired and this valt and monument to be made. . . .

There follow several stanzas praising the Viceroy who 'made this land late rude with peace to florish' and his worthy brother 'by base rebells slayn/ as he in martiall and brave warrelike feight/ opposde their furie in his countreys right'.

Many Irish hoped that the new King, as the son of a Catholic, might be lenient towards the Catholics; they therefore celebrated mass openly. However, in 1605 Chichester issued a proclamation making known the King's position against religious tolerance in Ireland. All seminary and other priests were ordered to quit the country before 10 December 1605, and forbidden to return. It was also forbidden to send children abroad for education. In 1608 the Irish Privy Council reported that priests and seminarians were landing secretly in every port and creek in the realm. The Crown appreciated the expediency of extinguishing Catholic power in Ireland, quickly and firmly. Six Ulster counties had fallen to the Crown through the forfeitures of the rebels O'Neill, O'Doherty, O'Cahan, O'Donnell, Maguire and others. These lands were systematically settled with English, Welsh and lowland Scots settlers, all staunch Protestants. The plantation was more successful in eastern Ulster, where the settlers came mainly from Scotland, than in western Ulster, where the former county of Coleraine (now Derry) was granted to London Companies; but in general the settlers had come to stay. In 1592, a university had been established in Dublin – Trinity College – whence came ministers for the churches of the growing number of Protestant settlers.

In Munster, an energetic adventurer, Richard Boyle, laid out the town of Bandon in Co. Cork, and two years after its foundation, built a new Protestant church there in a hang-over of the Late Gothic style. This church, Kilbrogan, of 1610, was in use until recently, but due to the paucity of Protestant parishioners it has now been dismantled. The reformers swept away stone altars along with the statues; a simple table, the 'Lord's Board', took their place. The Jacobean oak communion table in use in

Kilbrogan Church from 1610 is now in Ballymodan Church, Bandon, across the river. It is the oldest surviving communion table in the country. Bandon's founder, who became Earl of Cork, is buried at Youghal, Co. Cork, his principal residence. There he purchased the south transept of the parish church as a burial chapel for his family. The Earl's funeral monument, sculpted by Alexander Hills, 1619, is a handsome one. On each side of the recumbent figure of the great adventurer stand his wives, one holding a baby; below are effigies of the Boyle children, four sons and five daughters. Round the ruins of the thirteenth-century cathedral of Lismore, a few miles up the Blackwater from Youghal, the Earl built a new cathedral in 1633; it is still in use.

The old cathedral of Derry had been destroyed during the Ulster Rebellion. Derry, renamed Londonderry, was granted to a London Company. When the Protestant Bishop built a new cathedral for the growing immigrant population, the cost, £4,000, was defrayed by the Corporation of the City of London. The work began in 1628 and the rectangular building, 240 feet by 66 feet, was completed by 1633; it had a nave flanked by aisles with pillared arcades. One of the effects of the Reformation and the Book of Common Prayer was to emphasize corporate worship, bringing the minister into the body of the church and diminishing the importance of the chancel; rectangular hall-type churches were therefore found suitable. Architecturally, Derry Cathedral was already out of fashion when it was built, but the Gothic tradition died hard. In London a contemporary City church, St Katherine Cree, consecrated in 1631, was only partly classical; Derry, with its battlemented walls and octagonal spire on the tower at its west end, had the appearance of the older London City churches. The cathedral, still in use in the heart of bomb-scarred Derry, has undergone some changes. In the eighteenth century the Earl-Bishop added a pierced spire which, while elegant, was fragile, and became so dilapidated that a new tower and spire were built in the nineteenth century. Later in the last century a chancel was added to the east end, but it preserves the original east window. In 1910 a chapter-house and chapel were added to the north and south of the chancel, so the building is again rectangular.

About the same time as Bishop Hopkins built Derry Cathedral, settlers in South Ulster, at Belturbet, Co. Cavan, built themselves a parish church. The fact that it was a cruciform building may indicate that it was a remodelling of an earlier structure; the pointed east window with simple Gothic tracery of intersecting arcs may also have come from an earlier church, although it could be a product of traditionalism. The other windows are

Detail of the Earl of Cork's monument in St Mary's Church, Youghal, Co. Cork.

St Columba's Cathedral, Derry, the east end as it appeared in the eighteenth century before the addition of the chancel.

round-headed like those of Lismore, but at Belturbet they are grouped. The plain round-headed door to the transept at Belturbet resembles the original seventeenth-century one on the transept at Lismore. Another parish church in Co. Cavan, at Killeshandra, built later in the seventeenth century, had round-headed windows and a handsome Jacobean door, now hardly visible in the creeper-clad ruin.

The most perfect example of a seventeenth-century Church of Ireland church is the Middle Church at Ballinderry, Co. Antrim, built by Jeremy Taylor, Bishop of Down and Connor, for the settler community soon after the Restoration, in 1664. It was a simple rectangle, and as it stands today retains its original appearance to a remarkable degree. The gallery at the west end, lit by two oculus windows and entered by an outside stair, was added in the eighteenth century to accommodate more people, but it scarcely changes the effect. This charming little church is still lit by candlelight; the candlesticks are attached to each oak box-pew and to the three-tier oak pulpit and reader's desk. The church has many of its simple but elegant original fittings: the box-pews (whose doors have wooden latches), the communion table and chairs (made about 1666 from the oak roof-timbers of the ruined pre-Reformation church at Portmore), the treen chalice, the long-handled collecting-pans and the baptismal font. The old roof-timbers of the church were replaced by new oak ones in 1902.

Colonel Arthur Hill, Member of Parliament for Down, Antrim and Armagh, the local landlord, built a parish church for the settler community at Hillsborough, Co. Down, in 1663. It was in use for a century, until his descendant rebuilt it.

After the Restoration, especially under the Viceroy, Ormonde, Dublin throve and expanded. The Duke of Ormonde, a rich, brilliant, tolerant aristocrat, attracted to the city a cosmopolitan post-Restoration society: newly honoured Royalist nobles, gentlemen, merchants, civil servants, scholars, fortune-seekers, artisans. Head of the powerful Butler family, born a Catholic, he was raised as a Protestant by order of the Crown. He remained a convinced member of the Church of Ireland, but was a pronounced moderate, always on good terms with his own kinsmen and other Catholics. He promoted the growth of Dublin, including public building. The church of Dublin Castle, St Werburgh's, was rebuilt in 1662, but not very well, for it only lasted fifty years before being replaced. About 1670 the dilapidated medieval parish churches of St Audoen and St Michael-and-all-Angels were restored. In that year St Patrick's Cathedral got new bells; in the following year it was re-roofed. The rascally architect William Dodson, who worked for the Viceroy, rebuilt St Andrew's Church on a new site. The building was a hybrid, but probably the first church in Ireland to include classical elements, already established in England. The plan was elliptical. Dodson's church was jerry-

Ballinderry Middle Church, Co. Antrim.

built, due more to his avarice than his incompetence, and soon began to collapse. In the next decade St John's, Fishamble Street, and St Peter's, Aungier Street, were entirely rebuilt – the latter largely at the expense of the landlord of the area, Francis Aungier, Earl of Longford. St Bride's Church was rebuilt in 1684, and in 1685 work began on a new church for St Michan's parish, to serve the growing new suburb on the north side of the Liffey. St Michan's, which is still in use, is an unpretentious building. It is designed on a Renaissance plan, for the ideas which had reached England from Italy many years before had at last filtered into Ireland; however, its elevation is drab and unimaginative, scarcely affected by classical dictates. Beneath the church are the vaults, also built in the seventeenth century. They contain macabre mummified corpses, preserved by the unusual atmospheric conditions which prevail there.

At the same time some churches in provincial towns were repaired. St Nicholas, Galway, got a new pyramidal spire in 1683, and in 1685 the medieval parish church of St Nicholas, Dundalk, Co. Louth, was remodelled (pl. XI, p. 122).

The few churches erected frequently included pieces of earlier buildings, especially windows. One example, now roofless, is at Mansfieldstown, Co. Louth. It was rebuilt at the end of the seventeenth century, when a fifteenth-century window salvaged from elsewhere was inserted. The new church was a simple hall-type rectangle with a bell-cote and plain round-headed doorway at the west end. The report to the Episcopal Visitation in 1690 stated that £100 would be required to repair the church, and £40 for the chancel. By 1692 the windows had been glazed, the walls repaired, and the church painted and provided with 'a decent pulpit, good Communion Table, a decent carpet and also a Font of stone'.[6] The minister and the local landlord promised soon to provide a linen cloth and silver chalice. The church still had no parish chest, bells or books, but the landlord, Mr Tisdall, had promised an English Bible.

In the second quarter of the seventeenth century, a number of ministers of the immigrant Scots communities in Ulster were ejected from their parishes by the hierarchy of the Church of Ireland, intolerant of their Presbyterian tenets and keen to curtail their freedom. The Scots troops who were brought to Ireland to help quash the rising of 1641 helped their compatriots to form the first independent presbytery in the country, at Carrickfergus, Co. Antrim. Presbyterianism spread rapidly throughout Ulster; by 1665 it had a hundred thousand adherents. Under Charles II and James II the Presbyterians were harassed and persecuted. The ministers, who were ordained secretly, preached at night, in warehouses, barns or open fields. They were liable to a fine if they dispensed the Lord's Supper. Under these circumstances they could hardly build churches. The Presbyterian church at Urney, Co. Tyrone, was built in 1654 under Cromwell, and reconstructed after the persecutions in 1695, when the Presbyterians enjoyed a period of respite under William III, who was favourably disposed towards them. This late seventeenth-century building is still in use today. It is a rectangle with one entrance for the congregation and one for the minister; due to renovations and redecoration it has lost its original appearance. At Randalstown, Co. Antrim, the Drummaul Presbyterian congregation built a church about 1670 on land granted to them by the Marchioness of Antrim, born Rose O'Neill of Shane's Castle. This church was in use until 1790.

The members of the Society of Friends (Quakers), who had settled in Ireland in the seventeenth century, worshipped at first in private houses, or simple buildings of domestic appearance, like the thatched Meeting House at Lisburn, Co. Antrim, built in 1674; parts of this are incorporated in the present Meeting House.

Despite King James I's refusal to grant religious tolerance, the mendicant friars, to whom the people were particularly attached, persisted in their apostolate. In practice the authorities often turned a blind eye. The spirit of the Counter-Reformation was nourished by fervent clerics who returned to Ireland after studying on the Continent; Catholic resistance therefore stiffened. Pope Urban VII proclaimed a Bull exhorting the Irish Catholics to suffer death rather than conform, even for convenience. The Irish Franciscans at Louvain set up a printing-press with Irish type; they printed and circulated Irish catechisms from 1611.

It was reported in 1613 that the Catholics in Ireland had 're-edified monasteries wherein friars publicly preach and say mass'.[7] The Franciscan friary at Buttevant, Co. Cork, one of whose chalices is dated 1600, was repaired in 1604.[8] The Dowager Countess of Clanrickarde paid for Kilnalahan Friary, Co. Galway, to be re-roofed about 1615.[9] At Ross, Co. Galway, there were six friars active in that year. In 1621 the friars contrived to re-establish themselves at Kildare, for even in the Pale most of the old Anglo-Norman aristocracy remained Catholic. Multyfarnham Friary, Co. Westmeath, because of its isolated situation, was a haven for priests seeking refuge. Despite frequent raids, elderly and infirm friars and priests were hidden there. The Crucifixion plaque, dated 1625, at Turlough, Co. Mayo, belongs to this period of Counter-Reformation struggle.

In 1641 the troubled domestic situation in England, where Charles I was opposed by the Parliamentarians, provided the Irish with an occasion to rebel again. However, all the Irish Catholics were not united. Most of the old Anglo-Norman families were Catholic but Royalist, willing to fight against the Cromwellians for the King. The native Irish leaders persisted in refusing to acknowledge a heretic monarch, and looked abroad for help. Had both groups united to fight Cromwell, a common enemy, they might have been successful; but, unable to resolve their differences, they were utterly defeated by 1652. The Papal Nuncio Extraordinary, Cardinal Rinuccini, who came to Ireland in 1645, was intransigent: his faction could not be reconciled with the Royalists; Edmund O'Dwyer, the Catholic Bishop of Limerick, on the other hand, threw in his lot with them. He had had a life full of adventure: Turkish pirates had captured him at sea between England and France, and sold him into slavery in Smyrna; and when Limerick capitulated to Cromwell's besiegers, he had to flee in disguise to Brussels.

In 1642, at a provincial synod at Kells, Archbishop O'Reilly proposed a government composed of laymen and clergy, which would guide and prosecute a war with the Church's blessing. This resulted in the formation of a parliament at Kilkenny, whose members styled themselves 'The Confederate Catholics of Ireland'. Their aim was to restore the rights of the Catholic Church, while remaining loyal to the King of England as their monarch and maintaining the liberties of the Irish nation.

Catholic hopes revived in the 1640s. When Cardinal Rinuccini arrived in 1645 the Catholics were again in possession of Limerick and Kilkenny Cathedrals, and he celebrated mass in both. In 1647 the Catholic Bishop of Kilmacduagh repossessed the cathedral there, re-roofed part of it, and re-dedicated it in 1649. The monks of Meelick, Co. Galway, emerged from hiding and celebrated mass with a full procession.

When the Cromwellians were victorious most of the bishops went into exile; the Archbishop of Cashel was deported to Spain. Ireland was left practically without any Catholic hierarchy.

The Catholic Rising of 1641 was extremely ferocious. Many dispossessed Irish took the opportunity to settle scores locally, avenging old grievances. Several thousand unwelcome settlers were massacred, and many more relieved of their belongings. The unleashed fury of the Irish caused many Protestants to flee to England. Their arrival there provoked renewed anti-Catholic, anti-Irish feeling in England. The atrocities perpetrated by Cromwell and his soldiers in retaliation, with grim determination, bred a new spate of hatred and distrust in Ireland, with consequent further intransigence.

Church buildings fared badly again, often being used by the troops as quarters. The Catholics, once more dismissed from the churches they had managed to retake, could not build others, though at Ross Erilly, Co. Galway, where the friars were particularly persistent (they were expelled seven times between the Dissolution and 1753), Soracha Ionin did manage to erect a little chapel with mullioned windows off the south wall of the nave of the friary church, for herself and her family in 1678. Mass was celebrated secretly, usually in farmhouses or barns, sometimes in inns, often in the open air.

New Protestant settlers, Cromwellians, came to rural areas to enjoy lands forfeited by rebels. Many Confederate Catholics were removed from their homes and transplanted across the Shannon. Some of these unfortunate people were restored to their estates by Charles II; nevertheless by 1665 the imposed Protestant ascendant class was effectively installed. It held four-fifths of all the land in Ireland. Most of the remaining fifth, in Catholic hands, was in Connaught. In Charles II's reign an unpopular Act was passed to raise money for the payment of the Protestant clergy in Ireland by taxing the householders of Clonmel, Cork, Drogheda, Dublin, Kinsale, Limerick and Waterford (who were mostly Catholics), twelve pence in the pound annually.

The oppressed Catholics looked for improvement of their lot under the next King, James II, a professed Catholic, who appointed a Catholic Viceroy in Ireland in 1687, the Earl of Tyrconnell.

In 1688, King James was forced to flee, having lost his throne to his Protestant daughter, Mary, and son-in-law, William of Orange. In 1689, James landed in Ireland from France. This time the Catholics in Ireland were all able to unite in favour of a Catholic monarch. However, allegiances on the Continent had changed. The Holy See had quarrelled with France, and was now favouring the Grande Alliance – which included William of Orange and the Emperor – against James's ally Louis XIV. As a result, when the Irish Catholics were finally united, they did not have the help of the Vatican which tacitly supported their enemy. The French, embroiled in wars on the Continent, could afford scant support for James in Ireland. The Irish, though desperate, were ill-trained and poorly equipped. King James was a poor leader, half-hearted and lacking courage, diplomacy and sagacity. His son-in-law was an able leader with well-equipped and well-trained men. After the defeat of the Battle of the Boyne in 1690, King James returned to France. Limerick fell to King William's forces in 1691, and ten thousand Irish Catholics, the defeated officers and soldiers of the Jacobite forces, with some of their dependants, went into exile on the Continent. The estates of the Jacobites, totalling nearly one million acres, were confiscated by the victors.

CHAPTER 7

The years of the Ascendancy 1691–1799

IRELAND, AFTER THE JACOBITE DEFEAT, with the Catholic population debarred from wielding power, became an attractive refuge for French Protestants. When Louis XIV revoked the Edict of Nantes, which had granted some tolerance to the Calvinist minority, many were forced to emigrate, abandoning homes and property, and some settled in Ireland. There was one such Huguenot community in Dublin, weavers mostly, and artisans. They worshiped in the Lady Chapel of St Patrick's Cathedral, which became known as the 'French Church'. When their numbers increased, a new church, St Luke's, was built, mainly for their use, about 1708. At Waterford, the corporation turned over the chapel of the old Franciscan friary to refugees who arrived in 1693; it too became known as the 'French Church'. There were also two non-conformist French congregations in Dublin. One group of French Protestants was granted leases at Portarlington in Co. Leix, where they built their own church at the end of the century, named St Paul's. Services were conducted in French into the nineteenth century, but now St Paul's (rebuilt later in the last century) serves as the Church of Ireland parish church of Portarlington; the English-speaking community built their own church about 1700, but it fell into disuse.

Dublin continued to expand with the growth of parliamentary power and of the central government there. As well as continental immigrants, it received a steady flow from England, mostly civil servants, tradesmen and artisans. To meet the requirements of the growing metropolis, St Mary's Church in Mary Street was built about 1700–2. The architect, Thomas Burgh, was of old Norman stock, a son of Ulysses Burgh, Bishop of Ardagh. In 1700, still a young man, he became Surveyor-General. He was responsible for many handsome new buildings in the

capital, including the Royal Barracks, the old Custom House, the Library of Trinity College, the Infirmary of the Royal Hospital and Dr Steevens's Hospital. Burgh's concept of ecclesiastical architecture was based on the work of the classicists who rebuilt the London City churches after the Great Fire of 1666. Though competent, he lacked flair, and he was additionally hampered in his Dublin church-building by lack of funds. His are pleasant, practical churches, using classical elements based on English work. The exterior of St Mary's is unprepossessing; it is evident that funds for embellishment were limited, for a planned tower over the west end never rose above the first storey. The drabness of the exterior is relieved by the good classical west door and handsome east window surrounded with bolection moulding and flanked by pilasters beneath a scrolled moulding. The interior of St Mary's is narrower and higher than its late seventeenth-century English models. Like some London Wren churches it is galleried, the gallery running between orders of superimposed pillars, the upper of which support the vault of the nave. The aisles and galleries have flat ceilings. It was the first church to be built in Ireland with a gallery, a device which immediately proved popular, for it was economical, attractive and convenient. Throughout the eighteenth century the churches built in Dublin after St Mary's were all galleried. A galleried church was particularly suited for urban use, providing as it did maximum seating accommodation in a limited area. At St Mary's an additional gallery was even squeezed in above the main one, on both sides of the organ. This was not a comfortable place to sit or reach; the paupers who would have been obliged to worship so much closer to heaven must have gained their seats with panting resentment. The *hoi polloi* of the parish had to be content with the main gallery, while the gentry

St Werburgh's, Dublin, façade.

and burgesses had comfortable box-pews on the ground floor. The interior woodwork is quite lavish. The cornices are richly carved, and in a frieze on the organ-case are figures depicted in early eighteenth-century dress. Compared with London churches, St Mary's now seems mean, but in Dublin in 1700 it was the *dernier cri*, and much admired.

After St Mary's, Burgh designed a new church for St Werburgh's, the Castle parish; it was built in 1715. Burgh's interior with its compartmented ceiling and his original wooden tower and dome were destroyed by fire in 1754. However, as the tower built to replace the burnt one has since been demolished, the west front as it now presents itself is that of Burgh's original building of 1715. As might be expected of the parish which served the Castle, there was money available, and Burgh's three-bay front, while not magnificent, was certainly elegant. The pediment over the door rests on an entablature supported by Doric columns. In the outer metopes of the frieze are human skulls and crossed bones, which may have pleased puritanically inclined parishioners. On the inner metopes, correctly separated by triglyphs, are two bucrania.

William King, an energetic Archbishop of Dublin, initiated a programme of church-building and repairing in the city, backed by an Act of Parliament in 1707. The first church erected under this scheme was a new one for the Parish of St Nicholas Within, built in the year of the Act. It was an unpretentious classical church, possibly designed by Burgh. St Luke's, a simple galleried hall, plain and economical, was the next to be built.

Isaac Wills was the architect of St Ann's in Dawson Street, also built under the auspices of the 1707 Act. Wills had been employed by Burgh and may have worked for him on St Werburgh's. The ambitious original plan for the west front of St Ann's was an extravagant, ornate Baroque façade,[1] but it was never executed. Lewis reported in 1837 that the front was still unfinished, and consisted only of 'a portal with Doric half-columns'.[2] The front seen today was made in the last century, without regard to the style of the splendid interior, which remains much as Wills designed it, save for the insertion of stained glass in the windows, and modern lighting fixtures. The pews have been renovated. The gallery round three sides of the church rests on smooth, sober Ionic columns; the best carving, richly gilded, is in the apse. This apse appears to be the first reappearance of the form in Ireland since its use at Mellifont Abbey in the twelfth century.

The exact building date of the basilical-plan eighteenth-century church at Turlough, Co. Mayo, is not known, but it was probably also early in the century; it is now roofless.

The Protestants of Cork, who included many wealthy citizens, built Christ Church in 1720, followed soon after by St Nicholas, begun in 1720, St Anne Shandon in 1722, St Paul's in 1723, and the modest new St Finbar's (now demolished) in 1735. Christ Church, designed by the architect Coltsman, was a dull building, although the unostentatious galleried interior had considerable charm. St Anne Shandon, standing above a labyrinth of streets and alleyways, is a rectangular structure with an elegant graduated tower. The builders used silvery-white limestone for two sides of this tower, and purplish-red stone for the other two. Many visitors are attracted to St Anne's to hear the famous carillon.

The foundation-stone of Christ Church, Lisburn, Co. Antrim, was laid in 1708, but building continued for at least twenty years. The tower at the west end, contemporary with that of St Anne Shandon, bears a remarkable likeness to it, despite the dissimilar windows. The slender octagonal spire above the tower at Lisburn was added at the beginning of the nineteenth century.

The towers and belfries of St Anne Shandon, Cork (right), and Lisburn, Co. Antrim (left).

Moira Church of Ireland Parish Church, Co. Down, façade.

The Church of Ireland parish church at Moira, Co. Down, was built one year after St Anne Shandon, in 1723; it, too, is a simple rectangular church with a tower over the west end. The original spire was replaced by the present one in 1884. While it, and the rather graceless tower, tend to dwarf the façade, the over-all effect is naive and not displeasing. The lower part of the two-storey façade has been harmoniously conceived; the pedimented door flanked by finely executed Doric pilasters is handsome, and lends an air of distinction to the whole building.

At Downpatrick, Co. Down, the Church of Ireland parish church was rebuilt about 1733; it is the favoured rectangular hall-type building. The work may have been supervised by Ireland's leading architect of the day, Sir Edward Lovett Pearce, to whom the design of the Southwell School and Almshouse at Downpatrick, built in 1733, is attributed. The windows of the church have Gibbs surrounds. These were first used by the architect James Gibbs on the church of St Clement Danes, London, in 1719. In 1728 Gibbs published his *Book of Architecture* with illustrations; it was widely read and builders eagerly used the illustrations as patterns.

St John's, Ballymore, Co. Donegal, a window with a Gibbs surround.

Pearce (who had succeeded Burgh as Surveyor-General) or one of his assistants may have brought these window designs to Downpatrick. The church also has an accomplished Venetian window at the east end; this is a classical element at which Pearce excelled.

St John's, Ballymore, Clondehorky parish, Co. Donegal, also has a well-executed Venetian east window, and windows with Gibbs surrounds in the south wall. The architect of this rectangular church may have been Michael Priestley of Derry, who built the handsome courthouse at Lifford, Co. Donegal, in 1745. The Board of First Fruits gave £300 for building, prior to 1766, and possibly prior to 1745. The vestibule at the west end was added afterwards to accommodate the stair to the gallery; it too has been given a Venetian window. St John's has a light, pleasant interior. The architect created four niches on the north wall to balance the four windows in the south wall; the whole effect is one of tasteful simplicity. The walls are panelled to a height of about 6 feet. Unfortunately some well-meaning person armed with a paintbrush, some molasses-like paint, and possibly a comb, has dexterously attended to this wooden panelling, along with the box-pews and simple benches, painting and graining all as though they were made of some base material in need of disguise.

A Venetian window and a fine pedimented doorway were inserted in the tower of St Nicholas Parish Church, Carrickfergus, Co. Antrim, probably about 1740.

A number of ancient churches, such as Tuamgraney, Co. Clare, and Rahan, Co. Offaly, remained in use; though small, they could hold the Protestant parishioners of such rural parishes. Parts of medieval buildings were also converted for use. The Protestants of Kilmallock blocked off the chancel of the old collegiate church to serve as their parish church. At Kilfenora, Co. Clare, the nave of the old cathedral was enclosed for the same purpose. At Lorrha, Co. Tipperary, the Church of Ireland parish church is a part of an old monastic one. Where there was an energetic incumbent, or an interested and generous patron, a new church might be built; but such instances were rare in the first half of the eighteenth century. One, for example, was built in 1707 at Ballinderry, Co. Tyrone; another, at Freshford, Co. Kilkenny, built in 1730, incorporated a salvaged Romanesque door and window.

Despite King William III's debt of gratitude to the Presbyterians for their help at Derry, and his goodwill towards them, he was unable to secure an Act of Toleration in their favour. Consequently, during Queen Anne's reign, 1702–14, they were severely incapacitated by the Penal Laws. The doors of their

Meeting Houses were nailed up, and they, like the Catholics, were excluded from public office by the Test Act and disenfranchised. However, under George I their lot was considerably improved; he restored financial support in the form of the annual King's Bounty, which had been withdrawn, and in 1719 they were granted an Act of Toleration.

Even before this they managed to erect some new Meeting Houses, such as the one at Derry, built in 1690 and demolished in 1777, and the one in the Market Square at Lisburn, Co. Antrim, since rebuilt and enlarged. The original Presbyterian church at Rademon, Co. Down, was built in 1713, then more soundly rebuilt in 1723 after the Act of Toleration. The second building served the congregation for over sixty years. The Eustace Street Congregation in Dublin (founded by an ejected Provost of Trinity College) built a Meeting House which is now a commercial building. Its classical front with segmented pediments over the doors and bolection mouldings, was in keeping with the style of the contemporary parochial churches. At Armagh, the Presbyterians used some of the ruined masonry of the ancient church of St Peter and St Paul to construct their Meeting House in 1722. At Limerick, the Presbyterians rented the chapel of the old Augustinian nunnery in the 1690s and worshipped there until they built a church in Peter Street in 1775. The nature of Presbyterian belief and the form of the service called for a plain building without ornamentation. A T-shape was preferred, with the minister's place at the junction and the congregation disposed in three sections – to each side and facing him. An entrance for the minister was provided in the wall behind his desk, avoiding any procession. The early eighteenth-century Presbyterian church in Stream Street, Downpatrick, Co. Down, is a galleried T-shape building. The congregation opened their Meeting House there in 1711, but the appearance of the present building indicates later improvements.

In the second quarter of the eighteenth century the Presbyterian population of Ireland (which had increased due to immigration from Scotland) began to decrease due to emigration, mainly to North America. Frequently, when old leases expired, the landlords raised the rents exorbitantly, and this, combined with the insufficiency of available farming land, forced many to leave. About six thousand Scots-Irish, as they were called, left in 1729, and by the middle of the century as many as twelve thousand were emigrating annually. In 1726 there was a doctrinal schism in the Presbyterian Church. A minority of the ministers, who were unwilling to subscribe to the Westminster Confession of Faith, seceded with their flocks and formed the Presbytery of Antrim of Non-Subscribing Presbyterians. The

The Moravian church, Gracehill, Co. Antrim.

majority, who adhered to the recognized doctrinal articles, formed the Synod of Ulster. Each had their own Meeting Houses. In 1746, schismatic ministers from Scotland, who had seceded in an argument over patronage, came to Ireland. They collected congregations and formed three new seceding presbyteries, which grew and flourished.

The Quakers, also disenfranchised, built modest, practical Meeting Houses, in keeping with the sobriety and simplicity which their Society stressed, and unhampered by sacramental or liturgical requirements.

John Wesley preached his first sermon in Ireland in St Mary's, Dublin. The Methodists built simply, usually in the vernacular style. At Limerick the first Methodists rented the old church of St Francis Abbey and met there until they built a brick house, at a cost of £600, in 1763. The Methodist Chapel at Enniskillen, Co. Fermanagh, built in 1793, was a humble building indeed, with an earthen floor and thatched roof.

Another Nonconformist group, the Moravians, or United Brethren, built a church in 1765 at Gracehill,

Co. Antrim, where they had established themselves in 1746. It stands on one side of a delightful square, on two other sides of which stand the houses which were the quarters of the brethren and sisters. The rectangular chapel, with a gallery at each end and a central octagonal pulpit, has handsome twin doors with elaborate timber surrounds. One door was for the men of the community, one for the women; they sat at opposite ends of the chapel, and when they died were buried separately in the quaint cemetery at the rear. The Moravians built a church in Bishop Street, Dublin, in 1753.

Generally in the eighteenth century members of the Established Church and Catholics were buried in the same consecrated burial-ground. Funeral monuments of persons of both persuasions are to be found in and about most pre-Reformation churches, often with charming, naive stone-carving, sometimes classically chaste and elegant, frequently inserted into the ancient fabric with the same ruthless disregard that obtains today. The fourteenth-century church at Fenagh, Co. Leitrim, has a monument on the east wall, the work of a local mason named Price, with an inscription that reads:

> Our Hearts are Joyned
> Why not our Arms
> Love and Friendship
> have many Charms.

One half was commissioned by John Peyton of Laceen in memory of his parents, John Peyton and Jane Molloy, who died in 1741 and 1718; the other by George Reynolds of Loughscur, in memory of his sister Mrs Mary Taylor who died in 1751.

Peyton–Reynolds monument at the south church, Fenagh, Co. Leitrim.

The Catholics did not fare as well as the Presbyterians. The animosity engendered by the massacres of the seventeenth century, and the endless plots and frequent rebellions, came home to roost. Instead of enjoying relief and concessions, they were oppressed with severe restrictions aimed at ensuring their absolute social and civic impotence, and at exterminating the Catholic religion. King William III had promised his Catholic ally, the Emperor, that if he were victorious in Ireland in 1689, he would assure the Catholics religious liberty. Before the Battle of Aughrim he had proposed that the Catholics should be allowed to exercise their religion freely, be given back one-half of the churches, share in government, and have their former properties restored. The Treaty of Limerick in 1691 guaranteed the defeated Catholics the right to exercise their religion as they had enjoyed it in Charles II's reign, and also protection from religious persecution. These terms were soon repudiated shamelessly in order to placate Protestant opinion. The Emperor protested through his ambassador, but to no avail. The French could hardly protest against discrimination, having themselves just brutally expelled the Protestants from France. Bowing to anti-Catholic fanaticism, born of an unhealthy mixture of genuine religious conviction, genuine fear, greed and ignorance, the King, now secure on his throne, went back on all his promises. In 1697, freed of obligations to his Catholic allies by the Peace of Ryswick, he allowed the first of the Penal Laws to pass through parliament. This law ordered all the Catholic hierarchy to leave Ireland before 1 May 1698, on pain of imprisonment and transportation. The Act also expelled the Jesuits, monks, friars, and all regulars of the various orders. From 29 December 1697, these proscribed persons were forbidden to return to Ireland. Fines were imposed on persons concealing the proscribed clergy, part of which was given to informers. Although it would seem that such a law could not easily be enforced, it was in fact fairly successful. By the end of 1703 there were only two Catholic bishops left in Ireland, both in hiding; five years later one of these had been caught and imprisoned, and the other was too aged and infirm to officiate. Over four hundred regulars were shipped out of Ireland in 1698, and others were deported as they were captured. Some contrived to remain; they forsook their habits and hid in the homes of those who would risk fines to harbour them.

With no bishops in Ireland to perform ordinations, candidates for the priesthood had to go secretly to the Continent and be smuggled back. The Protestant Revenue men, mostly imported from England, who carefully watched the ports, failed to apprehend the little boats that slipped into quiet coves to land their

X Claregalway Friary, Co. Galway (pp. 69, 100) >

cargoes of forbidden priests. Despite the laws which forbade sending any child abroad for instruction, the illicit traffic continued with the help of fishermen and merchants. A steady flow of young men reached the seminaries in France, Flanders, Italy and Spain, returning to serve as undercover priests. The punishment for illegal entry, stipulated in an act of 1704, was imprisonment and transportation for the first offence, death for the second. The Catholic clergy remaining in Ireland were obliged by a penal law of 1704 to register, and to furnish their age, abode, pretended parochial jurisdiction, and particulars of ordination. They also had to produce two sureties of £50 each for their loyal behaviour and obedience to the law. One thousand and eighty-nine priests registered under this act, ostensibly all parish priests permitted to stay in Ireland; but among them were a number of friars and at least two prelates pretending to be parish priests. New priests who were secretly ordained in Ireland, and the greater number ordained abroad, could not, of course, register. Spies and informers were handsomely rewarded for turning in unregistered clerics, but the people willingly hid priests on the run, who often eluded capture by changing their names. A Franciscan friar is named in a Co. Leitrim Grand Jury presentment in 1714 as 'Owen O'Rorke alias Donell alias Robin the Juggler'.[3] In 1719, the exasperated Commons actually proposed that all unregistered clerics apprehended should be branded with a letter 'P' on their cheeks. The Irish Privy Council, which included two bishops and three peers, decided that castration of these celibates would be a more suitable measure than branding, and this they recommended to the English Privy Council, who did not, however, accept either suggestion.[4]

Catholics were prohibited from teaching or keeping schools, barred from the university, the Bench, the Bar and public office; they could neither vote nor sit in parliament; the laws governing land tenure were severely restrictive. 'Protestant Discoverers' could claim the property of Catholic landholders whom they could discover in breach of the laws. A Catholic son who conformed to the Established Church could claim all his father's estate. Mixed marriages were invalid if performed by a Catholic priest, and an attempt was even made in 1733 to invalidate all marriages performed by Catholic priests, and thus bastardize the entire future Catholic population.[5]

Through this period of persecution the Catholic Church continued to function as best it could. Adherence to the old faith was associated with patriotic and national sentiments, and this helped to discourage disaffection. The clergy lived close to, and with, the people. The Church finally emerged from the years of trial unshaken, indeed invigorated.

Mass was celebrated, at the best, in improvised chapels called 'Mass Houses'. These were not usually purpose-built; barns and warehouses were often used. At Portaferry, Co. Down, a Mass House was erected in 1704; this simple building served the community for nearly sixty years. About the same time a chapel was built in Waterford, opposite the present Catholic cathedral. In rural areas priests often officiated in the open air – behind hedges, in hollows and caves, or in the shelter of ruins. At Ballynacarriga, Co. Cork, the top floor of the sixteenth-century castle was used as a chapel. At Graiguenamanagh, Co. Kilkenny, a Mass House was erected against the south wall of the transept of the old Cistercian abbey in 1728. In Belfast, mass was celebrated on an oak table, in a sandpit in Friar's Bush graveyard. The surviving Catholic gentry allowed priests to celebrate mass in their houses, or sometimes (because these were more commodious) in the coach-houses. These gentlemen needed to exercise great care, for a number of them had conformed to the Established Church in order to keep their estates, and Protestant Discoverers watched to see if they received visits from priests.

In Connaught especially landowners protected friars who were in the country illegally. A letter concerning this situation written to the Primate of the Church of Ireland by Mr Eyre of Eyrecourt in Co. Galway, in 1732, is informative.[6] He reported that the only abbey in good repair was Ross, and that the friars were living only a mile away on the estate of a neo-Protestant. Other converts of convenience were harbouring friars of Kilconnell and Portumna, close to their old monasteries. The friars of Dunmore were at Galbally, but those of Esker, Athenry and Claregalway were all close to their old abbeys, the last-named building a new house. The friars of Meelick had almost completed the building of a spacious, slate-roofed brick house (whose ruins can be seen today beside the abbey church). The friars of Kinalahan had leased a house and eight acres adjoining their old abbey and built a commodious well-slated chapel.

At Quin, Co. Clare, the following inscription appears on a tomb in the cloister:

Here lies the body of the Revd John Hogan of Drim who depd this life AD 1820 aged 82 years. The last of the Franciscan Friars who had been residents of Drim the place of their refuge when driven from the Abbey of Quin, he was supported by the pious donations of the faithful and served as an auxiliary to his neighbouring parish priests in the Vineyard of the Lord he knew how to abound and to suffer want as the Lord was pleased

< XI St Nicholas, Dundalk, Co. Louth, the 'Green Church' (p. 113).

123

to send, he died in holy poverty respected for his strictness in religious discipling [*sic*] and venerated by all.

In the cities, Catholic merchants helped their priests. It was reported in 1732 that in Dublin, where Catholics were in the minority, there were several chapels to serve them.[7] The entrance to one Mass House was through a public-house named Adam and Eve's. The name has stuck to the Franciscan church which stands on the site, although all trace of the old buildings has long since been swept away.

By the middle of the century the laws against the clergy were no longer being so strictly enforced. The bitter memories of the seventeenth-century atrocities were fading. The failure of Bonnie Prince Charlie's attempt in Scotland and England in 1745 largely removed the Jacobite threat. Besides, a generation of educated Protestants, mostly graduates of Trinity College, had emerged. These men, influenced by the Age of Enlightenment, were impressed by the tenacity of the Catholics, who could so easily have conformed and reaped material benefits. They saw the injustice of Catholic suffering as a moral wrong, and were willing to help the Catholics evade the Penal Laws. In time these men, mostly third- or fourth-generation descendants of English settlers, had come to feel more Irish than English, in that they realized that the English interest was not necessarily their own. They saw how the English parliament passed laws beneficial to England and inimical to Ireland as a whole, regardless of religious affiliation. Thus a patriot element emerged, pressing for greater autonomy for Ireland and relief for the victims of the Penal Laws.

Under these slightly improved conditions the Catholics, especially in the cities where they had financial support from the merchants, cautiously built a few discreet churches. St Mary's in Limerick city was built on Little Island in 1749. A large but plain cruciform building, it has now vanished like most of the other eighteenth-century Catholic churches, demolished or cloaked in later buildings. St Patrick's, Ballyphilip, Co. Down, for example, built in 1762, was extensively repaired and renovated in 1831. A most interesting survivor is St Patrick's in the city of Waterford, the oldest intact post-Reformation Catholic church in Ireland. The exterior was even more unobtrusive when it was built (in 1764) than it is today, for the entrance was through a very narrow alley between shops and the church was hemmed in by dwellings. Some shops were demolished to create the present approach. The galleried interior is like a little theatre. A second gallery-tier has been squeezed in, to seat the maximum number; it is over the lower floors of the adjoining asylum for old ladies founded in 1754. The main gallery, with an attractive balustrade, runs round three sides of the rectangular church, supported by slender fluted Doric columns on plinths. The altar, which is flanked by fluted pilasters and surmounted by a Neoclassical pediment, has above it, and to each side, eighteenth-century paintings, apparently imported from Italy. A handsome door leads from the chapel into the former residence of the priest, behind the altar.

The two principal Mass Houses in Cork, the original North and South Chapels, were built in 1729.[8] Several more Catholic chapels were built there in the second half of the eighteenth century. The old South Chapel, St Finbar's, rebuilt in 1776, survives. St Mary's was rebuilt in the nineteenth century. The Augustinian chapel, Brunswick Street, was built in 1780, St Peter and St Paul in 1786.

At Limerick none of the eighteenth-century Catholic churches has survived: St Munchin was built in 1744, St Mary's, 1749, St Patrick's, 1750, St John's, 1753 and St Michael's in 1779.[9] St Mary's had above its altar a painting presented by a local merchant in 1760, described as a 'copy of Michelangelo's Crucifixion'.[10] The little chapel of the Augustinians in Creagh Lane was erected in 1778; Timothy Collopy, a Limerick boy who had been sent by them to study painting in Rome, painted an Ascension for it in 1782,[11] and a Crucifixion for St John's. The Dominicans' chapel in Fish Lane, erected as early as 1730, was 60 feet long and 30 feet wide, with galleries supported by Corinthian columns.[12] Many non-Catholics contributed towards the chapel of the Franciscan friars in Newgate Lane, Limerick, built in 1782.

A Catholic chapel at Armagh was built in 1750, at first as three small adjacent buildings, later amalgamated as one. St Catherine's, Meath Street, Dublin, built in 1780, was an unusual octagonal brick building with galleries. At Waterford, the first Mass House, built early in the century, was a galleried building with carved and gilded panelling; it boasted a number of paintings, and statues of saints stood in niches round the walls.[13]

The refined taste of the educated class of the Anglo-Irish (as the descendants of the settlers were known) combined with the affluence of the gentry to produce a number of gracious Protestant places of worship after the mid-century. Dr Bartholomew Mosse, born at Maryborough, Co. Leix, in 1712, is a good example of an enlightened eighteenth-century Anglo-Irishman. Maurice Craig aptly describes him as 'a man who combined to a rare degree the love of architectural magnificence with that of his fellow men'.[14] In 1748 he leased land in Dublin for a maternity hospital, which was built

St Patrick's Church, Waterford, the interior from the altar.

between 1751 and 1757 to a design by the leading architect in the country, Richard Castle. Castle, an immigrant from Germany, of Huguenot extraction, died just before the work commenced, so that it was executed under the supervision of his assistant, John Ensor. The Rotunda Hospital Chapel, 86 feet square and 30 feet high, is unique in Ireland. The lavish and joyous Baroque decoration is reminiscent of the theatrical churches of Bavaria and Austria, although a slight restraint overlies it, as compared with some continental work. Its ebullience is somehow expressed in a peculiarly Irish manner. Were it not the sole example in Ireland of such work, the term 'Irish-Baroque-Rococo' might have been coined to join Irish-Palladian and Irish-Romanesque. The decoration of the Rotunda Chapel was not, in fact, the work of an Irishman, but of an immigrant craftsman, Bartholomew Cramillion, probably a Walloon or a Huguenot from France. Within Richard Castle's pristine framework Cramillion placed his stucco allegories, drape-swathed *putti*, winged cherubheads, trumpet-blowing angels, festoons of plump purple grapes, green vine leaves and olive branches. A gallery supported by fluted Corinthian columns (mahogany, like the handsome pews and Chippendale communion table) runs round three sides of the chapel. Access to it is by two doors opening from a

Stucco-work Allegory of Faith in the Rotunda Hospital Chapel, Dublin.

The Cobbe family gallery in the Church of Ireland parish church, Donabate, Co. Dublin. Below, a detail of the stucco-work in the corner over the chimney-piece.

corridor in the hospital, so an internal stair did not have to be accommodated. Between the upper doors, over the main entrance, is the organ. In an alcove over one side-gallery is a superb allegory of Faith, blindfolded and seated with a cross held up in one hand, in the other a plummet; beneath her a snake lies coiled, and a lively fox is crushed under her sandal. In the niche over the other gallery is an allegory of Hope with an anchor. Above the ornate altar (which is set in a Venetian window on the south wall, and surmounted by a curtain held by flying *putti*, and hanging from a canopy) is an allegory of Charity suckling one babe and embracing another – very suitable for a maternity hospital. The chapel was intended to be even more sumptuous, with more gilding, and paintings by Cipriani ordered for the ceiling oval and four panels.[15] Cramillion's fee for the stucco-work was £568 15s 0d.[16] Dr Mosse died before all his plans were carried out, and the paintings were never done.

The parish church of Donabate, Co. Dublin, a few miles outside the city, was built in 1758 under the auspices of Archbishop Cobbe, the principal landowner in the parish, who had a magnificent house there, Newbridge, built for him by Richard Castle. The entrance to the church is in the south wall; at the west end is an arcaded private gallery for the Cobbe family, still used when they attend. It was made cosy with a chimney in the corner and cushioned benches around, so that some faced the fire with their backs to the preacher and the altar, unless they lolled sideways triclinium-fashion. Unlike the rest of the church, which is simple, the ceiling and frieze of the Cobbes' gallery is decorated with delicate swirling Rococo plasterwork. In the corner over the fireplace the stuccodore has worked in the family motto: 'Moriens Cano'; heraldic charges: two swans; and crest: a pelican's head rising from a ducal coronet. This Rococo stucco-work was the rage in the houses of the wealthy; Archbishop Cobbe had commissioned it to decorate the principal rooms of his seat, and clearly he wished his family's place in church to be equally refined.

In St Patrick's, Tickmacreevan, Glenarm, Co. Antrim, there was a separate door to the south transept; the presence of a chimney there indicates that it accommodated a private gallery for the Earls of Antrim, who rebuilt Glenarm Castle about 1756.

The local landlord, Hugh Boyd, bore the entire expense of the building of the gracious church at Ballycastle, Co. Antrim, in 1756. This church, still in use, is built of stone quarried in the parish. The pleasing three-bay façade is well proportioned; a classical pedimented door in the breakfront centre bay is flanked by smaller doors on the outer bays, with windows above them and Old Testament quotations in panels. Above the eaves-line of the centre bay is the clock-tower, with a Venetian window; it terminates in a balustrade which surrounds the base of an octagonal spire. The interior is equally agreeable, the pedimented west door being repeated on the inside.

Another 'landlord' church of this period is Villierstown, Co. Waterford, built by the Earl of

Ballycastle Church, Co. Antrim. Above façade; below, the interior, west end.

Church of Ireland cathedral, Cashel, Co. Tipperary.

community. The tower and spire were added towards the end of the century by Francis Johnston, who built Townley Hall, a few miles away, in 1792. The original interior is not intact; the box-pews and fine chandeliers have gone, but excellent eighteenth-century plasterwork monuments and woodwork remain. The spacious rectangular church has a gallery; the substantial octagonal oak columns with Corinthian capitals rise to the roof. The stucco ornamentation is of the highest quality. High up at the east end, plaster eagles in high relief, amid swirling foliage, hold open a Bible with the inscription 'Holy-Holy-Holy' in Hebrew characters. Ornate stucco cartouches frame the more important wall-monuments; the windows are flanked by stucco panels surmounted by eagles displayed. The church-yard enclosure has excellent wrought-iron gates. These and the elegant lanterns which crown the gate-piers are splendid examples of eighteenth-century Irish ironwork. St Multose Church, Kinsale, Co. Cork, also has attractive eighteenth-century iron gates, but there the piers are topped by stone urns.

The Neoclassical movement which began in Europe in the 1750s was largely a reaction against Baroque and Rococo extravagances. In Ireland, in ecclesiastical building, save for an occasional exuberant trend in stucco-work, the architectural tradition had remained conservatively close to the English classical revival of the preceding century. The new cathedral at Cashel, Co. Tipperary, begun in 1763, was unaffected by any new spirit; the western porch and tower, added twenty years later, were unashamedly old-fashioned. It is said that the tower and spire were based on a rejected design of James Gibbs for his London church, St Martin-in-the-Fields, built 1721–26;[17] they are certainly in the same vein. Unfortunately most of the eighteenth-century interior furnishing of the cathedral, including the carved stalls which lined the nave, the canopied pulpit and the box-pews, were banished in 1867 when the interior was tastelessly renovated.

The intellectual spirit which prompted the Neoclassicists caused them to reject the mere use of an assembly of classical elements drawn from Renaissance sources; they sought an historical truth by going back to the world of Antiquity. In this search they also rediscovered and appreciated the medieval world, so that the revival of the latter half of the eighteenth century embraced not only Roman and Greek, but also Gothic.

In Ireland, where architectural fashions lagged notoriously behind England, church-building was still wedded to seventeenth- and early eighteenth-century models; a long time elapsed before the appearance of churches where the architect sought a genuine classical integrity. By the time they did

Grandison, who lived at Dromana, for the community of Protestant weavers he brought down from Ulster and settled on his lands. The Protestant population eventually diminished, and a few years ago the attractive church was given to the Catholic diocese, who failed to make use of it. It has now been repaired and was reopened for use as a community centre in 1974, in the presence of the President of Ireland, representatives of both religious communions, the Irish Georgian Society and the Villiers-Stuart family.

The parish church of St Thomas, Wicklow, Co. Wicklow, which had been rebuilt and reconsecrated about 1700, was renovated and improved by local landowners, the Eaton family, in 1777. They added the four-storey clock-tower over a porch at the west end; it is crowned by a quaint angular copper cupola, on top of which is a weather-vane in the form of the Eaton crest: a lion bearing a sheaf of straw. The prettily glazed oculus window in the gallery, through which a splendid view of the town can be seen, probably dates from the time of the Eaton renovations. A stained-glass window in the south wall of the south porch shows the church as it was before the addition of the chancel in 1912.

St Peter's, Drogheda, Co. Louth, is an exceptionally fine mid-eighteenth-century parish church, built in 1753 to serve a prosperous and flourishing

St Malachy's Church of Ireland Parish Church, Hillsborough, Co. Down >

Ballymakenny Church, Co. Louth. Below, the reredos.

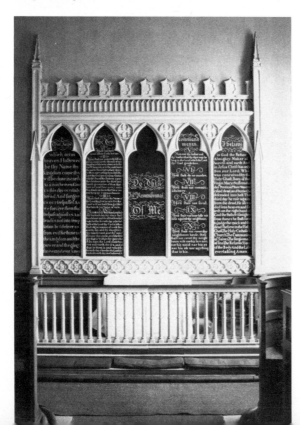

arrive, the movement was already enfeebled elsewhere, so they reflect the outward signs of Neoclassicism but lack its earlier authority and conviction. The few examples of the eighteenth-century Gothic Revival in Ireland are far better products of the movement, undoubtedly because the designs were free from adulteration, representing as they did a clean break with current fashions.

St Malachy's, Hillsborough, a cruciform parish church in Co. Down, rebuilt by the landlord, the first Marquess of Downshire, in 1773, has a remarkably competent Gothic Revival interior. Lord Downshire was a cultured and travelled man, and it is to his taste that this 'import' is due. The superb pulpit, the dark oak box-pews and the curved organ-loft, are all in the manner called 'Gothick', with delicately carved tracery. The beautiful little marble font with a brass liner stands on a finely carved wooden clustered column. Great attention has been paid to the details.

The Irish architect Francis Johnston was competent in both classical and Gothic Revival work. He was the architect of the small but delightful parish church at Ballymakenny, Co. Louth, built between 1785 and 1793. This church was commissioned by his patron, the Primate, Archbishop Robinson, who had his seat, Rokeby Hall, in the parish. The Primate's arms and archiepiscopal insignia are over the pointed west door; it is flanked by slender pointed windows with 'Gothick' glazing and hood-mouldings. The interior, which is quite unspoiled, is most attractive. A canopied three-tier oak pulpit, with readers' desk below, rises above the plain box-pews. Behind the altar-table (which is enclosed by a balustrade) is a delightful entablature with the Lord's Prayer, the Ten Commandments, and the Creed, in Gothic-style gold lettering on a black background. The stuccowork of the entablature, niches, dado and chair-rail is all beautifully executed.

Francis Johnston also designed the superb pulpit with 'Gothick' decoration (pl. XII, p. 139) for St Werburgh's, Dublin. After the fire of 1754, in 1759, the interior of St Werburgh's was rebuilt with a new ceiling, new pews and gallery. In 1767 another gallery was added at the west end, on either side of the organ, to accommodate schoolchildren; this was designed by the architect John Smyth, who may also have designed the organ-case. The Royal Arms on the front of the viceregal pew were added in that year. The sumptuous pulpit was carved by Richard Stewart who worked for Francis Johnston in other Dublin buildings. The supporting pillar of the pulpit, composed of clustered columns, terminates in four splendidly carved heads of the Evangelists, on each of which lies a tome; these form a platform, from which spring the ribs of the pedestal under the

St Werburgh's, Dublin.

polygonal pulpit-box. The sides of this box, the ribs of the pedestal, and the sides of the free-standing stair which leads up to the pulpit are all magnificently carved.

John Smyth was the architect of two other Dublin city churches, St Thomas, Marlborough Street, and St Catherine, Thomas Street. St Thomas, built in 1758 with a grant of £5,000, was badly damaged in the Civil War in 1922, and subsequently demolished. It was in the old-fashioned classical style, its façade, with pilasters and engaged Composite columns supporting an entablature and enclosing niches, was based on Palladio's church of the Redentore at Venice. St Catherine's was built of mountain granite in 1769, with a grant of £4,490, and survives.

The tower planned for it was never built. The Palladian pedimented five-bay two-storey front is finished off with a balustrade; giant Doric pilasters divide the bays. The interior has been repaired and redecorated by a volunteer group. The galleries are supported by eight Ionic columns, above which a second order with Corinthian capitals rises to the roof. The galleries stop one bay short of the east end, thus creating a sort of internal transept on each side.

St Mark's, Dublin, was built with a grant of £2,000 made in 1758. It has a ponderous classical façade with pedimented breakfront, a lunette above the door, and an oculus. The stark effect is now heightened by the full exposure of the side-elevation, originally closed in by a street of houses, but now

St Catherine's, Thomas Street, Dublin, prior to cleaning done for European Architectural Heritage Year, 1975.

bleakly confronting a main road. St John's, Fishamble Street, was built with a grant of £3,000 made in 1771. It was demolished in the last century. Designed by George Ensor, it showed the effects of the Neo-classical movement, having a temple-front with a recessed portico, and Doric columns supporting a pediment. Ensor (who was Clerk of Works to the Surveyor-General) and his brother John were capable architects, both active in the second half of the eighteenth century.

The architect of Wilson's Hospital near Multy-farnham, Co. Westmeath (a privately endowed Protestant school built in 1759), was John Pentland. Its appearance is that of a substantial country house in the Irish Palladian manner, with pavilions joined by wings to a central block. It has a chapel which has changed little in two hundred years, the principal addition being Victorian tiling on the floor in which the names of the headmasters appear. The chapel is a delightful galleried room, with a curved end which accommodates the altar. The balustraded gallery on three sides, over a frieze with triglyphs, is supported by Doric columns. The low pews were specially designed for small boys.

The interior of Wexford Parish Church, dating from about 1775, is a cool, grey, white and wedgwood-blue surprise behind a drab hybrid façade on the busy main street. It, too, is galleried on three sides, but here the supporting pillars are disproportionately slender. The gallery above the entrance is deeply bowed to accommodate the organ and the soloists of the choir; in the two corners under this gallery are twin flights of stairs. The sanctuary is separated by a lofty arcade whose columns have

grand Corinthian capitals. Round the walls of the galleries are chaste Late Georgian monuments, mostly with draped Grecian urns. The stucco frieze has a row of these joined by garlands and bows, while the frieze in the sanctuary has harps and floral festoons.

There were excellent masons in Ireland, and these were kept busy by the minor and major gentry, who commissioned stone and marble memorials, often bearing grandiloquent epitaphs. Ireland has a rich collection of eighteenth-century funerary sculpture by both Irish and foreign craftsmen. It is perhaps unfair to single out for attention any particular favourites. These monuments provide a distinct decorative feature of many Irish churches. A charming one in Killaloe Cathedral, commissioned in 1730, has a Latin epitaph in a fanciful cartouche. Kilnasoo-lagh Parish Church, Co. Clare, has a fine assembly of Georgian monuments, as does St Peter's, Drogheda, Co. Louth (see p. 128). The very rich commissioned grand monuments and cenotaphs of such celebrated sculptors as Van Nost, Nollekens and Scheemakers, by whom there is an elaborate example in St Peter's, Ballymodan, Co. Cork. Some important pieces were made by fashionable London sculptors, such as the tomb of Lady Matilda Bermingham (who died in 1788) in the ruined chancel of Athenry Friary, signed by Coade of London, 1790.

St Mark's, Dublin.

Wexford Church of Ireland Parish Church.

Another London-made monument, signed by William Hickey, 1790, is surely the most pompous in Ireland. It stands in a specially constructed south chapel of Delgany Parish Church, Co. Wicklow, to commemorate the rich banker David LaTouche. Mr LaTouche, the descendant of Huguenot refugees, died in 1789; the church was built that year by his bequest. The gigantic monument with figure-sculpture contains the following epitaph:

He added a rigid integrity of principle to a mild and benevolent nature and the most amazing gentleness of manner, but the purity of his mind was most strongly evinced in his constant and unaffected piety. His life though long and pros-perous appeared alas transitory. Riches in his hands became a general blessing, his profusion was a disinterested liberality to the deserving: his luxury the relief and the protection of the poor and defenceless.

Delgany Church is otherwise modest, built in the Gothic Revival vein, with narrow pointed windows which are attractively glazed. The interior has been renovated and restored.

Waterford Church of Ireland Cathedral, built between 1773 and 1779, on the site of the medieval one, is by a local architect, John Roberts. Roberts' other work shows his liking for Baroque, and his attachment to the work of Inigo Jones. The interior of Waterford Cathedral is astonishingly similar to some of Wren's London churches built almost a century earlier, such as St James's, Piccadilly, built 1683, and St Bride's, Fleet Street, completed in 1684. The conclusion that Roberts copied them as in-escapable. The similarity to St James's, Piccadilly, extends to the black and white floor. Eighteenth-century engravings show the interior as it was originally, with galleries along the aisles. The giant columns are placed on tall pedestals to avoid conceal-ment by the pews, a device first used by Wren in London in 1677 at Christ Church, Newgate Street. The galleries were able to rest on the top of the pedestals, thus becoming an organic part of the whole design. Without the galleries, which have been removed, the interior is curiously out of proportion. The present restoration and redecoration, munifi-cently paid for by Mr Ambrose Congreve, may perhaps provide an opportunity for their replace-ment. Unfortunately the first stages of redecoration

Waterford Church of Ireland Cathedral interior, left, as it appeared in the eighteenth century before the removal of the galleries, and right, as it appears today. Below, St James's, Piccadilly, London, built almost a century earlier.

have disimproved the appearance, rather than re-stored it; the water-gilding on the pedimented reredos, for example, has been replaced by garish gold paint.

Another provincial architect, John Morrison of Midleton, Co. Cork, father of the more famous Sir Richard, designed Kingston College (a half-square of almshouses with a chapel), at Mitchelstown, Co. Cork, endowed by the Earl of Kingston and built about 1765. The chapel is the centre of a well-planned architectural ensemble – a small rectangular building with a projecting porch under a discreet bell-tower.[18]

Sir William Chambers was an architect of quite different calibre. Born in Sweden in 1723 of Scots parents, he visited China and India, studied architecture in Paris and spent a period in Rome at the time when Piranesi, Soufflot and Winckelmann were there. In his mid-thirties he returned to take up architectural practice in England, where he became architect to the King, helped to found the Royal Academy, and, with his contemporary Robert Adam, dominated the architectural scene for three decades. In Ireland he built Charlemont House, Dublin, and the Casino at Marino (1769) for his friend the Earl of Charlemont. He also designed the Theatre (a public examination hall, begun in 1779, finished 1791) and the chapel for Trinity College, Dublin. The chapel, on the north side of the quadrangle, is entered through an imposing recessed portico of four Corinthian columns. Behind the portico is a spacious vestibule with doors to the chapel proper, and a stair to the organ-loft. Internally, the chapel is 80 feet long (plus a semicircular apse, 20 feet in radius) and 40 feet wide; as the walls are 40 feet high, the body of the chapel, excluding the apse and the vault of the ceiling, is a double cube. The organ, in a beautiful gilded case, is in a gallery over the entrance. This gallery is curved, forming a semicircular recess which matches the apse at the opposite end; under it are the seats of the Provost and other dignitaries. The walls are panelled to a height of about 10 feet; above the panelling is a plinth, from which paired fluted Ionic pilasters rise to the cornice. In the spaces between the pairs of pilasters are tall round-headed windows or matching niches. Some of the windows have been refitted with nineteenth-century stained glass, which, while a good quality (the central window of the sanctuary is by Mayer and Co. of Munich), detracts from the unity of the chapel. Above the cornice, over each window or niche, in the vault of the roof, is a lunette window. The ceiling has splendid stucco decoration by the Dublin architect and stuccodore Michael Stapleton. Bands of rosettes in octagonal frames divide the bays, between them are huge but exquisitely worked stylized rosettes in low relief.

James Gandon, born in London in 1743, served his architectural apprenticeship under Sir William Chambers. He settled in Dublin in 1781 to become Ireland's greatest resident architect. He was responsible for some of Dublin's most impressive buildings, such as the Custom House, the Four Courts and King's Inns. Gandon's friend and protector, the Earl of Portarlington, who had persuaded him to come to Ireland, commissioned him to build a magnificent new seat on his estate in Co. Leix, and a new parish church. The church at Coolbanagher, Co. Leix, can be seen in a view attributed to James Malton, as it was before the removal of the bow front to the little gallery and the additions of both the Victorian chancel of 1870, and the unsuitable openwork timber roof in place of the barrel-vault. The barrel-vault was divided into three compartments; the bands on the vault which divided these were of equal width with the piers in which they were continued. The piers now end abruptly, and the sense of Gandon's design is lost. The interior has been neatly restored, though the use of colours is rather alarming.

At the entrance end of the church Gandon created a small vestibule and a vestry. Lord Portarlington took an active interest in the building, which was

Trinity College Chapel, Dublin, the provost's box, the entrance and gallery.

Coolbanagher, Co. Leix, Church of Ireland Parish Church as it was planned at the end of the eighteenth century.

135

consecrated in 1785;[19] save for the rough-cast, and possibly the later spire, the front of the church appears now as it did then. Those who rail against the plastic flowers and plaques which spoil many old churches and abbeys in Ireland, may observe at Coolbanagher that such visual intrusions are confined neither to this century nor to the *hoi polloi*. In 1874 the Duchess of Marlborough immortalized her lack of visual taste and her sister, the Countess of Portarlington, by having inserted on the wall of Coolbanagher Church, not a classical urn or a swathed sarcophagus, but an alien polychrome mosaic in a heavy black frame.

At the middle of the eighteenth century, the Church of Ireland diocese of Waterford had only 9 churches in repair and 22 ruinous.[20] The situation was analogous in many other dioceses; Ardfert and Aghadoe had 15 churches in repair and 54 ruinous; Cork diocese had 30 in repair and 46 in ruins.[21] This state of affairs caused the hierarchy of the Church of Ireland to take a hard look at the situation, and eventually a church-building programme was promoted by the Irish Parliament. An act of 1720, which provided that in any parish where there were a considerable number of Protestant parishoners more than six Irish miles from a church, one or two chapels-of-ease might be erected, had proved ineffectual. There were a number of non-cures, where the incumbent, having neither church nor residence, had abandoned his cure altogether.

The best agricultural lands in Ireland had been abbey lands, and most of their tithes had passed at the Dissolution into lay hands. Therefore, even in prosperous rural areas which had a sizeable Protestant population, it had become necessary to unite several parishes in order to have enough revenue to support even one church and one minister. These amalgamations, called 'Unions', were also necessary in poorer regions where the tithes, albeit not impropriated, were meagre.

The First Fruits or annates are the first year's revenue of a benefice, bishopric or other dignity. Prior to the Reformation annates were remitted to Rome. The Board of First Fruits was established in Ireland in 1711, when it was decided to use the income from annates to buy back impropriate tithes from lay owners. The Board was also empowered to use its surplus revenue to build and repair churches and to purchase and build glebe houses. As the total revenue of the Board was meagre, the building activities were very limited. The number of churches in disrepair was so great by 1777 that the Irish Parliament voted an annual grant to the Board of First Fruits for the church-building programme. These grants, £6,000 in 1777–78, £1,500 in 1779–80, £6,000 in 1781–82, £3,000 in 1783–84, and £5,000

per annum from 1785 until the end of the century, were considerably larger than the Board's revenue from annates.[22] With this money the Board made grants for building and repair. The standard grant, £500 for a new church, was made to benefices which had been without a church for at least twenty years.

In connection with this building programme, a survey was made in 1787 which revealed that Ulster with 626 parishes, 395 benefices and 417 churches, had the highest number of churches per benefice in the country. Leinster had 658 parishes, 254 benefices and 217 churches; Munster, 839 parishes, 362 benefices and 254 churches; Connaught, 313 parishes, 111 benefices and 113 churches.

Unless the £500 building grant was augmented by a gift from a benefactor, these churches could not be more than small, unpretentious buildings. The economy in materials was such that many soon required further grants for essential repairs. Ballyphilip Parish Church at Portaferry, Co. Down, built in 1787 at a cost of £883 18s 9d of which £500 came from the Board of First Fruits, is typical of these unassuming buildings. It originally had a spire, which had to be removed in 1810 as it had become perilous. Eventually the churches built on Board of First

Ballyphilip Parish Church, Portaferry, Co. Down.

Fruits' grants came to be built almost all to a similar plan in the Gothic style. Most of these easily recognizable sturdy little churches belong, however, to the first quarter of the nineteenth century.

In the Diocese of Derry, the Bishop, the Earl of Bristol, an irrepressible builder, promoted the construction of new parish churches in the simplest Gothic style. His builder, Michael Shanahan of Cork, built two in 1775, Desertoghill and Banagher. Desertoghill cost £383, raised by subscription among local landowners. The Bishop himself gave £95, and the Ironmongers' Company of London, £100.[23] It had a square tower at the west end, a three-bay nave, and the east end was railed off to serve as a sanctuary. The furnishings were of the plainest kind: pine pews, a stone-flagged floor and no decorative plasterwork or other ornamentation. Banagher Church, which is larger and has an octagonal spire above the tower, cost £883 of which the Bishop gave £50 and the Skinners' Company of London, £500.[24] Several other churches in the simple Gothic vein were built in Co. Derry during the Earl-Bishop's jurisdiction: Clonmany, Tyanee. Ballyscullion, Tamlaghtfinlagan; other churches were embellished with spires, such as Maghera and Aghadowey.[25]

The Presbyterians did not receive money from Parliament to build churches. The annual Royal Bounty was used to support ministers; it was increased in 1784, and again in 1792. Their civil position was improved by the repeal of the Test Act in 1780, and by an Act of 1782 which validated marriages between Presbyterians performed by their own ministers. Another Act of 1782 permitted Seceders to swear by raising the right hand instead of kissing the Bible. Seceders were more active than the Synod of Ulster, which was apathetic in the last third of the century, no new congregations at all being formed between 1769 and 1789, while the Seceders set up forty-six congregations between 1740 and 1792.

Dunmurray Non-Subscribing Presbyterian Church, Co. Antrim, was built in 1779 when the congregation adhered to the Synod of Ulster. It is a simple rectangular stone building with attractive pedimented twin doors, and windows with Gibbs surrounds. When the minister and congregation seceded from the Synod of Ulster in 1829 they kept the church. Rademon Non-Subscribing Presbyterian Church, Co. Down, was built, as an inscription commemorates, 'in the year of Our Lord 1787 which was the twenty first year of the Reverend Moses Nelson's ministry in This Place'. It is a long T-shaped stone building; the façade might be that of a very substantial farmhouse. The three galleries are entered by outside stairs at the sides and back.

Dunmurray Non-Subscribing Presbyterian Church, Co. Antrim.

Rademon Non-Subscribing Presbyterian Church, Co. Down.

As might be expected in a larger town, the First Presbyterian Church, completed in 1783 in Rosemary Street, Belfast, by the leading Belfast architect Roger Mulholland, was a stylish building, although carefully kept within the bounds of Presbyterian propriety. The wealthy and cultured Earl of Bristol, Bishop of Derry, generally remembered as the Earl-Bishop, contributed fifty guineas in 1781 towards the cost of this building, which he greatly admired.[26] The Earl-Bishop was an enthusiastic builder, and it is not impossible that his predilection for oval forms influenced Mulholland in his design of the oval interior. The design is a composition of beautifully articulated curves. The entrance hall and stairs are outside the oval, contained in a two-storey, three-bay rectangular pedimented vestibule joined to the west end. Externally this once attractive front was ruined by alterations in the nineteenth century, and

Randalstown Presbyterian Church, Co. Antrim. The porch and upper storey with oculus windows are both additions to the original building of 1790.

further disimproved by bomb-blast damage in recent years. The interior, extended in the last century at the east end to accommodate an organ, is otherwise intact. The Second Belfast Presbyterian congregation built their Meeting House, a balconied classical building, just behind that of the First, in 1790.

The oval interior of the Belfast Church may have inspired the oval Presbyterian church at Randalstown, Co. Antrim, built in 1790. The congregation, previously known as Drummaul, had been formed in 1655. The oval church of 1790 lacked the gallery inside, and the hexagonal vestibule crowned by a lantern outside, which were added in 1829. In 1929 the walls were raised to make the gallery loftier, the row of oculus windows inserted to light it, and the building re-roofed. This was done so judiciously that the external appearance of the building was not impaired. The pulpit was also remodelled at this time, and the pews renovated. A small organ has been neatly fitted in under the pulpit. No place was arranged for an organ in early Presbyterian Meeting Houses, for the congregation sang without accompaniment, taking their pitch from the precentor's pipe. Neither was there a font; a small bowl sufficed for the sprinkling of infants.

Catholic churches had to be built with the contributions of the faithful, most of whom were desperately poor. Exceptionally an enlightened Protestant landlord generously helped his Catholic tenants to build their church, or donated the ground. The Marquess of Headfort, for example, donated the ground for the handsome Catholic church at Kells, Co. Meath,[27] designed by the skilled Francis Johnston, and built in 1798. The Marquess also contributed liberally towards the cost of building, and presented an altar-painting of the Assumption attributed to Raphael. Such paintings, often imported from Italy through the Irish seminaries, were popular.

The Earl-Bishop was well disposed to Catholics; he allowed the lower part of the Mussenden Temple, on his estate at Downhill, Co. Derry, to be used as a Catholic chapel. Through the Rector of Desertmartin, Co. Derry, the Earl-Bishop donated £22 15s 0d for the Catholic chapel there in 1787.[28] In 1784, when driving through Co. Down, the Earl-Bishop saw a partly finished Catholic chapel. When he learned that the people were too poor to pay for it to be roofed, he called on the priest, and, in the words of a reporter in the *Hibernian Journal* of that year, 'laying aside the pomp of greatness, entered his

XII St Werburgh's, Dublin, detail of the pulpit (p. 130) >

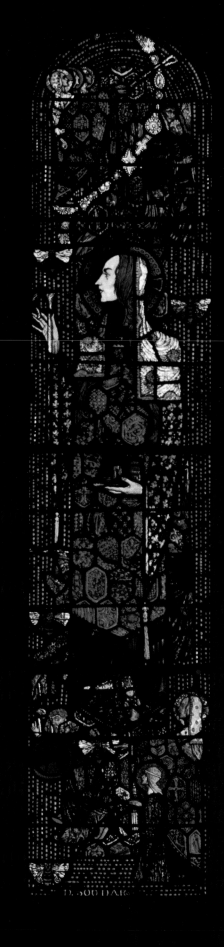

humble cabin and generously presented him with ten guineas to enable him to prosecute the work'.[29] The Earl-Bishop contributed £210 towards the new Catholic church at Derry[30] on the site of the ancient Dubh Regles; it was completed in 1786. Such was the ecumenical spirit in Belfast at the end of the eighteenth century, that the Protestant inhabitants contributed generously to the building of St Mary's Catholic Church there; when the church was opened in 1784 the First Belfast Volunteer Company, all Protestants, under the command of their Captain, and in full dress uniform, formed a guard of honour in the forecourt and presented arms to the priest as he entered to celebrate mass.[31]

Waterford had a prosperous Catholic merchant population, as well as a few old Catholic families, like the Wyses of the manor of St John, who had contrived to hold on to their lands. The Waterford Catholics built a handsome cathedral between 1792 and 1796. The Catholic and Protestant bishops were on good terms: when beautiful medieval vestments were found while demolishing the twelfth-century cathedral, the Protestant bishop presented them to his Catholic counterpart; they are now preserved in the Catholic cathedral. The same architect, John Roberts, designed both cathedrals. The sanctuary was lengthened 1829–37, the apse added 1854, and the west front erected 1893. The organ is set in a bow-fronted loft over the entrance; on both sides are bow-fronted galleries supported by fluted Ionic columns. Giant columns set in groups of four with gilded Corinthian capitals, support the roof; on these are painted the Stations of the Cross.

Few places in Ireland in the eighteenth century could afford so grand a Catholic cathedral as Waterford, or as grand a Catholic parish church as that of Kells. St Columba's, Derry, completed in 1786, cost £2,800; it had an earthern floor.[32] Latlurcan Old Church, Monaghan, Co. Monaghan, built about 1790, served as the parish church and pro-cathedral. This modest rectangular building with 'Gothick' glazing in the pointed windows is representative of the better late eighteenth-century Catholic churches. The galleried chapel at Newry, Co. Down, built in 1789, was another such simple building.

Even the most optimistic Catholics in Ireland in 1799 could hardly have imagined what magnificent cathedrals and parish churches would be built within the next seventy years.

Latlurcan Old Church, Monaghan, Co. Monaghan. It was the pro-cathedral until the new one was built in the latter part of the nineteenth century.

< *XIII–XVI Stained-glass windows. Above, Tuam Cathedral, Beatrice Bernard memorial window (p. 163); below left, St Carthage, Rahan, Co. Offaly (p. 164); below centre, Loughrea Cathedral, St Brendan by Sarah Purser (p. 178); right, Honan Chapel, Cork, St Gobnet by Harry Clarke (p. 179).*

CHAPTER 8

From the Union to Disestablishment 1801–1869

BY THE ACT OF UNION, on 1 January 1801 the Kingdom of Ireland created by King Henry VIII ceased to exist, and Ireland became a part of the United Kingdom. The economic effects of this change were eventually deleterious to Ireland, as were the far-reaching political effects. Both the aristocracy and the rank and file of the Church of Ireland had been divided on the issue, but a number of its political representatives were bought over by those anxious to secure the Union. Some who still cherished the independent and patriotic principles of Grattan, Tone and Lord Edward Fitzgerald naturally opposed the Union. On the other hand a number of Protestants, alarmed by the activities of the Whiteboys, the brutalities of the Rising of 1798, especially in Co. Wexford, and the French attempt on Bantry (1796) and landing at Killala (1798), felt that union with England would safeguard their interests. The Catholics, who had finally been enfranchised in 1793, but were still not admitted to Parliament, were also in favour of the Union; their hierarchy had been led to believe that Catholic Emancipation would be granted in return for their support. Their hopes were soon dashed. King George III himself was set against emancipating the Catholics, and the bulk of English public opinion was also opposed to it. Within three months of the Union, Pitt, the British Prime Minister who had achieved it, resigned. The promises made during the campaign were broken, and the Catholics of Ireland, left without any relief, swiftly turned against the Union and sought to repeal it. The Presbyterians, on the other hand, at first unsure about the Union, soon favoured it. The members of the Orange Order, founded in 1795 principally to combat Papism, once they saw that Catholic Emancipation did not materialize, became staunchly Unionist, and Unionism flourishes in Ulster today as it did at the time of the Union.

After the Union the Presbyterians were rewarded by the Government; their annual Royal Grant was increased to £14,000. Their ministers were divided into three classes: the first class received £100 per annum, the second, £75, the third, £50. In 1809 the Seceders obtained a grant too, also in three classes, but at £70, £50 and £40 per annum, respectively. These distinctions and classifications were abandoned in 1838, when the Government granted all Presbyterian ministers an annual stipend of £75. This continued until Disestablishment. In 1829 there was a further schism in the Synod of Ulster; a dissident faction, the New Light group, seceded. However, in 1840 the General Assembly of the Presbyterian Church in Ireland was formed, uniting the Synod of Ulster and the Seceders; the Synod of Ulster contributed 292 congregations and the Seceders 141.

The principal object of Presbyterian church-building was to provide preaching-houses. In the nineteenth century the congregations passed from being content with a plain building in the vernacular style to preference for a preaching-house with a smart façade. Overwhelmingly the architectural choice for the façade was Greek Revival, deemed beautiful, chaste and austere. In 1828 the First Presbyterian Congregation at Derry added a temple-front to their Meeting House, built in the preceding century in Magazine Street. It cost £700; the pediment and corners are of freestone quarried at Dungiven, Co. Derry. The church of the Belfast Third Congregation, designed by John Miller and completed in 1831 at a cost of £10,000, had an imposing Doric portico. This Greek Revival *chef-d'œuvre* so delighted Samuel Lewis that he wrote of it in 1837 that it was perhaps 'the most elegant edifice of its kind in the three kingdoms', and enthusiastically described its 'beautiful attic balustrade composed of a series of pedestals and light pierced work having a novel and pleasing effect', and the 'especially grand staircase' which led to the gallery.[1] This church was destroyed by enemy action in the Second World War. The church of the Belfast Sixth Congregation in May Street, built in 1829, survives. This cost £9,000; its solid classical façade with a recessed Ionic portico now looks rather shabby, but it is evident that its appearance was once better. The interior is attractive: the box-pews are curved, and twin curving staircases lead up to the mahogany horseshoe-shaped gallery. Another important Belfast Presbyterian church of that period, that of the Fifth Congregation in Fisherwick Street, now demolished, was a Greek Revival building. It was completed in 1827 at a cost of £7,000. About the same time an accomplished Greek Revival Presbyterian church was built in Dublin, in Gloucester Street (now Sean McDermott Street). The Adelaide Road, Dublin, Presbyterian church, built in 1840, is less distinguished.

A late but excellent example of a nineteenth-century Ulster Presbyterian church in the Greek Revival manner may be seen at Banbridge, Co. Down. The First Presbyterian Church there, built in 1846, is a rectangular building with a handsome pedimented prostyle Ionic portico. The temple-front, as was usual, is stuccoed. As in many similar churches in Ulster, the box-pews survive; some are upholstered. The U-shaped gallery is supported by painted cast-iron columns. Double curved flights of stairs with cast-iron balusters lead up to the pulpit. The First Presbyterian Church in Antrim town, built 1834–37, has an unusual façade with heavy Doric columns in a recessed portico. Oblivious to the dictates of orthodox revivalism, Kilmore Presbyterian Church at Drumaghlis, Co. Down, built in 1832 to serve the congregation established in 1712, was given a three-bay façade with giant Doric pilasters and a door with a Gibbs surround. Crumlin First Presbyterian Church, Co. Antrim, built in 1835, is a delightful octagonal building with a projecting vestibule which contains the stair to the gallery.

By 1850 the Ulster Presbyterians were being weaned of their predilection for Greek and Roman Revival buildings. They were reluctant at first to consider even a restrained flight into Gothic. Perhaps they distrusted gargoyles, tracery and triforia for their papist associations. The Dunluce, Co. Antrim, Presbyterian congregation was one of the first in Ulster to risk a Gothic essay. The T-shaped building, a five-bay hall with a Gothic vestibule across the front, built in 1845, is pleasing. Its appearance is now enhanced by the white and light-blue painting of the stucco. Dunlop, the biographer of the Ulster architect W. J. Barre, considered that Barre's Decorated Gothic-style Unitarian church at Newry, Co. Down, marked the commencement of

Banbridge, Co. Down, First Presbyterian Church.

Bushmills Presbyterian Church, Dunluce, Co. Antrim.

143

Elmwood Presbyterian Church, Belfast.

Outside Ulster, at Fermoy, Co. Cork, a market-town whose growth and importance in the nineteenth century was due to its military barracks, there is a delightful small Presbyterian church, built in 1839 and still in use. This is in the manner of the inexpensive smaller Gothic Church of Ireland parish churches financed by the Board of First Fruits, and has a pinnacled tower. Its diminutive size and neat appearance lend it considerable charm.

After the middle of the century, when a serious return to Gothic became fashionable and the best architects were ecclesiologists, Presbyterian taste veered towards eccentricity rather than historicism. Elmwood Presbyterian Church, on the corner of Elmwood Avenue and University Road in a prosperous suburb of Belfast, is an example. This church, designed by John Corry, an amateur architect, is now an auditorium of Queen's University. The interior is an unexceptional Victorian medley of Gothic windows and a compartmented ceiling, decorated with frothy stucco motifs. The finely executed plaster frieze combines in its design running chevrons, Neoclassical foliage, brattishing, quatrefoils and Baroque consoles; Corinthian columns support the gallery on the entrance wall. The impression, however, is one of spaciousness and light. The exterior is pervaded by the same exuberant spirit. Generically Italianate, with an arcaded portico and a tall three-tier tower of Lombard-Gothic inspiration, it is finished off with a spire.

Bannside Presbyterian Church, Castlewellan Road, Banbridge, Co. Down, built in 1866, has a distinctly weird exterior, vaguely Italianate. It combines a very tall pediment and a small Baroque belfry. Other odd hybrid churches are not hard to find. Few sources of inspiration were left untapped; the results are occasionally disarming, usually uninspiring, sometimes monstrous.

The *Dublin Builder* ran advertisements in 1861 for tenders for the Unitarian church to be built in St Stephen's Green, Dublin, to designs by Lanyon, Lynn and Lanyon of Belfast. The building in their version of Decorated Gothic included boys' and girls' schools with separate entrances, a committee-room and offices, all in the basement. Other extra-ecclesiastical refinements included a ladies' retiring-room under the organ-gallery but not, apparently, one for the Unitarian gentlemen.

One of the earliest surviving Methodist churches in the country was built in 1800 in Great Charles Street, Dublin. It is now a Church of Ireland church, having been purchased from the Methodists in 1828. At Bandon, Co. Cork, where the Methodists gained a number of converts among the predominantly Protestant population, there is an early nineteenth-century Methodist church, still in use as

the change in style patronized by the Dissenting churchmen,[2] though it was not in fact the first.

Liberation from temple-fronts did not always lead to Gothic, nor to felicitous alternatives. The façade of the small rectangular Presbyterian church at Strangford, Co. Down, built in 1846, is decidedly spurious. Nevertheless, the effect of the medley of debased and disparate classical elements is quaint rather than ugly. The church is kept in excellent repair; inside it has attractive tall brass oil-lamps with spherical glass bowls, attached to the box-pews. At Maghera Presbyterian Church, Co. Derry, no attempt has been made to articulate component units of the building. The bastardized façade, which must have a Palladian architectural pattern-book somewhere in its ancestry, is too low to mask the gable behind it. Above its central bay rises a disproportionately tall louvred turret, crowned with a little metal cupola.

Broomfield Presbyterian Church, Co. Monaghan, erected in 1842, is uncompromisingly plain and neat. It has a prim ogee-headed door with a fanlight, and slender lancet windows, elegantly glazed.

such. Samuel Lewis described it in his *Topographical Dictionary* in 1837 as 'a large and handsome edifice'.

The Methodists, like other denominations, had their own architects. The leading one was Isaac Farrell of Dublin, designer of the Dublin Savings Bank in Abbey Street, built 1839. Farrell's work was sound, but visually uninspiring. His Wesleyan Centenary Church, built in 1843 to commemorate the centenary of Irish Methodism, still presents a massive classical front to St Stephen's Green in Dublin. He also designed the large Methodist church on Donegall Square in the centre of Belfast, with a ponderous Corinthian portico. This church, like the one in Dublin, is still in use; it was built in 1850 to replace an earlier one of 1847, destroyed by fire in 1849. The Methodist church at Coleraine, Co. Derry, built in 1854, with a recessed Corinthian portico, was also designed by Farrell. Portadown, Co. Armagh Methodist Church, built in 1861, has a tall Corinthian portico; this church, with an adjoining house for the minister and a schoolhouse, cost £5,000. The Methodists continued to favour Classic Revival buildings for several years after the Presbyterians had given up their long-cherished temple-fronts. The tail-end of a genre, these Methodist churches were dull if not ugly, and lacking in authenticity. The Methodist church at Enniskillen, Co. Fermanagh, still in use, is a typical example. Designed by W. J. Barre and built in 1865, its Victorian plate-glass sash-windows stare morosely out on to the street, through the giant Corinthian portico: a solid and sullen memorial to the death-throes of the Classic Revival. In the same year, in Belfast, a Methodist church was built in a different style by the same architect. A native of Newry, Barre was then an active man in his mid-thirties, described by C. E. B. Brett as 'the evangelist of ornament and of the decorated Gothic style'.[3] He had been in the vanguard of persuading the Non-conformists to adopt Gothic, and the modest polychrome brick and stone church he built for the Methodist bourgeoisie of Belfast, in University Road, is loosely based on the twelfth-century architecture of Lombardy. In the same quarter Barre built homes for the newly rich textile magnates: ostentatious urban châteaux near which an Italianate place of Evangelical worship was not amiss. Barre's Gothic Methodist church at Portstewart, Co. Derry, built in 1861, had flying buttresses, a crow-stepped tower, and a Scots Baronial turret with a conical roof corbelled out at one corner. All these trimmings have since been removed.

A group of Methodist churches all on the same pattern, with a surprising neo-Romanesque doorway, were built in Ulster about 1855–61; there is one at Newtownards, Co. Down, others at Donegal, Co. Donegal, Cookstown, Co. Tyrone, and Ballymoney, Co. Antrim. The doors are flanked by engaged columnettes with simple Romanesque capitals and have a zigzag ornamental dressing over the arch.

With the Act of Union the Established Church lost its clerical boroughs. The Government paid compensation of £46,863 for this loss, a sum at first invested at 5 per cent for the benefit of the Board of First Fruits, then in 1808 merged with the Board's general funds. The Parliamentary Act of 1808, which consolidated all of the Board's sources of revenue into one account, also removed most of the restrictions on its operations. The Board was thereafter free to make gifts and loans for building as it pleased, and grants could be made to build churches even for parishes which had not been churchless for twenty years. From the Union to 1807, the Board had received £5,000 annually from the Government. In 1808 this was raised to £10,000, and from 1810 to 1816 inclusive the Board received £60,000 a year from the Government. In 1817, this annual payment was halved; and in 1822, after a glut of church-building, the amount was cut back to £10,000 again. Over and above this, the Treasury was empowered to loan the Board up to £50,000, free of interest. Even after 1823, when the annual grants ceased, the Board had an annual income which ranged from £3,000 to £16,000. Only a few hundred pounds of this came from the actual First Fruits, the rest being derived from the Board's holdings and the repayment of building loans. Between 1800 and 1823, over one million pounds passed through the Board's hands, of which £149,269 was spent in outright gifts for church-building and £281,148 on loans.[4]

By 1832 there were 1,293 Church of Ireland churches in use, of which 1,182 were parochial. Over half this number, 697, had been built, repaired or enlarged, in the preceding decades, by gifts and loans from the Board. Many a parish with hardly any Protestant parishioners got a church, and the majority of surviving rural Church of Ireland parish churches date from the period 1810–21. The prevailing style was overwhelmingly a simplified Gothic, with square towers, crude pinnacles, walls with clumsy battlements, and pointed windows with elementary tracery. So widely was this genre used, and in such a condensed form, that it represents a style on its own, First-Fruits-Gothic. The size and quality of the churches depended, of course, on whether they were built exclusively with the Board's grant, or whether more money was available from a benefactor or public subscription. In those balmy years of the Regency, the Board's usual gift for building a church was £800–£900; on top of this a substantial loan, often as much again, was usual. In

St George's, Hardwicke Place, Dublin.

Francis Johnston, designed St George's, Dublin. He was as much at home working in the classical vein as the Gothic. At the same time that St George's was being built, he completed the Chapel Royal in Dublin Castle with an Early Gothic Revival exterior, and an elaborate interior with rich oak carving and marvellous fan-vaulting.

A new orthodoxy slowly overtook the Neo-classical school of architecture at the beginning of the nineteenth century in England. Its leaders were Thomas Hope, the champion of pure Greek, William Wilkins, who published his *Antiquities of Magna Graecia* in 1807, and Robert Smirke, who built the new Covent Garden Theatre in London in 1808. Francis Johnston was not yet influenced by this current when he designed St George's (it became evident in his General Post Office, Dublin, built 1814–18). St George's has a prostyle Ionic portico, but in many ways it harks back to Gibbs' St Martin-

St George's, Hardwicke Place, Dublin, keystones on the front.

some instances much larger sums were given. The following churches received a total of £3,000 or more:

		Gift	Loan	Total
1814	St George's, Dublin	£500	10,000	10,500
1817	St George's, Belfast	4,500	1,000	5,500
1815	Birr, Co. Offaly	—	5,000	5,000
1818	Newtownards, Co. Down	900	4,000	4,900
1815	Collon, Co. Louth	3,800	700	4,500
1818	Taney, Co. Dublin	—	4,300	4,300
1822	St Peter's, Mount Street, Dublin	4,100	—	4,100
1818	Mallow, Co. Cork	—	3,500	3,500
1812	Roscrea, Co. Tipperary	—	3,500	3,500
1808	Fermoy, Co. Cork	500	3,000	3,500
1822	St John's, Sligo	—	3,500	3,500
1812	Templemichael, Co. Longford	—	3,490	3,490
1820	Kilmud, Co. Down	900	2,500	3,400
1822	Derryloran, Co. Tyrone	—	3,000	3,000

The two most expensive churches were both named for St George, in honour of the King and England's patron saint. The eminent Irish architect,

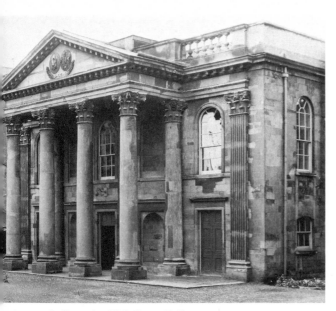

St George's, High Street, Belfast.

in-the-Fields, London (1721–26), especially the tiered tower and spire. Altogether the design is not well articulated, but the appearance of the church is nevertheless striking, especially as it enjoys a superb site in Hardwicke Place, at the spacious junction of three streets. The interior has fine wood-carving, executed by Richard Stewart. A cantilevered gallery runs round three sides. The stone heads on the keystones inside the portico are in the same vein as Johnston's designs for wood-carving.

St George's in High Street, Belfast, completed in 1816, was designed by John Bowden of Dublin, architect to the Board of First Fruits. The grandiose portico came from the Earl-Bishop's magnificent seat, Ballyscullion, Co. Derry, built for him by Michael Shanahan in 1788. This house was broken up by the Earl-Bishop's executors in 1813, when the magnificent façade was purchased for St George's, Belfast; Bowden fitted it on to a pathetically plain and insignificant hall.

John Anderson, who introduced the mail-coach system in Ireland, purchased two-thirds of the manor of Fermoy, Co. Cork, in 1791. In 1797 he donated land to build military barracks, which brought prosperity to the town. A philanthropic landowner, he also donated a site for the Catholic church and gave £500 towards its construction. With John Hyde of Castle Hyde he promoted the building of a new parish church in 1802, to a design by the Cork architect Abraham Hargrave, who had rebuilt Mr Hyde's splendid mansion. Anderson contributed no less than £3,000 towards the parish church, Hyde

£1,500, and the Board of First Fruits, £500; the Board also made a loan of £3,000. The church stands in a commanding position, and has an elegant silhouette. The tower is reminiscent of that of Hargrave's own parish church, St Ann Shandon in Cork City. Hargrave rather timidly incorporated some Gothic elements together with the Palladian ones which he employed in his country-house work.

Birr Parish Church, Co. Offaly, was built to ornament a carefully laid out town, as well as to serve its Protestant population. The landlord, the Earl of Rosse, was an intelligent, enlightened man, who, to the immense benefit of the town, devoted much of his energies to its improvement and development. He laid out a broad tree-lined mall opposite the main gates of his castle, and at the end of it the church (for which the Board of First Fruits loaned £5,000 in 1815) was built. It was designed by John Johnston, who did other building work for the Earl. The Gothic details do not stand up to scrutiny: Johnston only had a superficial knowledge of medieval architecture; but there is charm in his self-conscious and naïve use of details, while his good sense of over-all proportion gives the church character. It is one of the best-looking bogus Gothic churches of this building phase.

Holy Cross Parish Church, Co. Tipperary, for which the Board loaned £600 in 1821, is more

Birr Church of Ireland Parish Church, Co. Offaly.

Holy Cross Church of Ireland Parish Church, Co. Tipperary.

typical of Board of First Fruits' churches of this period, and Crossmolina Parish Church, Co. Mayo, is a more substantial example. The latter was completed in 1810, following the Board's loan of £1,000 in 1809. Seen along the river from outside the town, its tower makes a fine impression.

Inch Parish Church, Co. Down, was built in 1742 and its tower and spire were added in 1784; but its present appearance is mostly due to the renovations, enlargements and repairs carried out in 1826 and 1831.

Nantinan Parish Church, Co. Limerick, for which the Board made a loan of £800 in 1817, is a departure from the norm. It has more the appearance of an English country parish church of the Norman period, with a squat tower.

The architects of these early nineteenth-century churches showed a preference for Perpendicular in the towers, and Early English in the window forms. Generally they eschewed tracery and complicated decorative details. Kilcooly Parish Church, Co. Tipperary, is a pleasing essay in this generic simplified Gothic, built about 1825. The architect of St Munchin's, Limerick, rebuilt in 1827 at a cost of £1,460, concentrated on the tower for effect.

Cahir Parish Church, Co. Tipperary, is much more ambitious, built in 1817 to the design of the famous English architect John Nash, who was procured for the project by the local potentate, the Earl of Glengall. Nash was as ignorant as most of his contemporaries of the refinements of Gothic; his pinnacles, battlements and attempts at tracery are

elementary, but he made up for his lack of knowledge with flair. At Cahir he used elements which he employed for the Revival castles of his country-house practice, and in much the same way. Derryloran Parish Church, Co. Tyrone, for which the Board made a loan of £3,000 in 1822, was almost certainly designed by Nash, who had been employed as the architect of Killymoon Castle in that parish. This church was rebuilt in 1861.

The brothers James and George Richard Pain first worked in Ireland for Nash; they acquired an extensive architectural practice mostly in Munster, designing churches and country-houses as well as civic and commercial buildings. Carrigaline Parish Church, Co. Cork, is a felicitous example of their work, built in 1828. The tower is surmounted by an elegant pierced octagonal spire. The church was enlarged in 1835 by the addition of a north transept. Rather than attempt tracery, the Pains glazed the windows in the 'Gothick' tradition of the eighteenth century.

Parishes which numbered among their faithful a wealthy resident peer were likely to get a smarter church than others, especially if this lord had an architectural bent. The Earl of Charleville, for example, who had employed Francis Johnston to build his great castellated pile, Charleville Forest, retained the architect to make the new parish church at Tullamore, Co. Offaly, also in the Gothic style. This spacious and rather dull building cost just over £8,000, of which the Earl donated £4,523.[5] Within twenty years, several hundred pounds had to be spent on its repair. Lord Talbot de Malahide's parish church at Malahide, Co. Dublin, was not in the same class. Built in 1822, it cost only £1,300, of which Lord Talbot donated £100;[6] most of the cost was defrayed by a gift of £900 from the Board of First Fruits.

Early nineteenth-century restorations suffered from the very superficial knowledge of medieval architecture of those who undertook them. Appreciation of pre-Reformation work led to the repair in 1803 of the fifteenth-century tower of the ruined parish church of Trim, Co. Meath; behind it a new inexpensive church was built. The restoration of the ruined fourteenth-century cathedral at Downpatrick, Co. Down, was initiated after an Act of Parliament of 1790 granted £1,000 for the purpose. The Earl of Hillsborough donated a further £568, and £300 per annum of the deanery tithes were appropriated.[7] The long chancel, which survived from the late medieval cathedral, was repaired and transformed into an aisled nave and chancel for the new cathedral. The restoration, directed by Charles Lilly, was so drastic that many details of the original building disappeared. Lilly was uninterested in details in his

Cahir Church of Ireland Parish Church, Co. Tipperary.

St Mary's Chapel-of-Ease, the 'Black Church', Dublin.

restoration; he aimed at reproducing an over-all medieval effect. The heavy-handed plastering on the capitals of the arcade all but obscures the original decoration. Work was completed and the cathedral ready for use in 1818. In 1826 an octagonal vestibule and a Perpendicular Gothic tower were added to the west end. The cathedral looks best seen on top of its little hill from the marshy lands beside the ruined abbey of Inch.

Another English architect, Lewis Cottingham who had restored St Alban's Abbey, Hertfordshire, was brought over to superintend the restoration of Armagh Cathedral in 1834. The Primate subscribed £8,000 towards the work. What remained of the ancient fabric had been severely manhandled in the seventeenth century, and again when repairs were carried out in the eighteenth century. The clustered columns of the nave had been encased to strengthen them, and much of the decoration thickly coated with plaster. A study of drawings of the cathedral, and of a model made before Cottingham started work, shows that a great deal of it as seen today was added by him.

After John Bowden's death, the Board of First Fruits appointed an architect for each of the four Archbishoprics. John Semple, who became the architect for the province of Dublin, was unaffected by the current movement towards orthodoxy and historicism in Gothic building. His work is at once accomplished and highly original. Semple's eccentricity is by no means a mere urge to startle; his strange designs were a real *tour de force* combining uncommon engineering skill, intellectual curiosity and aesthetic sensitivity. An isolated figure in his time, Semple must rate as the most interesting architect in Ireland in the first half of the nineteenth century. St Mary's Chapel-of-Ease, Dublin, usually known as the 'Black Church', and Monkstown Parish Church in the suburbs of Dublin, illustrate the extraordinary variety of his work and the virtuosity of his imagination.

The 'Black Church', so named because it is built of black Dublin culp, stands on a plot presented by Lord Mountjoy. Built in 1830 to serve as a chapel-of-ease, it is now deconsecrated and serves as the head-quarters of the city's traffic wardens. The interior is even more original and surprising than the exterior; it has a wonderful parabolic vault constructed on the Mycenaean principle.

Semple's Monkstown Church is a glorious extravaganza; it would be less amazing if it were in Portugal than in alien majesty in the middle of genteel Monkstown. The retired judges and conservative ladies and gentlemen who worshipped there must have felt out of place inside their Lusitanian marvel, the subject of much criticism (pl. XVII, p. 173).

Balloughton Church of Ireland Parish Church, Co. Wexford.

Balloughton Parish Church, Co. Wexford, built in 1822, has a variation on the usual conservative ingredients of the period. A slender Tudor corner-turret runs up one corner of the battlemented tower. Kilcolman Parish Church, Miltown, Co. Kerry, built in 1820 of red brick with red sandstone dressings, has four little castellated Tudor turrets at the corners of its tower.

The original chapel at Old Court, Strangford, Co. Down, built in the seventeenth century, was extensively altered and repaired between 1835 and 1848 by the owner of the estate. The front has a crow-stepped porch and gable; there is a crow-stepped gable at the east end too, with a very unconvincing window. In 1848 the three-tiered miniature Round Tower with a conical cap was added at the south-east corner of the nave. This appears to be the first revival of this antique Irish element in ecclesiastical building, an early sign of the search for a Celtic dimension in revivalism, contemporary with the reawakening interest in Ireland's literary past. The carving in the interior is the heartiest sort of Victorian Gothic, its inaccuracy offset by its self-assurance.

The financial arrangements which obtained in the Church of Ireland were altered by the Church Temporalities Act of 1833. The Ecclesiastical Commissioners were established, and the Board of First Fruits ceased to function. Tuam and Cashel were reduced to bishoprics, their archiepiscopal jurisdictions passing to Armagh and Dublin. The number of bishops was drastically reduced by creating ten unions of sees. The revenue of the Ecclesiastical Commissioners came from these suppressed bishoprics, from a tax on the rich Bishopric of Derry and later on the Archbishopric of Armagh, from the sale of episcopal perpetuities, from an income-tax on benefices above £300 per annum, as well as the income from the balance turned over by the obsolete Board of First Fruits. One of the responsibilities of the Commissioners was the repair and construction of churches. The two archbishops were *ex officio* members, along with the Chancellor, Chief Justice and four Irish bishops. Three paid laymen served with them, two appointed by the Government and one by the Archbishops. The Commissioners employed a salaried staff, which in 1837 included seven architects at between £500 and £516 per annum, plus 4 per cent of the outlay on buildings. By 1860 there were only two architects. The Commissioners had to approve all the estimates of the provincial architects for new buildings or repairs. One of their first decisions was to demolish the parish church of St Nicholas Within, Dublin. They sold the pews to a publican for his tavern, the communion table, altarpiece and windows to the parish priest for the new Catholic chapel at Baldoyle. The annual revenue of the Commissioners was never less than £100,000, and sometimes over £200,000.[8] Despite the building activity of 1800–30, they had 90 new churches built between 1833 and 1865, and sanctioned repairs to 198 others.[9]

Ulster with its predominantly Protestant population still provided plenty of scope for new church-building. Charles, later Sir Charles, Lanyon, an English architect who settled in Ireland as a young man, built several churches for the United Diocese of Down and Connor after being appointed Surveyor of Co. Antrim in 1835. Drumtullagh Parish Church, typical of these, was built in 1841. Lanyon's Church of Ireland parish church at Lisburn, Co. Antrim, with a 72-foot-high tower, and his Trinity Church, Belfast, were both much admired. Trinity Church was destroyed by enemy action during the Second World War.

Among the last churches built before Disestablishment, with the aid of the Ecclesiastical Commissioners, is St Bartholomew's, Elgin Road, Dublin; it was built to seat 555 persons in a prosperous suburb. The site, on the Pembroke Estate, was granted by the guardians of the Earl of Pembroke, and the cost of building, about £7,000, was met partly by the Estate and partly by the Commissioners. The foundation-stone was laid in May 1865; the church consecrated two days before Christmas 1867. The consecration ceremony and the arrangements caused some furore; accusations of ritualistic practices were made.[10] The architect was Thomas H. Wyatt of London; his plan consisted of a nave and choir with apsidal chancel and double transepts, which disconcerted some visitors. Externally the main feature is a pinnacled octagonal tower over the choir; an Irish Round Tower complete with stone stair, bell-chamber, and conical cap rises at its north-east angle. The intended spire was never built. The choir and chancel were paved with patterned encaustic tiles, then the rage, imported from England. The fashionable fittings included a massive brass lectern, plenty of pseudo-medieval brass, gaslighting, and a ventilated heating apparatus made in England, placed under the vestry.

In 1868 Sir Thomas Deane's graceless and insensitive neo-Romanesque front was added to St Ann's, Dublin, probably the first full revival of the style in the country. St Ann's was a rich parish; in the 1860s Messrs O'Connor of London supplied it with expensive stained-glass windows which shut out the light, and some brass memorials.

In 1795 the Irish Parliament had sanctioned the opening of a college to train Catholic priests in Ireland, at Maynooth, Co. Kildare, and awarded it an annual grant of £8,000, which continued after the Union. By 1800, home-educated priests were coming out of Maynooth, and several religious orders had discreetly surfaced or returned. In Limerick several orders had their own chapels; in Dublin the Discalced Carmelites had their first church, in Clarendon Street, just before the Union.

In 1810 the Augustinians at Callan, Co. Kilkenny, built a church costing £4,000, with apartments in the basement for the community. The Franciscans returned to their ruined friary at Multyfarnham, Co. Westmeath, and built a church in 1827, incorporating the nave, south transept, and tower of the fifteenth-century building. Some orders found it easier to procure a private house for their community and convert a room for use as a chapel, like the Dominican nuns who moved into Much Cabra House, Co. Dublin, in 1819. In 1831, sixty-four English and Irish Trappists expelled from France, accused of treason and rebellion, established themselves at Mount Melleray, Co. Waterford.

As the money for building had to be raised by the parishioners, the rural Catholic churches of the first decades of the nineteenth century were usually unpretentious; most of them have vanished, having been replaced by more substantial buildings. A pretty and unusual Catholic church, in use until 1972,

The old Catholic church, Johnstown, Co. Wicklow.

at Johnstown near Arklow, Co. Wicklow, was built in 1803. It is a vernacular building in the picturesque 'Gothick' manner then popular for small houses and gate-lodges. When the smart new church was opened in 1972 the old one was deconsecrated and sold, with the parochial residence, to a smallholder. Its future seems very uncertain; part of it is used as a piggery. This little church, a touching memorial to the faith, achievement and sacrifice of the men who built it in the difficult times before Catholic Emancipation, surely deserves a better fate.

St Mary's Catholic Church, Aldergrove, Co. Antrim, built in 1816, is a delightful small church in the same vein as the old Johnstown Church. It is T-shaped, with pretty 'Gothick' glazing and a little rose window.

Father John Milner, an English Catholic priest, in his *History of Winchester*, published in 1798, promulgated the idea that Gothic was essentially a Catholic, as opposed to an Anglican style, and therefore eminently suitable for Catholic churches. The Catholics in Ireland, however, when they could afford an architect and a definite style, usually opted for a classical building. This may have been due to a desire to assert their respectability, for their better churches vied with Neoclassical public buildings. (The best buildings of the Regency in Ireland were Classic Revival, ranging from Cork gaol, with its Doric portico, of 1818, to Dublin General Post Office, with its hexastyle Ionic portico, completed in the same year.) The plethora of First-Fruits-Gothic Protestant churches, which covered Ireland like a rash at the time when Catholics began serious building, may also have turned them against Gothic.

Work began on St Mary's Metropolitan Catholic Chapel, Dublin, now called the 'Pro-Cathedral', in 1816. It was intended to be the most impressive Catholic church in Ireland (which was not difficult as there was scant competition), and to vie with the best Protestant churches in the country. The Catholics, emerging from the dark years of subjugation and humiliation, were beginning to realize

St Mary's Pro-Cathedral, Dublin.

the older chapels, but that of the church of Saints Michael and John,[12] built in 1815, with an exterior by J. Taylor in the half-hearted Gothic manner of the Protestant churches of that decade. It cost £10,000.

At least three Irish architects, Thomas Duff, Thomas Cobden and Bernard Mullen, made serious attempts at Gothic Catholic edifices. Mullen's St Brendan's, Birr, Co. Offaly, is a very creditable effort, built in 1817, less bogus than its Established Church counterpart, which had just been completed. Cobden's aisleless cruciform cathedral at Carlow, begun in 1820, is pleasing. The Perpendicular Gothic tower, rising to a height of 151 feet, and crowned by an elegant octagonal lantern, has a very authentic air. Cobden probably found it in the illustrations to contemporary English publications by Britton or Rickman,[13] disciples of the more serious approach to Gothic architecture which had been fostered by John Carter, who died in 1817. The attractive interior of Carlow Cathedral is far from orthodox; this is the Gothic of Wyatt and Nash – pretty, with tall slender clustered columns, triple lancets, and diagonal rib-vaulting with stuccoed bosses and ribs. The building was made possible by the energetic James Doyle, Bishop of Kildare and Leighlin from 1819 until his death in 1834; there is a fine white marble statue of

St Brendan's Church, Birr, Co. Offaly.

the force of their numbers. They were no longer willing to be discreet in their building. Dublin County Catholic gentry like the Nettervilles and Barnewalls, who had survived the penal degradation, wealthy urban Catholics – shipbuilders, shipowners, builders, bankers and traders – and Irish-educated priests coming out of Maynooth, all wanted the best that money could buy in the way of churches. The site of the Pro-Cathedral detracts from its appearance, for it is impossible to view the monumental building from a sufficient distance. While work was in progress Francis Johnston's General Post Office with its great hexastyle portico was being built a few yards away, and John Sweetman decided on a huge hexastyle portico for his building too. It took more than twenty years to complete the work (which cost in the region of £50,000), and by 1837 the west front was not finished – the heavy portico with its fluted Doric columns had still to be added.[11] The interior, which is basilical, is splendid; it has a great internal colonnade of twenty-two fluted Doric columns, which continues round the curve of the apse, creating an ambulatory. Over the nave there is a handsome coffered dome.

According to Dr Craig, the first Catholic bell to toll in Dublin after the Reformation was not, however, that of the new Pro-Cathedral, nor one of

him by John Hogan in the nave. Cobden's practice was mainly in Co. Carlow and Co. Kildare; another of his Catholic churches is at Naas, completed in 1833, with the adjoining Presentation Convent. The towers and spire were added twenty-five years later.

In 1820, the same year that Cobden started Carlow Cathedral, George Richard Pain rebuilt the interior of St Mary's, the Pro-Cathedral of the city of Cork. The ceiling has fancy lierne vaulting, stuccoed like the delightful bogus tabernacle-work and bishops' heads. The gothicization of the exterior, which continued over many years, is not very successful.

Pain abandoned his customary restrained 'Gothick' in his unusual portico for Holy Trinity Church, Cork, begun in 1832. The tower and spire were added fifty years later.

Thomas Jackson, a native of Waterford who practised in Belfast, was the architect of the most romantic Catholic church in that city, dedicated to St Malachy and completed in 1844. The style is Tudor Revival, with slender castellated turrets at the corners and flanking the central gable. But it is the interior that is most impressive. This has a prodigious fan-vaulted ceiling, based on the Henry VII Chapel in Westminster Abbey, complete with icing-sugar pendants and drop-tracery on the reredos.

The Cathedral of the Assumption, Carlow, Co. Carlow.

St Malachy's Church, Belfast.

Newry Cathedral, Co. Down.

The Catholic cathedral at Newry was built by Thomas Duff of Newry, who also worked in partnership with Thomas Jackson. Its rather romantic Gothic is very accomplished. The nave is separated from the aisles by a lofty arcade with granite clustered columns. Over the arcade and round the clerestory windows is mosaic-work, with the names of the parishes of the diocese worked in Gothic lettering on shields, between floral designs and medallions with busts of saints. Along the walls of the aisles are ogee-headed cartouches with portraits of favourite saints, all in mosaic, part of the work done later in the century. St Patrick's, Dundalk, is another fine church by Duff.

The Catholics were organized in their struggle for Emancipation by Daniel O'Connell, the Catholic Association was formed, and largely due to its agitation, Emancipation was granted in 1829. The Catholic Association also campaigned for tithe reform, to remedy the injustice of the Catholic peasantry paying tithes to the Established Church. Crops were assessed in July, and a bargain struck between the farmer and the tithe-collector shortly before harvest-time. The tithes were predial: on fruits of the ground; personal: on profits of labour; mixed: on produce from both. In theory the tithe was 10 per cent, but this was not always so in practice. The money went to the Church of Ireland clergyman of the parish unless the tithes were impropriate to some other person or body. The Catholic house-holders of Dublin, Cork, Limerick, Waterford, Drogheda, Clonmel and Kinsale continued to be taxed towards the support of the Established Church ministry. The injustice of this levy, which was collected by the churchwardens of the Church of Ireland parishes, caused much resentment. The amount raised in Minister's Money was £15,000 per annum until the tax was finally abolished in 1857, after having been reduced by 25 per cent in 1854.

In the years between the Union and Emancipation, some Protestant landlords, aware of the plight of their Catholic tenants, donated sites and sometimes money to build a church for them. Thus, at Mallow, Co. Cork, the thatched Mass House was replaced in 1818 by a new church on a site donated by Mr Jephson-Norreys of Mallow Castle;[14] at Doneraile, in 1827, Lord Doneraile gave a site for the pretty church of St Mary's, and £50 towards the building.[15]

After Emancipation, Catholic church-building proceeded apace. In Dublin, Patrick Byrne was the most prominent Catholic architect. His church for the Franciscans on Merchant's Quay (still known by its name of penal days: 'Adam and Eve's') was built in 1830. It has a severe Neoclassical façade, with two orders of pilasters, the lower, Doric, the upper, Corinthian, and for a belfry on top of the tower, a complete Greek temple. The main interior features are the arcaded aisles and large cupola. Across the Liffey is another of Byrne's churches, St Paul's, Arran Quay, built 1835–37. It has a very pleasing silhouette, with triumphant statues above the pediment of the prostyle Ionic portico, and a green cupola surmounting the tower. Three other Catholic churches were being built in Dublin in 1832. The

The Franciscan church, Merchant's Quay, Dublin (known as 'Adam and Eve's').

St Nicholas of Myra, Dublin.

St Audoen's Church, High Street, Dublin, plasterwork on the ceiling.

largest, St Andrew's in Westland Row, designed by James Bolger, was completed in 1837. The cruciform St Francis Xavier's in Gardiner Street was built for the Jesuits (Father Bartholomew Esmonde SJ is credited with the design, probably in collaboration with Joseph B. Keane); St Nicholas of Myra was the work of John Leeson: it has an Ionic portico very similar to Byrne's on St Paul's, but the pilastered tower, originally intended to have a spire, has a hemispherical dome like that of St Stephen's, Upper Mount Street, a classical Church of Ireland church built in 1825. St Andrew's façade is flush with the adjoining houses, its Doric portico recessed and flanked by outer bays with doors under the same broad pediment, which is crowned by a statue of St Andrew.

The best of this group of Dublin churches is St Audoen's, High Street, designed by Patrick Byrne, begun in 1841. It presents to the street a gigantic prostyle Corinthian portico added in 1898, its pediment topped with three statues. Behind, and best seen from below, is Byrne's immense hall built of black Dublin culp. Dr Craig aptly described it as 'an impregnable fortress of the faith'.[16] The inside, now pleasingly painted in yellow and white, is not as fine as it was, for the dome over the crossing collapsed forty years after it was constructed, and was never rebuilt; in its place is a large flat plaster circle. Nevertheless this is the most beautiful interior of the Neoclassical Dublin Catholic churches. It is barrel-vaulted, each bay coffered and divided from the next by a broad cross-band with a running design,

Belfry of St Patrick's Catholic Church, Cork.

St Mary's, the Dominican church, Pope's Quay, Cork.

in stucco, while the compartments are elaborately treated with rosettes in high relief. The only windows, lunettes, are cut into the barrel-vault, above an elaborate cornice. The bays of the nave and transepts are marked by giant fluted Corinthian pilasters; the reredos is composed of a white and gilt pediment, resting on pairs of Corinthian columns with richly gilded capitals.

Cork has a distinguished Classic Revival church, St Patrick's, built in 1836 by the architect George Richard Pain. It has an attractive belfry. The interior was remodelled at the end of the century. Kearns Deane designed the handsome St Mary's on Pope's Quay, Cork, for the Dominicans. It was built between 1832 and 1839, with an impressive Ionic portico and a rich interior with a coffered ceiling.

In smaller towns where less money was available, parish priests economized by dispensing with the services of an architect. Some priests tried their hand at drawing the plans themselves, with the help of a pattern-book, or, worse still, based their design on what they had seen in the cities. The Catholic church at Callan, Co. Kilkenny, begun in 1836 and finished in 1843, is an example of this home-made Neo-classical. The interior, which Samuel Lewis described in the year after it was built as 'very neat, the ceiling chastely and handsomely carved',[17] is now alarming. The application of gold, crimson, pink, tomato-red

Fethard Catholic Church, Co. Tipperary.

and mauve paint makes an astounding effect, something between a theatre-set and a circus. The façade of the church at Fethard, Co. Tipperary, is imaginative, with a fanciful bell-cote decorated with urns. St John the Baptist, Cashel, in the same county, was built by Father Edmund Cormack between 1792 and 1804; the stone façade was added in 1850. The mosaic decoration is modern. The church dedicated to the Blessed Virgin at Clonmel, Co. Tipperary, was also built in 1850 – good provincial Neoclassical; the tall prostyle Corinthian portico has an unusual sculpted tympanum, and statues of the Virgin, St Bridget and St Patrick on the pediment.

Father Justin Foley who was parish priest at Kinsale, Co. Cork, built the church of St John the Baptist there in 1834. The building is cruciform, with galleries over the west end and the transepts. The church is very well lit by a series of handsome round-headed windows, finely glazed and flanked by Corinthian pilasters. The exterior is a discreet, old-fashioned Neoclassical, with handsome urns on the pediment.

Arklow Catholic Church is another pleasing example of conservative Late Georgian Neoclassical.

Augustus Charles Pugin was one of the prominent early exponents of serious Gothic Revival, and his technically accurate *Specimens of Gothic Architecture*, 1821–23, was a work of considerable influence. His son Augustus Welby Pugin was converted to Catholicism in England; his visits to, and study of, the Gothic churches on the Continent had drawn him towards Catholicism. He fervently believed that building Gothic churches was a religious duty, and his serious research into Gothic included the devotional, sacramental and liturgical uses of buildings. A. W. Pugin's rigid principles resulted in a new doctrinaire approach to church-building in England, which spread through the English-speaking world. His first important church, St Marie's, Derby, in England, was built in 1838, two years after the publication of his influential *Contrasts*. Pugin's principal patron, the Earl of Shrewsbury, a rich, cosmopolitan Catholic peer, had married an Irishwoman, Miss Maria Teresa Talbot, the daughter of a Catholic landowner in Co. Wexford. Because of this connection Pugin was commissioned to build a number of Catholic churches in Co. Wexford. Ramsgrange and Bree churches, both built in 1837–38, are attributed to him;[18] certainly his, is St Michael the Archangel, Gorey, Co. Wexford, begun in 1839. In the same year he made the design for the chapel of the Loreto Convent, Rathfarnham, Co. Dublin, for which there are dated drawings. His next Irish church, St Peter's, Wexford, was started in 1840. In 1841 Pugin made drawings for the Presentation Convent at Waterford. The foundation-stone for

Church of St John the Baptist, Kinsale, Co. Cork.

Tagoat Catholic Parish Church, Co. Wexford.

Birr Convent of Mercy, Co. Offaly.

St Mary's Cathedral, Killarney, Co. Kerry. Opposite, the view down the nave towards the east end as it now appears.

St Aidan's Cathedral, Enniscorthy, was laid in 1843; mass was celebrated there in 1846, but the building was then only partially finished, and the tower was not built until 1850. The foundation-stone of St Alphonsus, Barntown, Co. Wexford, was laid in 1844. The last of the Pugin churches in Co. Wexford, Tagoat, was opened in 1846. This is an example of Pugin's best work on a small church: it has excellent proportions, fine clear lines and careful detail. In 1848 the *Irish Catholic Directory* published illustrations of Pugin's scheme for the convent at Birr, Co. Offaly, then being constructed. Here Pugin employed an element from Ireland's own architectural heritage: the Round Tower attached to the corner of the building.

The most important and best of Pugin's Irish churches is Killarney Cathedral, Co. Kerry. According to the architect's son, Killarney was the nearest to Pugin's heart of the more than sixty churches he designed. When the building committee engaged Pugin in 1840, they had only collected £900. By 1846 they had raised £6,000. Lord Kenmare, the local magnate, himself a Catholic, gave £2,000, and bequeathed a further £500. By 1842 the first drawings were made, and the ground was laid out. It was an extremely ambitious undertaking: when the cathedral was consecrated in 1855, £20,000 had been spent.[19] A reporter writing in the *Tralee Chronicle* described the event as 'more like a dream of the Middle Ages than a thing of modern reality'.[20] Pugin was not there – he had died, mainly of strain and overwork, in 1852 – but his son Edward W. and J.J. McCarthy, who together had carried on after 1852, were both present. Pugin had been unable to come often to Killarney, so had accepted the commission on condition that Richard Pierce of Wexford, whose work he knew and trusted, should be the Superintendent of Works. Pugin drew some inspiration for Killarney Cathedral from the ancient ruined cathedral of the diocese, at Ardfert. Between 1908 and 1912 further work was carried out, including the addition of the spire, which reaches 285 feet, and cost £11,000.[21] In 1972 extensive repairs were made (to be discussed in the last chapter). Stripping off the plaster and cutting back to the stone has revealed the strength and masterful beauty of Pugin's design.

Killarney was the precursor of several splendid Irish cathedrals, the best of them by J.J. McCarthy, Pugin's Irish architectural heir. Even as a young man, McCarthy's work was of high standard; his private chapel, built at Bellevue, Co. Wexford, for the Cliffe family, was for a long time wrongly attributed to Pugin.[22]

The famine in Ireland, caused by the failure of the potato crop in 1846 and 1847, brought dire distress

St Alphonsus, Limerick, west door.

and poverty. The Catholics had to rely on voluntary contributions for their building work, and these ceased almost entirely. Those who could afford to give, diverted their donations to the relief of the hungry. At Killarney work stopped in 1846. The partly built cathedral was boarded up, and remained so until the resumption of building in 1853. St Mel's Cathedral at Longford, commenced in 1840, was not completed until 1893.

After the bleakest years, contributions for building in the old country began to trickle in from the United States, Canada, South Africa, Australia, New Zealand, England and Argentina. These were the offerings of the Irish who had been forced to emigrate.

A number of important Catholic churches were begun after the worst famine years had passed. The foundation-stone of St John's Cathedral, Limerick, was laid in 1856,[23] and five years later the work was completed, save for the tower and the spire – one of the most beautiful in the country, designed by Maurice Hennessy, a Limerick-born architect. The cathedral was the work of P. C. Hardwick, assisted by William Corbett.

Hardwick was from England, where, with his father, he had built the Hall and Library of Lincoln's Inn, London. He came to Co. Limerick to work for the Earl of Dunraven on Adare Manor, after Pugin, and had also been commissioned by the Earl to repair the Trinitarian abbey church there for use as the Catholic parish church. At the same time, assisted by Corbett, he was engaged on another Limerick church – St Alphonsus, built for the Redemptorists. The foundation-stone was laid in 1858, the church dedicated in December 1862.[24] The style is thirteenth-century Gothic; in the tympanum over the west door is a Christ with adoring angels, under the inscription 'Copiosa Apud Eum Redemptio' on one of the red marble bands which decorate the front. The church is 173 feet long, terminating at the east end in an apse. A great novelty at the time of building were the varicoloured encaustic tiles of the sanctuary floor, designed by Minton and Co.

Maurice Hennessy and George Goldie, who were responsible for the additions to St John's Cathedral after Hardwick left, remodelled another Limerick church with J. J. McCarthy: the Dominican church, St Saviour's, enlarged and remodelled in 1860.

An English architect, John Hungerford Pollen, was brought over to Dublin by Dr (later Cardinal) Newman, to build the Catholic University Church in St Stephen's Green, Dublin, in 1855. Pollen made a departure from Gothic, apparently at Newman's instigation. The style is Byzantine, and it caused a furore. One Puginite critic described it as 'a horrid monster of a building'.[25] An anonymous pamphlet entitled 'A Word to the Goths' appeared, offering a rebuttal. Newman, then Rector of the Catholic University, was accused of being the author of this pamphlet. This he denied, stating that he never set himself against the adoption of Gothic architecture in churches, and even contemplated its use in this case, considering it the most beautiful of architectural styles; but claimed the liberty of preferring for worship and devotion, 'a building which, though not so beautiful in outline, is more in accordance with the ritual of the present day, more cheerful in its interior, admitting more naturally of rich materials, of large pictures or mosaics, and of mural decorations'.[26]

Newman got what he wanted, but in general the Puginites held the day. In 1858 Pugin's disciple J. J. McCarthy built St Saviour's Catholic Church in Dominic Street, Dublin. Architects and ecclesiologists were quick with criticisms, even insults. In a letter to *The Dublin Builder* of 1 February 1863, 'An Architect' queried whether McCarthy himself designed any of St Saviour's, and implied that it was the work of the late A. W. Pugin. Murphy and Son, Builders and Contractors (whose restoration work at St Patrick's Cathedral had been assailed by

McCarthy), accused McCarthy of 'slavishly copying a cross from Brandon's book of examples, and placing it on the summit of St Saviour's', and decorating its gable with 'a poor window from St Clotilde's at Paris'.[27] According to Messrs Murphy, the columns at St Saviour's had crumbled with their own weight; and the Dominican symbol, 'two dogs in stone with jaws desperately clenched on something like mutton-bones while they grinned in ghastly unity from each side of the doorway', had had to be removed quickly because passers-by were so amused or disgusted by them.[28] A fortnight later a correspondent signing himself 'Truth', denied that the pillars at St Saviour's crumbled, and moreover declared that they carried the clerestory walls and roof of the highest church in Dublin. As for Messrs Murphy, 'Truth' pointed out that having successfully built the Guinness breweries was no qualification for restoring St Patrick's Cathedral.

Pugin's son E. W. Pugin and his partner G. C. Ashlin had a busy architectural practice in Ireland. One of their most elaborate churches is St Augustine and St John in Thomas Street, Dublin – full-blown French Gothic, begun in 1862. Thomastown, Co. Kilkenny, has a good Puginesque Catholic church, built 1857–69.

The Murphy's virulent attack on McCarthy included criticism of his work on the new Catholic cathedral at Armagh. The foundation-stone there had been laid in 1840, the original design being by Duff. Work was discontinued in 1848 due to the Famine, and McCarthy took over.

The cathedral, which was not dedicated until 1872, will be discussed in the next chapter, with other McCarthy churches.

By 1870 the disastrous economic situation caused by the famine had begun to improve. Emigration continued, but a new Catholic bourgeoisie was emerging, anxious to assert its presence and importance. The churches of the last decades of the century were to reflect this new social order.

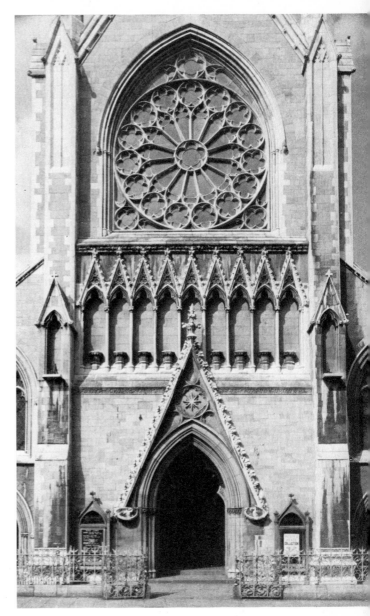

St Saviour's, Dublin, the west door and rose window.

Catholic University Church, Dublin, detail of carving on front doorway.

161

CHAPTER 9

The end of the Old Régime 1870–1922

AFTER MORE THAN A YEAR of fierce discussion, hard bargaining and broken promises, the Bill for the Disestablishment of the Church of Ireland was passed in July 1869. 'Now you see, My Lord,' said an Irish Catholic bishop to the Protestant Primate on that night, 'what the English are really like.' The Primate had been coerced into co-operating with Gladstone on the issue, and by the time the promises made to him had been broken, it was too late for him to retract and consolidate the opposition. The Catholics were delighted that the anomaly of an Established Church of the minority was finally ended. The State handed over £7,581,075 to the disestablished Church, which from thenceforth was on its own. The annual grant to the Presbyterian Church also ceased; its ministers compounded their life-incomes to set up a capital fund of £580,000.

The magnificent new cathedral of St Finbar at Cork was begun before Disestablishment. William Burges, an English architect (who, in 1855, had won the competition for the new cathedral at Lille, France, in collaboration with Henry Clutton) won the competition for St Finbar's, Cork, in 1863. This choice was the subject of bitter polemic, with disappointed competitors seeking legal advice.[1] One of the building-committee's conditions was that competitors must submit a design at a cost not exceeding £15,000. Burges's design could not be executed at less than £25,000–30,000, and some competitors angrily protested that they could have submitted more beautiful designs had they not adhered to the rules. Others complained that Burges had not provided a chapter-house as required by the committee, only a poky room he called the 'Consistory Court', 12 feet square, and separated from the nave by an openwork screen. Another complaint was that the seating capacity stipulated by the competition rules was 700, while Burges's plan only allowed for

466 pew sittings, at 5 square feet per person.[2] Burges's reply to these accusations was that no cathedral was ever executed for £15,000, with towers and spires complete; so he had never imagined that the committee meant that sum to cover the whole design, but merely everything essential for carrying on divine service. He also declared himself ready to show how 738 adults could be seated by making use of the transepts.[3]

The building work began on St Finbar's in 1865, and it was completed in 1876. The first impression of the triple-towered cathedral on its hill, is of something quite alien to Cork; the second is surprise that this is a Protestant church, for in its elaborate Revival splendour it rivals contemporary continental churches like Viollet-le-Duc's parish church at Saint-Denis, in the suburbs of Paris, completed in 1867. Basically the style of the exterior is that of the twelfth century in France. The interior, however, at once lavish and vigorous, less delicate than McCarthy's work, has a more English air, largely due to the fine wooden roof in the Early English Gothic manner. Burges's approach was more intellectual than aesthetic, and this is evident in the strength of his design. St Finbar's is one of the most unusual and interesting Victorian Gothic churches. Some of the interior furnishing is quite sumptuous, especially the bishop's throne.

The building of the Church of Ireland cathedral of St Mary, Tuam, Co. Galway, also began before Disestablishment. On 27 August 1863 the second Baron Plunket, Bishop of Tuam, laid the memorial-stone with a silver trowel presented by the architects Sir Thomas Deane and Son; at that time some of the walls had already been raised to the eaves-line.[4] For centuries the fourteenth-century church to the east of the present chancel had been used as the cathedral. Sir Thomas Deane built the new one on to the west

St Finbar's Cathedral, Cork; elaborate Revival splendour.

of the ancient chancel, incorporating the latter with its magnificent Romanesque chancel arch. The old church behind the chancel was converted into a chapter-house. Both Bishop Plunket and Sir Thomas Deane died before the work was finished in 1878, when the Honourable Charles Broderick Bernard, second son of the second Earl of Bandon, was Bishop. Limestone from Kilroe, Co. Galway, was used for the building, but the walls were lined inside with sandstone, brought from near Castlebar, Co. Mayo. A space of 2 inches was left between the outer wall and this lining, to prevent the penetration of damp. Deane based his design for the nave on the Gothic of St Patrick's Cathedral, Dublin. Tuam Cathedral, which now usually enjoys a Sunday congregation of less than a dozen persons, has some fine High Victorian fittings. The lectern before the throne in the choir, the throne, the pulpit, font and stalls are of Caen stone and Irish marble. There is some splendid stained glass. The windows at the west end were put up in 1919 by the family and friends of the Bishop's son, Percy Broderick Bernard, who died in 1912. The most westerly window in the south wall is exceptionally pretty (pl. XIII, p. 140). It was given by Bishop Bernard, his wife and younger son, in memory of the Bishop's young daughter-in-law Beatrice, who died in 1876.

St Mary's Cathedral, Tuam, Co. Galway. Left, interior; right, the lectern in the choir before the episcopal throne.

Memorial window in St Multose's Church, Kinsale, Co. Cork.

The Bandon Bernards were great memorial-makers. In the Victorian Gothic church of St Peter's, Ballymodan, Bandon, Co. Cork, the parish of their seat, Castle Bernard, are funeral monuments in the best nineteenth-century tradition. At the west end of the nave, all in white marble, the sleeping figure of the second Earl of Bandon lies with his feet against his coronet, on a sarcophagus sculpted with his armorial bearings; the window behind him, also with the Bernard arms, was put up in 1881. His Countess, who died in 1870, is commemorated by a trumpeting angel under a decorated Gothic canopy with abundant crocketing. A mural to the side of the east window, an angel holding a lily, is dedicated to Colonel Richard William Aldworth who died in 1899, after having 'served his Queen and Country . . . and married Lady Mary Catherine Henrietta, daughter of the 3rd Earl of Bandon' – equally praiseworthy achievements in the opinion of Anglo-Irish Victorian society. The companion mural depicts a helmeted angel in armour.

In Rahan Church, Co. Offaly, is a delightful window (pl. XIV, p. 140) portraying St Carthage who had a monastery there in the seventh century, before going to Lismore. The window bears the inscription: 'The gift of a wayfarer'. The Victorians did not usually hide their good works, heraldic achievements or aristocratic connections under a cloak of anonymity. A monument to a Miss O'Looney bears the epitaph:

> She was bland, passionate and deeply religious, had several watercolours hung in the Royal Hibernian Academy of Arts, and was a first cousin of Lady Jones: Of such is the Kingdom of Heaven.

Mr John Carry of Cloughog, Duneane, Co. Antrim, erected a monument in memory of his parents in the Presbyterian churchyard: several panels are inscribed with wordy moral exhortations, proclamations of the family's long-standing loyalty to the Crown, and details of their better connections. 'For further information', the inscription ends, 'see Burkes' landed gentry.' John Dillon MP, to express his gratitude to his cousin Mrs Anne Deane, 'to whom he owed everything', ignominiously ruined the superb Flamboyant Gothic tomb-niche at Strade, Co. Mayo, by inserting in it a very ugly memorial to her memory.

Loyalty to the Crown and military valour, revered by the Anglo-Irish gentry, are portrayed in a window of St Multose Church, Kinsale, Co. Cork. Under a label inscribed 'I have fought the good fight', Lieutenant Stephen Henry Lewis of the Connaught Rangers, killed in action in 1915 at Gallipoli, is depicted with short-back-and-sides haircut, armour, a halo round his head, flanked by angels and surrounded by his regimental emblems and armorial bearings.

Church of Ireland Parish Church of the Good Shepherd, Urney, Sion Mills, Co. Tyrone.

Apart from repairs to existing churches, and the major restoration of St Brigid's Cathedral, Kildare, by G. E. Street in 1875, Church of Ireland building activity dwindled after the Disestablishment. The Church authorities, who retained all churches in actual use, had a large number to maintain, on a drastically reduced income. The rural Protestant population in Connaught, Munster and Leinster began to diminish, largely due to the effects of the Land League agitations of the 1870s and 1880s. Outside Ulster, only the growing suburbs of Dublin required new churches.

Of the churches built in Ulster in this period, few can claim architectural merit, but two are unusual and worthy of note. The church of Urney parish, Co. Tyrone, at Sion Mills, dedicated to the Good Shepherd in 1909, is in the Byzantine style. The sanctuary in the apse has an inlaid marble floor and steps. On either side of the chancel arch are twin pulpits, also of varicoloured panelled marble. The rest of the church is agreeably plain: parquet flooring, whitewashed walls, no stained glass. St Matthew's, Woodvale Road, Belfast, was designed by Welland and Gillespie of Dublin. It is a curious trefoil shape, built in polychrome brick, dirty yellow, banded with red. An Irish Round Tower in yellow brick rises above the church; it has an elongated conical roof and tall unconvincing lancet windows. Courses of red brick round the tower indicate the line of the treads of the winding stair within.

A number of Presbyterian churches were built in Ulster between 1870 and the First World War,

mostly economical buildings of little interest. Gransha Presbyterian Church, Co. Down, is a fairly typical example of what was required. The contracted price was only £1,500, and when the church was opened in June 1879, the minister happily declared 'there was not a single six pence of an extra on the contract.'[5] This bargain was designed by Henry Chappell of Newtownards, and built by Hutcheson Keith of Belfast. Accommodation was provided for four hundred persons, but six hundred managed to squeeze in for the opening ceremony. Everyone marvelled at the moderate cost of this neat Gothic church, built of local stone, complete with tower, pinnacles, window tracery and chiselled dressings. The price even included the internal fittings, pulpit and seats, all in pitch pine. Chappell also designed Fortwilliam Presbyterian Church in Antrim Road, Belfast.

Crescent Presbyterian Church, built in 1887, in University Road, Belfast, is altogether grander, and is considered one of the best-looking churches in the city. The architect, John B. Wilson of Glasgow, based his design on thirteenth-century French forms; the result is contained, agreeable, and improved by the colourful effect of the two shades of sandstone, red and beige. The campanile design is original: eight tall, slender square columns, with pointed arches to the interstices.

In Belfast during this period most of the Presbyterian churches were by a firm of architects, Young and Mackenzie, who also built at Derry, and elsewhere in Ulster. Their output was large and mediocre.

Carlisle Road Methodist Church, Derry, buttresses and drainpipes.

St Peter's Pro-Cathedral, Belfast, was designed by a native Belfast priest, Father Jeremiah McAuley. When he went to Spain, the work was successfully completed in 1866 by John O'Neill, who thereby established his reputation. He built a number of Catholic churches, usually in the French Gothic style, including St Patrick's, Downpatrick, Co. Down, opened in 1870, which has an elegant spire, and the successful St Michael's, Enniskillen, Co. Fermanagh, completed in 1875, best viewed from the lower ground to the south-east.

The firm of Pugin and Ashlin of Dublin (founded by E. W. Pugin) specialized in Catholic ecclesiastical work. Their most successful undertaking was St Colman's Cathedral at Queenstown (now Cobh), Co. Cork. The foundation-stone was laid on 30 September 1868, but progress was slow, and the external walls and roof were not completed until 1879, when the cathedral was opened for mass. Work on the interior recommenced in 1895 and went on until 1919, when the solemn consecration took place.

St Colman's Cathedral, Cobh, Co. Cork.

An example of their clumsy, undistinguished work is Townsend Street Presbyterian Church, Belfast, completed in 1878.

Alfred Forman, a capable but eccentric architect who practised in Derry, built the Methodist church there in Carlisle Road in 1901. The façade is disconcerting, although the architect concentrated on creating a visual effect. He achieved this by uniting a number of striking non-functional elements: a hexagonal turret with a tiled pyramidal roof, gables, flying buttresses, and decorated finials. The whole would be less bizarre were it not for the drainpipes which punctuate the gabled bays. This church has excellent acoustics, as does Ballynafeigh Methodist Church, also by Forman, built on Ormeau Road, Belfast, in 1899. The *Belfast News Letter* of 13 January 1899 announced to a puzzled readership that the style was adapted from 'American-Romanesque'. This is a bold attempt to classify the queer-looking building, with its protuberances and fussy arrangement of disparate forms. It is redeemed by its well-lit mock-Elizabethan interior, an adaptation of the plan of a Shakespearean theatre, with a fretwork roof supported by tall wooden columns. C. E. B. Brett inclines to award the prize for Belfast's ugliest church to another Methodist church,[6] the graceless Carlisle Memorial Church in Carlisle Circus, completed in 1875 and designed by W. H. Lynn, who until 1872 had been a partner in the prestigious firm of Lanyon, Lynn and Lanyon. Lynn was capable of much better designs.

It is to Catholic churches and cathedrals that one must look for impressive architecture after 1870.

The total cost of the cathedral was £235,000. The later work (directed by Pugin and Ashlin's successors, Ashlin and Coleman) included the stately limestone spire, started in 1912,[7] 128 feet high and reaching a height of 300 feet from the ground. It is felicitous that the cathedral has such a beautiful silhouette, for it stands in a prominent position overlooking the harbour. The building is cruciform, with an aisled nave and two eastern chapels in each transept. The dark-red marble columns of the seven-bay nave arcade have richly sculpted capitals with foliage and human heads. The tall, slender, clustered columns of the triforium rise to the springing of the arch over the clerestory windows; winged angel-heads crown these pointed arches. The chancel arch, which is extremely high, is also supported by clustered columns. Both the pulpit and the altar are extravagantly carved.

Several capable architects received their training with Ashlin and Pugin, among them the promising Thomas Hevey, who died in his early thirties. He designed St Joseph's, Prince's Dock Street, Belfast, completed after his death by Mortimer Thompson in 1881; and with Thompson he designed and saw completed St Patrick's, Donegall Street, Belfast.

The grey spires and silhouettes of Late Victorian Puginesque churches are attractive features of the rural landscape in Ireland. They were often advantageously sited on the edge of the town, like St Joseph's, Carrickmacross, Co. Monaghan. The Catholic church at Ballina, Co. Mayo, though built in the town, looks very fine from afar.

The dominating figure of Catholic architecture in the latter part of the century was J.J. McCarthy, an enthusiastic and learned ecclesiologist. One of his best works is St Macartan's Cathedral at Monaghan, begun in 1861 and not quite complete when he died in 1882. It was completed by William Hague. It is sited on high ground just outside the town. The approach is now neatly landscaped, and the cathedral, built of hard local limestone, is impressive at the top of the flights of stone steps. The exterior, which has rich carving, just avoids being over-ornate. In niches on either side of the main door, on the west front, are statues of Saints Peter and Paul in white Carrara marble, the work of Pietro Lazzerini, one of a family of prolific artist-masons at Massa Carrara, Italy, who did a roaring trade exporting competent but bland Catholic statuary in great quantities. In the tympanum is a carving in high relief of Christ giving the keys to St Peter. The beautiful stained-glass rose window in the west front is largely obscured on the inside by the organ. Over the door to the south transept is a figure of Christ; in the tympanum is a carving of the Virgin and Child surrounded by very un-Gothic *putti*, and in an arcade below the

St Macartan's Cathedral, Monaghan. Below, sculpture on the south transept.

rose window a statue of Saint Dympna wearing the martyr's crown of victory, flanked by statues of nineteenth-century bishops of Clogher (McNally and Donnelly), an ancient one (the soldier-bishop Heber McMahon), and of Saints Tiarach, Ultan and Columcille – three on each side, all in trefoil-headed niches. The dignified interior is imposing. The nave is very high, covered with a finely joined hammer-beam roof; the corbels of the supporting beams are carved with naturalistic heads. The bishop's throne and the lofty pulpit are lavish; there is a painted dado, sky-blue and beige, round the pointed arches of the nave arcade, and some excellent High Victorian stained-glass memorial windows.

McCarthy also employed, very effectively, an arcade of niches containing statues at Armagh, over the west door. He had taken over work on this cathedral, and, not without opposition (see p. 161), he radically changed Duff's plan, discarding the intended central tower in favour of twin towers flanking the west portal, surmounted by spires with lucarnes (pl. XVIII, p. 174). The cathedral is built of local limestone and Dungannon freestone. It is cruciform, 212 feet in length, 120 feet across the transepts, the nave 114 feet long. It was dedicated in 1872, almost twenty years after McCarthy had taken over the

St Patrick's Cathedral, Armagh.

St Patrick's Cathedral, Armagh, Angel holding a stoop. Opposite, Archbishop Daniel McGettigan with a model of the cathedral. In the distance is the Church of Ireland Cathedral.

work. By the time he died in 1882, the exterior was finished but the interior was still bare. Most of the decoration of the interior was done between 1887 and 1904, largely financed by a mammoth charity bazaar in 1900 which raised the amazing sum of £30,000.[8] The cathedral was consecrated in 1904. A great deal of Italian marble was used, mostly carved by Italian sculptors, for the ornate main altar, reredos, side-altars and statuary. An Italian was imported to paint the ceiling of the nave with scenes from the lives of Irish saints. The walls of the nave are decorated with mosaics; in fancy medallions are romantic portraits of twenty Irish saints, made to drawings by John Early, a Dublin artist who specialized in religious subjects and stained-glass work. Most of the stained glass was ordered from Mayer and Co. of Munich. On the terrace in front of the cathedral, facing the city and the hill of Druimsaileach (where St Patrick sited his first cathedral), are marble statues of the Primate who initiated the work, William Crolly, with the plan in his hand, and the Primate under whom the exterior was completed, Daniel McGettigan, beside a model of the cathedral.

McCarthy employed a different style for the cathedral at Thurles, Co. Tipperary, the seat of the Catholic Archbishop of Cashel. The building, which

took over ten years, was completed in 1872. The style is Lombard-Romanesque, with three storeys of blind arcading on the façade and a rose window. A circular domed baptistery is attached to one side of the west front, and a four-storey rectangular tower to the other. Inside, the arrangement is basilical, with massive marble columns. Marble has been used abundantly throughout, the ambulatory being particularly sumptuous; beneath the windows which light the apse is a blank arcade faced with inlaid polychrome marble panels. The ceiling is painted with a High Victorian floral pattern. The late sixteenth-century Italian marble tabernacle on the high altar comes from the Baroque church of the Gesù at Rome; it was probably designed by Giacomo della Porta who designed that church. The Jesuits brought it as a gift to the Synod of Thurles in 1850.

The foundation-stone of St Eugene's Cathedral, Derry, was laid in 1851. The Gothic building, designed by McCarthy, was dedicated in 1873, by which time £40,000 had been spent.[9] This price did not include the spire, which was erected 1903–4, the statues in the niches, or some of the interior

Saints Peter and Paul, Kilmallock, Co. Limerick. Above, interior; opposite, the marble and mosaic decorations.

Cathedral of the Assumption, Thurles, Co. Tipperary.

furnishings. Bishop's throne by Mayer and Co. of Munich, pulpit and reredos were added in 1905.

McCarthy also designed parish churches, of which one fine example is St Patrick's, Dungannon, Co. Tyrone, dedicated in 1876. His most interesting parish church, however, is Saints Peter and Paul, Kilmallock, Co. Limerick, dated 1879. McCarthy studied the thirteenth- and fourteenth-century ruins of the Dominican friary on the edge of the town, and used several elements from these in his design, especially for the windows. The tall nave with a clerestory is flanked by one-storey aisles which terminate in side-chapels; the sanctuary at the east end is lit by a five-light window copied from the magnificent one in the friary. It has been fitted with undistinguished stained glass out of the bequest of Father Thomas Downes who died 1890, the parish priest at the time the church was built. The nave is lit by paired lancets in the aisles and ten sexfoil windows in the clerestory, also copied from the friary. An impressive fifteenth-century window with reticulated tracery in the south transept of the friary was the model for the south window of the chapel at the end of the south aisle. The flower-bud stone-carving in the friary was adapted for the capitals of the reddish-brown marble columns of the six-bay arcades between the nave and aisles. Above the columns, as corbels for the moulding of the arches, are heads of the Twelve Apostles. The roof timbers rest on plain corbels. There is rich

Maynooth College Chapel, Co. Kildare, stalls in the nave and one of the Stations by Westlake, 'Christ falls for the first time'. Below, inner doors of the chapel, seen from the inside.

Victorian mosaic and tiling in the church, including a mosaic of the Crucifixion with gold stars in a bright blue sky, all surrounded by floral patterns and fleurs-de-lis; the wooden ceiling of the sanctuary is painted with stylized flowers and foliage. The rose window at the west end is attractive, and there are stained-glass windows in the aisles by Mayer and Co. of Munich. As an example of Irish conservatism, a notice still indicates that the south aisle (to which there is a separate door) is for 'women only'.

The Irish Parliament had passed an Act in 1795 to open a place of study in Ireland for young men intended for the Catholic ministry. The French Revolution and consequent upheavals had prevented students attending their usual places of study on the Continent, and the Government, more astute than their predecessors, saw the necessity of enabling them to study at home, and the advantage of keeping them away from revolutionary doctrines. The Duke of Leinster generously offered a house and fifty-two acres of his estate at Maynooth, Co. Kildare, on a lease renewable for ever at only £72 per annum; the college opened there for fifty students in 1795, principally supported by an annual parliamentary grant of £8,000, later raised to just under £9,000.[10] By 1840 the college accommodated 450 students and had received a number of donations. One benefactor was John Butler, Catholic Bishop of Cork, who, when well past middle age, unexpectedly succeeded to the family title of Baron Dunboyne. He then applied to the Pope for permission to marry, on the grounds that he ought to produce an heir. The permission was not granted and the Baron-Bishop resigned, conformed to the Established Church, and married. His marriage proved childless, and he was received back again into the Catholic Church before his death. He left his entire estate to the Trustees of Maynooth College, but after litigation they compromised and accepted an annual income. The Maynooth Trustees were able, thanks to another Government grant, to commission A. W. Pugin to built a new college in 1842. After Pugin's death in 1852, McCarthy continued the ambitious project. The foundation-stone of the handsome chapel designed by McCarthy was laid in 1875, and the exterior work was finished in 1882 – the year of McCarthy's death. The interior work continued under the direction of William Hague. It was finished in 1893 and the chapel was consecrated in that year.

The interior, solemn and dignified without being oppressive, is a fitting complement to McCarthy's superb building. The long aisleless nave with a figure-painted ceiling is lined on each side by four tiers of beautifully carved stalls, comprising 454 seats, the work of a family of Irish carvers named Moonan.

XVII Monkstown Parish Church, Co. Dublin (p. 149) >

Maynooth College Chapel, Co. Kildare.

Above them, beneath the stained-glass memorial windows fitted 1891–93, are Stations of the Cross painted by Nathaniel H. J. Westlake, an English decorative painter, writer and stained-glass designer who specialized in biblical subjects. He also painted the ceiling. The great rose window above the organ-loft at the west end is extremely fine.

The ambulatory behind the rose-coloured marble altar, which was erected in 1911, has five chapels, of which the central one is richly decorated in blue and gold mosaic. One chapel, which has a delicate pale mauve and purple window of St Brigid, is even more colourful; the floor and altar steps have been carpeted with three carpets in varying shades of green, each with a different floral pattern. The Irish have become great carpet-lovers, with a special penchant for all-over patterns.

Curiously, the coloured glass in the swing-doors between the chapel and the vestibule bear the inscription 'Porta Coeli' written to be read from *inside* the chapel as one goes out.

Many embellishments were made to churches in the closing decades of the century. Italian firms which manufactured religious statuary exported a

< *XVIII St Patrick's Cathedral, Armagh (p. 168).*

Pulpit in the Cathedral of the Assumption, Carlow, Co. Carlow.

Limerick has two Late Victorian Catholic churches built with ultra-conservatism in the Neoclassical style of the first half of the century. The Franciscan church of the Immaculate Conception in Henry Street, with a giant pro-style Corinthian portico, was begun in 1876 and completed by 1879. It was built to encircle the old church, so that services could continue during the period of construction. The apse envisaged in the architect's plan could not then be built because the ground on that side was not in the hands of the Franciscans. When they did get control of it, in 1896, there was no money available to build; the extension was made thirty-five years later, and the reconstructed edifice solemnly consecrated in 1931. The laying of the foundation-stone in 1876 was accompanied by a panoply of civic pride; the Mayor and Corporation attended in state and the Congregated Trades' Guilds of Limerick and the Pig Buyers' Association marched in procession behind their respective bands.[11] The basilical interior, including the additions of 1931, respects the original plan.

St Joseph's, Limerick, cruciform with an apse, has another Late Victorian Neoclassical interior. The Jesuits' Church of the Sacred Heart at Limerick, next to their school, Crescent House, purchased in 1862, is fitted into a row of domestic buildings. The façade is unattractive – early seventeenth-century

Church of the Immaculate Conception, Limerick.

considerable quantity to Ireland. The Redemptorists' church at Limerick has a copy of the famous bronze statue of St Peter in St Peter's, Rome, a gift of the Sodality of the Holy Family in 1893. The ornate pulpit in Carlow Cathedral was erected in memory of the Bishop, Michael Comerford, who died in 1895; below are figures of St Victor (with wings), St Conleath and St Laserian; above, in panels, Brigid and other saints.

Not every parish could raise the money for a steeped Gothic or marbled Lombard church. Our Lady of the Wayside at Kiltiernan, Co. Dublin, for example, is built of wood with a wooden belfry. Brightly painted in blue and white, it has a neat appearance. The old Catholic church at Rathkenny, Co. Meath, in use until 1974, has a home-made Gothic façade, not without naive charm. St Columba's, Kilmacrennan, Co. Donegal, was built in 1903; a hall-type church with a little entrance porch and an angular apse. The plain interior has a pleasing timber ceiling in dark and light wood, and a scrubbed deal floor, but was disimproved by painting the walls, up to the chair-rail, raspberry colour, and the apse, vivid turquoise. The outside of the church was painted green.

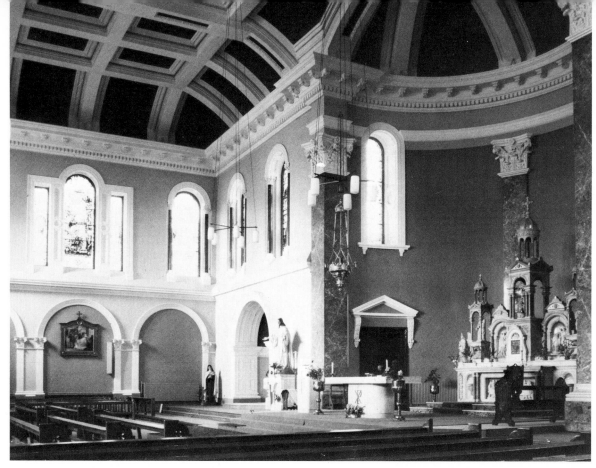

St Joseph's Church, Limerick.

Church of the Sacred Heart, Cloghoge, Co. Down.

revival in red brick, with giant grey-stone Corinthian pilasters rising from the string-course below the second storey. The third storey has tall windows, quite out of proportion to the squat ones of the second. The glazing bars of the giant upper window of the central bay have been rearranged to show the statue placed there. The inside is more successful, with Classic Revival decoration, giant Corinthian pilasters on the walls and rather elegant Corinthian pilasters on the confessionals.

Ashlin and Coleman of Dublin built the Church of the Sacred Heart of Cloghoge, Co. Down. Work began in 1911; the church was blessed and dedicated for divine service on Easter Sunday 1916, the day before the Rising in Dublin, and consecrated by the Primate in 1930. It was mainly financed by the testamentary bequest of Father Thomas Hardy, parish priest of Upper Killevy, who died in 1901. The style is broadly Italian Romanesque. The aisles of the long nave terminate in chapels on either side of the sanctuary, which has splendid mosaic decoration, the gift of Miss Betty M'Gurk of Cloghoge. It depicts scenes from the New Testament, portraits of St Brigid and St Patrick, and angels in medallions amid floral and geometrical patterns.

The Celtic cultural revival was popularized by the Gaelic League, founded in 1893, the Gaelic Athletic Association, founded in 1885, and the National Literary Society. These organizations, and a galaxy of writers involved in the Gaelic literary movement, promoted an interest in the Irish language, myths and legends and in Celtic art and lore; in general they sought to re-establish an Irish identity. Sarah Purser, an accomplished painter who was born in 1849 and lived to be ninety-four, founded her stained-glass studio in Dublin in 1903; she called it *An Tur Gloine* (The Glass Tower).

She and other artists involved in the Gaelic Revival contributed works to the Catholic cathedral at Loughrea, Co. Galway, built between 1897 and 1903. The building itself is not noteworthy, but the works of these artists have made it almost a museum of early twentieth-century Irish art and artisanry. The Stations of the Cross in *opus sectile*, with inscriptions in Irish, are by Ethel Mary Rhind. The three stained-glass windows in the apse, two of those in the baptistery, and three others in the cathedral, are by A. E. Childe. Michael Healy, born 1873, an excellent watercolourist and an artist of Sarah Purser's group, did six of the windows; Hubert McGoldrick, one; Patrick Pye, one; and Sarah Purser herself, two, including the delightful St Brendan (to whom the cathedral is dedicated) in the porch (pl. XV, p. 140). Evie Hone, who emerged from the group as Ireland's greatest stained-glass artist, did the magnificent rose window on the west front depicting the Creation (unfortunately largely masked by the organ), and a window of St Brigid in the nave. The Madonna and Child in marble was sculpted by John Hughes. Jack B. Yeats, the painter, designed the sodality banners made by Mary Cottenham Yeats and Pamela Coleman Smith. The ironwork, including the lamps with inscriptions in Irish, is by Michael Scott; the altar rail and the capitals were carved by Michael Shortall, and Francis O'Donohue painted the Sacred Heart.

The stained glass fitted in the five lancet windows of Kilbrogan Church, Bandon, Co. Cork, is another example of design of the Dublin School, differing from the figurative work of Mayer of Munich and his imitators. Another Church of Ireland church in Co. Cork, at Castletownshend, has some excellent windows by Harry Clark, a Dublin artist, born in 1889. John Early, who designed the mosaics in Armagh Cathedral, is the artist of the beautiful windows now standing as a screen in the modern Catholic church at Cong, Co. Galway.

A fervent interest in the early Irish saints accompanied the literary, linguistic and artistic revival. A statue of St Fursey or Fursa, who founded the church at Killursa, Co. Galway, in the seventh

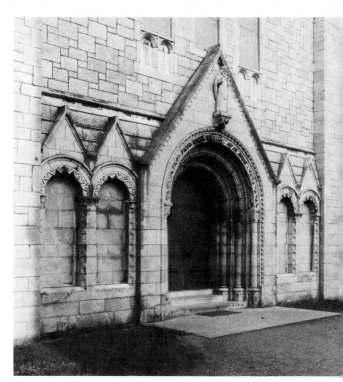

The Honan Chapel, Cork, the front inspired by the Romanesque front of St Cronan's, Roscrea.

century, was erected in the graveyard there. According to the inscription, 'his visions are said to have inspired Dante's *Divina Commedia*'. Catholic ecclesiastical art of this period is replete with romantic representations of rediscovered saints and scholars.

A number of not very successful attempts at Hiberno-Romanesque Revival churches were made. The Catholic church at Newport, Co. Mayo, is one unhappy example, built with a bequest of £10,000, left for the purpose by Martin Carey of Newport, who died in 1909. The pink and red stone façade has a recessed doorway with a gabled hood in the Cormac's Chapel tradition but with paltry and unconvincing low-relief carving; the hood cuts a blind arcade awkwardly; above this is a tall round-headed three-light window which looks top-heavy. The interior arrangement is a ribbed barrel-vaulted nave separated from the aisles by a plain arcade of undecorated columns with cushion capitals; at the east end is the sanctuary with side-chapels. The white marble altar in the Gothic style, with crocketing, is ornate; the sanctuary has a marble rail and metal gates; but Mr Carey's money seems to have run out, for the church has a bare wooden floor, and the Stations of the Cross are crudely painted. The stoop is an aluminium kitchen stock-pot complete with lid and faucet and marked 'Holy Water' with stick-on black lettering.

Isabella Honan, who died in 1913, bequeathed her estate to build the Honan Chapel of University College, Cork. It embodies much Celtic Revival art. The memorial-tablet to Matthew, Robert and Isabella Honan, in fancifully adapted Gaelic script, states that this collegiate chapel dedicated to 'St Fin Barr', for the use of the scholars and students of Munster, was built with part of the Honan family riches 'acquired during several generations of commerce in the City of Cork'; the foundation-stone was laid in 1915. The architect, James F. McMullen, plunged into the Irish past and produced a neo-Hiberno-Romanesque nave-and-chancel church; the lower storey of the west front is copied from the ruined façade of St Cronan's, Roscrea (see p. 34). The interior is interesting, not so much for the reproduction of an Irish Romanesque chancel arch and sedilia, as for the mosaic floor, the Stations of the Cross in *opus sectile* in the tympana of the Cormac's Chapel-type blind arcading of the nave, and the magnificent stained-glass windows. The floor, inspired by the Canticle of the Three Children in the Fiery Furnace, depicts a great beast with the River of Life flowing from his mouth. Round the beast are animals from all parts of the world, exotic birds and plants surrounded by the sun, moon, stars, planets and signs of the zodiac. There are nineteen stained-glass windows: eleven by Harry Clarke (pl. XVI, p. 140), eight by artists working in *An Tur Gloine*, including a splendid east window – a St Fachtna, a St Aillbe and a St Colman – all by A. E. Childe. Others are by Catherine O'Brien and Ethel Mary Rhind. The processional cross inscribed in Latin and Irish is a fine replica of the twelfth-century Cross of Cong. Irish Catholics had discarded classical and Gothic and claimed Hiberno-Romanesque as their own true style; it seemed well suited to a people bound for Independence.

Neo-Hiberno-Romanesque front of the Catholic church, Newport, Co. Mayo, by Rudolph Butler.

CHAPTER 10

Modern Ireland

TWICE IT APPEARED, before Independence, that Ireland would achieve its own government by legal and parliamentary means. The likelihood that the ninety-year-old Union was about to end seemed high in 1890, but then Parnell, the leader of the Irish party pressing for Home Rule, was sued as co-respondent in a divorce case. He thereby lost the essential support of Gladstone, the leader of the English Liberal party, who, in order to assuage shocked English Nonconformist opinion, was obliged to dissociate himself from the adulterous Irish politician. In Ireland, Parnell, himself a Protestant, had enjoyed the support of the Catholic majority; but the Catholic hierarchy withdrew their backing and assailed him with ferocity. In their wake the priests persuaded the masses that a man whose sexual morals were not impeccable was not fit to be a leader. Politically defeated and disillusioned, Parnell died in 1891. Gladstone's second Irish Home Rule Bill was defeated in the House of Lords in 1893. The Government then embarked on a programme of agrarian reforms for Ireland, hoping that social improvements would extinguish the fire of the Irish nationalist movement. In 1910 the Liberals, who were returned to power with a limited majority, required the support of the Irish party, and were prepared to pay the price for this by introducing another Home Rule Bill. By July 1913 this third Bill to give Ireland limited self-government had been twice approved by the House of Commons, and twice rejected by the Lords. As the Liberal government together with the Irish party had a safe majority in the Commons, it looked as though the Home Rule Bill must run its course and eventually become law in 1914, for the power of the Lords had been curtailed by the Parliament Bill. However, the extra-parliamentary opposition to Home Rule marshalled its forces, led by the Ulster Protestants and those who sympathized with their determination to resist becoming a minority group. Para-military groups formed in Ulster, and, as tension mounted with the formation of the Irish Volunteers in the South and the illegal importation of arms to both North and South, civil war seemed imminent. But in 1914 the First World War broke out and the Home Rule issue was postponed.

On Easter Monday 1916, at the instigation of the Irish Republican Brotherhood (who hoped to profit from England's involvement on the Continent), some Irish Volunteers with some of the Irish Citizen Army (a militant, working-class, revolutionary group), came out in open revolt, took the General Post Office building in Dublin and proclaimed the Republic. When reinforcements arrived from England, the British Army put down the rising and its leaders were executed.

Many Irish people, while basically committed to Independence, actually disapproved of the revolt at a time when Irishmen were serving in the British forces, but the intransigence of those who were determined to delay Independence and the harshness of the executions exasperated public feeling, so that when a general election was held after the war, in December 1918, 70 per cent of the seats in the country went to Sinn Fein candidates. As half of the newly elected members were in gaol, the party decided to ignore Westminster and set up their own Republican parliament, the *Dail Eireann*, in Dublin, in January 1919. Two and a half years of bitter strife followed, during which the British forces, the Royal Irish Constabulary and the specially imported 'Black and Tans' fought a guerrilla war with the Irish Republican Army.

In 1920 the London parliament passed the Government of Ireland Act which established two separate parliaments, one at Belfast for six of the nine counties of Ulster, and one at Dublin for the remaining twenty-six counties. General elections were held in May 1920 following this Act; the Unionists won a solid majority in the six counties they had carved out to create Northern Ireland. In the remaining twenty-six counties Sinn Fein candidates were returned unopposed for all but one seat. The guerrilla war continued. In 1921 King George V opened the Northern Ireland Parliament in Belfast, but *Dail Eireann* had not accepted the partition or the Government of Ireland Act. In the summer of 1921 peace talks were held in London, and in December a treaty was signed whereby the *Dail Eireann* representatives accepted partition; they were led to believe that the Boundary Commission's findings would reduce the size of the separated North. They also accepted the oath of allegiance to the Crown. Most Irish people acquiesced; they were weary of internal warfare and keen to see the last of the British troops, especially the cruel 'Black and Tans'. Some, however, refused to accept the Treaty; the *Dail* itself split into pro-Treaty and anti-Treaty factions. The Irish Republican Army also split, forming the pro-Treaty Free State Army and anti-Treaty Republican Army, each occupying separate headquarters in Dublin. Thus the Irish Civil War broke out in 1922. The Free State forces, armed by the British, attacked the Republican forces in the Four Courts. The Catholic authorities who had backed Sinn Fein now gave their moral support to the Free State, and excommunicated Republican fighters. Nevertheless resistance continued until May 1923 when, undermined by the fierce reprisals of the Free State government, and lacking enough popular support, the Republicans threw in the sponge.

Both sides left their martyrs and neither could claim any achievements; Ireland was divided as Ulster Protestants had wanted it to be in 1916. In 1926 the Republican opposition itself split; the less intransigent faction, *Fianna Fail*, won some seats in the *Dail*; in 1932 they won a majority. De Valera, the *Fianna Fail* leader, unilaterally revoked some of the Treaty provisions, which were obnoxious to his party, and in 1938 negotiated the abrogation of the defence clauses, thus substantially affirming Irish sovereignty. The link with the Crown was ultimately severed by Ireland's secession from the Commonwealth in 1949.

After partition, the Irishness of Ireland was stressed in the twenty-six counties by emphasis on the teaching of Irish, which became an official language. The relics of Anglo-Irish ascendancy were found distasteful and so were shunned. English names of towns were replaced by Irish ones or substituted by the original Irish names; place-names with Crown connotations such as Kingstown, Queenstown, Kings Co., Queens Co. and Maryborough became Dun Laoghaire, Cobh, Offaly, Leix and Portlaoise. Irish names for children were patriotically preferred: Declan, Aillbe, Attracta, Kevin, Kieran and Nuala, long out of use, became fashionable and popular. Those most committed to the revival of the national language resumed the Irish form of their surnames, Reilly, Higgins and Kelly, for example, became O'Raghallaigh, O'huiginn and O'Ceallaigh. Some Irish enthusiasts of more or less distant English origin even translated their names and adopted the Irish form, so that Williamson, Wall and Smith became MacLiammoir, de Bhall and MacGabhann.

This insistence on an Irish cultural dimension, and rejection of everything English, implied a return to pre-Norman times. Norman art was all right if it could be assumed to have come direct from Normandy, but not if it had arrived via England and Wales. Scandinavian cultural influences, brought by the barbarous Vikings, were admitted.

Early in the century pre-Norman-invasion Romanesque architecture had been accepted as a glorious national style; if it had any roots in England this fact was not recognized. The style was considered eminently suitable for the churches of the New Ireland. It was not a happy choice from an aesthetic standpoint, for no one managed to copy or adapt the twelfth-century examples with distinction or real sensitivity, or devise a practical form of building in which Romanesque doorways, windows and chancel arches looked right. The fact that Romanesque remains in Ireland consisted largely only of decorative elements (save the unique and impractical Cormac's Chapel) was, of course, a disadvantage to those who tried to develop a neo-Hiberno-Romanesque building style. Nevertheless most parish priests able to consider a new church wanted 'Irish Romanesque'. The Catholic church at Ederny, Co. Tyrone, is an example of the unsatisfactory buildings which resulted.

The years of struggle for Independence and the Civil War left Ireland economically debilitated. Then the economic depression in the United States of America caused a decrease in emigrants' remittances and donations from Irish-Americans. Even through the 1930s, when matters improved a little, cash for building churches was still scarce.

St Patrick's, Donegal, known also as the 'Church of the Four Masters', was built in 1935; the architect was Ralph Byrne. The exterior, of pinkish-red Barnesmore granite, is striking because of the attached Round Tower; from close-up it is disimproved by a quantity of unsightly external drainpipes. The west door is heavy-handed neo-Romanesque, with chevron decoration in the arch-rings. The Romanesque style has also been attempted

St Patrick's, Donegal, the 'Church of the Four Masters'.
Cavan, Co. Cavan, the Catholic cathedral, by Ralph Byrne.

St Thomas, Dublin.

inside, in the columned arcades between the nave and aisles. The otherwise sober effect of the grey ashlar interior is marred by the contrast of the too-bright stained glass in the roses at the east and west ends, and in the side-windows. The Irish marble altars were paid for from the testamentary bequest of a local solicitor, Patrick M. Gallagher, who died in 1927.

The Protestant population in the twenty-six counties decreased due to emigration. A number of both large and small country-houses had been burned or damaged during the Troubles, and in many cases their owners, discouraged or scared, and unable to envisage the future, emigrated. Others, ruined by the economic consequences of the Troubles, were obliged to sell up and leave. As the Protestant population dwindled, the Church of Ireland found itself considerably over-churched in the Republic. Nevertheless, St Thomas, Dublin, which was badly damaged in the fighting and had had to be demolished, was rebuilt. The replacement is a neat Italianate red-brick church designed by Frederick Hicks, with a low pro-style five-bay arcaded portico across the front.

When it was decided to build a new cathedral at Cavan for the Catholic diocese of Kilmore in 1942, the architect, eschewing chauvinistic Irish cultural nationalism, rather surprisingly produced a Neo-classical cathedral with a front inspired by Francis Johnston's Protestant church of St George, Dublin, of 1802, plus domes. The plan is, however, cruci-form, and the interior basilical. The dome over the crossing is supported by four marble columns, and the clerestory storey by rows of grey and white marble columns. These have Corinthian capitals and ox-blood marble bases, standing on black marble plinths. The Stations of the Cross are pristine grisaille panels.

Due to the departure of many landowners, large country-houses came on the market; a number were purchased by religious orders and adapted for their use. Chapels were usually arranged in the former reception-rooms. With so many large houses available there was little incentive to build among the orders, although sometimes a new chapel was constructed next to or adjoining the house.

A notable exception, a massive monument to the generosity of the Irish people, is the enormous St Columban's College Missionary Society, Dalgan Park, Co. Meath, purpose-built in 1941. Destined to accommodate over two hundred trainees for the missions, with its own printing-press, television studio and language laboratories, it is now an impressive white elephant, with long stretches of empty parquet-floored corridors, and only a few students. The chapel is large and expensive, with plenty of Connemara marble, green carpeting and neo-Hiberno-Romanesque motifs. To each side of the sacristies are seven individual chapels, so that fourteen priests could celebrate mass separately, as was required.

St Stanislaus College was founded by the Jesuits in 1818 at Tullabeg, near Rahan, Co. Offaly, described in 1837 as 'a college for young gentlemen';[1] it is now a busy Jesuit retreat house. Its glory is the chapel with magnificent windows by Ireland's greatest stained-glass artist, Evie Hone. Miss Hone, born in 1894, studied painting first under Sickert, Meninsky and Glen Byam Shaw, then in Paris under André Lhote and the Cubist Albert Gleizes; when she returned to Dublin in 1932 she joined Sarah Purser's *An Tur Gloine*.

Evie Hone's most famous stained-glass composition is the great east window in the chapel of Eton College in England. Her series of windows in the chapel of St Stanislaus, Tullabeg, is the best of her work in Ireland. In the superb large window Christ is surrounded by six Jesuit saints, Francis Xavier, Aloysius Gonzaga, John Berchmans, Ignatius Loyola, Stanislaus Kostka and Robert Bellarmine (pl. XX, p. 192). Four other windows depict respectively the Nativity and the Adoration of the Magi, the Beatitudes, the Last Supper and Christ washing his disciples' feet, the Pentecost and a miracle of St Stanislaus. Sensibly, the chapel has practically no other decoration to detract from these windows; the

effect when the room is lit by sunlight through the brilliant glass is wonderful.

Economic conditions improved after the Second World War, during which the Republic of Ireland had remained neutral. By the end of the 1950s there was a renewed interest in church-building within the Catholic Church, to provide churches for the new urban housing-estates, as well as rural areas, where farmers were pleased to see reflected in a new church the prosperity they were enjoying.

In Galway city a large and imposing new cathedral was built with a made-to-last-for-ever look, and in an unidentifiable hybrid style. The Iberian effect may have been intended to recall Galway's bygone links with Spain, but it is reminiscent of twentieth-century Hispanic buildings in South America, and looks magnificently alien in Connaught, especially on a gloomy day.

The cathedral, designed by John J. Robinson, was dedicated to Our Lady Assumed into Heaven and St Nicholas, in 1965. The cruciform interior, replete with greenish-grey limestone and Connemara marble, seats two thousand people. Its stoniness

Galway, the Catholic cathedral.

Church of Christ the King, Cork, doorway.

suits Galway building tradition (even the Stations by Gabrielle Hayes are in Portland stone), but as the design lacks plasticity the effect is rigid.

The very North American-looking Church of Christ the King at Turner's Cross, a suburb of Cork city, is built entirely of concrete. This is the work of a Wrightian architect of the Chicago School, Barry Byrne (on whom there is a monograph in *The Prairie School Review*). The design is reminiscent of P.V. Jensen Klint's unusual Grundvig Church at Copenhagen, designed in 1913 and finished in 1926; it has a stepped outline, rising in ten graduated recessed levels on each side, to the top of the central bay. The whole façade is dominated by a gigantic, purposefully modern statue of Christ, crowned and bearded, his long body in a colobium separating the twin doors, his arms outstretched above them; it is the work of an American sculptor, John Storrs. The effect of the interior, a huge rectangular auditorium, is unusual, for it is lit by eight slender windows gradually increasing in height on each side, in the wall behind the three altars. The windows are glazed with coloured glass ranging in shade from indigo-blue through turquoise and sea-green to yellow, like graded chiffon.

St Theresa's, Sion Mills, Co. Tyrone, begun in 1962, was finished in 1966, the work of a Belfast-

based architect, Patrick Haughey. The frontispiece, etched in white on grey stone, was carved by one of Ireland's best-known modern sculptors, Oisin Kelly. His religious work is often inspired by medieval examples, here used with excellent effect. The cool grey interior with a timber ceiling is very agreeable; the plastic flooring muffles sound, and nothing intrudes on the spacious simplicity. The stair to the gallery is in the glazed vestibule, as is the font; the confessionals are concealed in a recess. The stained-glass lights with cubist designs in a combination of blue, grey, yellow and white, are the work of Patrick Pollen (another artist associated with *An Tur Gloine*), as are the figurative panels in the screen.

The church of Our Lady of the Rosary, Ennis Road, Limerick, was conceived as a temporary structure in wood, but is more pleasing than many permanent ones of the 1960s. The sculpted Annunciation on the outside is also the work of Oisin Kelly.

St Dominic's, Athy, designed by John Thompson and Associates of Limerick and Dublin, and completed in 1965, caused considerable comment when it was built, as it was arranged to accord with the latest directions of Vatican II. 'Church in Revolutionary Style Displays Spirit of Council', reported *The Irish Press* in their headline the day after the opening of the new church on 17 March 1965.[2]

St Dominic's Church, Athy, Co. Kildare.

St Theresa's Church, Sion Mills, Co. Tyrone, frontispiece carved by Oisin Kelly.

Under the headline 'Unique Dominican Church Blessed' the *Irish Times* reporter enthusiastically announced: 'Yesterday [March 17] Athy took its place among the most up-to-date towns of the world when its ultra-modern Dominican church was blessed and opened.'[3]

The opening was also an ecumenical event; clergy of the Church of Ireland, the Methodist Church in Ireland, and the Presbyterian Church in Ireland all attended the first solemn High Mass, and heard Father Patrick Deegan's sermon in Irish and English. 'We are now in the process of changing from traditional styles of church-building to radically new ones,' said Father Deegan; and continued:

> Now a great Council of the Church is approaching its ultimate session. It has again introduced many far-reaching reforms in the public worship of the Church and has given instructions that the new liturgy is to be celebrated in churches adapted to its use. The Constitution on the Sacred Liturgy states that the Church has not adopted any particular style of art as her own; she has admitted styles from every period according to the natural dispositions of the people and the needs of various rites. The art of our own day, coming from every race and region, is also to be given free scope, provided it adorns the sacred buildings and holy rites with due honour and reverence. Bishops must see to it that the design of these churches is such as to facilitate the celebration of the liturgy and the active participation of the faithful. This is a building of our time, in an age of little or no ornamentation, an age of questioning of old values and old ways, of change, and of experiment – and the Church is meeting this age on its own ground. We no longer live in a world of castles and Gothic spires, God does not belong only in Romanesque buildings and in the Middle Ages. He belongs just as much in our modern age. What perfectly expressed the beliefs, feelings and aspirations of one generation might not fulfil the genius of another.[4]

One of the innovations promulgated by Vatican II is that the altar should be the very centre of the church. *The Instruction of the Implementation of the Constitution of Sacred Liturgy* states categorically that the altar 'should be so placed that, automatically, it becomes the true focus of attention for the entire congregation of the faithful'. Article 90 of the Constitution insists on the necessity of considering the participation of the people in the religious ceremonies; it states, 'In erecting new churches, or in restoring or adapting existing churches, care should be taken that they are suitable for the performance of sacred actions, as befits their true nature, and for the promotion of the active participation of the faithful.' Such instructions encouraged architects to make the altar the focal point of the church visually, to arrange the seating so that as many people as possible should sit close to the altar, and to dispense with the old-fashioned distant railed-off sanctuary.

The decisions of the Council of Vatican II regarding the renewal of the liturgy and lay participation have had an immense effect on Catholic ecclesiastical architecture in the last decade, and will continue to do so, as they present architects with an exciting challenge to create new forms adapted to suit the Council's spirit and instructions.

Part of this challenge was summed up by Canon J. G. McGarry of Ireland's National Liturgical Commission: 'The sanctuary is the meeting-place of God and man, and however we try to do it, we must, artist and priest alike, try to suggest the holiness of that place.'[5]

Despite the publicity which it received, it is doubtful whether St Dominic's, Athy, really achieves this aim, for notwithstanding the excellent intentions of those concerned, it desperately lacks artistic co-ordination. A dramatic hyperbolic paraboloid concrete shell roof spans 147 feet between the abutments which carry its weight; they are tied by a concealed pre-stressed concrete beam under the floor, and when the walls were raised, a one-inch gap was left at the top to allow for the deflection of the roof in low temperatures. The appearance of the remarkable exterior has not been enhanced by uninspired landscaping. Inside, the fan-like arrangement of the seats in four wedge-shaped sections allows for none to be more than eighty feet from the altar; thus every one of the six hundred persons who can be accommodated should be able to see what is happening at the marble altar and ambo. The altar-rail, however, creates a physical barrier between the sanctuary and the body of the church, spoiling the over-all unity.

Suspended over the altar is an elongated T-shaped crucifix, the work of Brid Ni Rinn of Kildare. The altar frontal, a Deposition sculpted in bronze, is the work of Breeda O'Donoghue Lucci, a Cork-born artist who lives in Rome, and whose altar for the International Basilica at Nazareth represents Ireland's contribution there.

Cumulatively, decorative elements which could be delightful on their own detract from the harmony of the whole. Grouped on two of the side walls, George Campbell's Stations of the Cross in black, red, blue and grey stained travertine marble, and his vivid multicoloured non-figurative windows, conflict with the chipped-glass panels in bright and pale blue, yellow, orange, red, lilac, purple, turquoise, green and white, designed and executed by the

Dublin Glass and Paint Company. There are many jarring notes, such as the multicoloured floor tiles, the peg-board with red and white letters for announcements, the fussy-looking metal rail of the balcony and votary candle-stands. It is a shame that this first valiant effort at a new type of church was not better co-ordinated. The *Irish Independent*, reporting the opening of St Dominic's, mentioned that the Dublin Glass and Paint Company designed, executed and erected 'the coloured antiques'.[6] Such lack of understanding may also be a clue to the uncertain taste of some of the decoration.

In contrast to the rest of the interior is the delightful small chapel with four seats, intended for meditation. It has calm colours, copper panels depicting scenes from the life of St Martin of Tours, and a distinguished grey marble statue of that saint by H. Flanagan.

St Mary's, Melmount, Co. Tyrone, designed by Patrick Haughey, in some ways resembles his earlier St Theresa's at Sion Mills; but the liturgical changes introduced by Vatican II were taken into consideration. Despite the arrangement of the benches in six wedge-shaped sections with the altar-table as the focal point, the church lacks intimacy; it is large but it seems vast. The decorations are agreeable, albeit a little stark. The Stations are marked by a plain metal cross and the name; a crucifix is suspended from the ceiling above the altar. The colour scheme is sombre: outside, dark brownish brick and a brown metal roof; inside, brownish brick walls and beige flooring. Like St Theresa's, St Mary's is lit by a line of windows high in the walls; here, glazed with frosted glass, they are just below the ceiling.

St Cooey's, Portaferry, Co. Down, was built in 1968 by McLean and Forte of Belfast. This church is lit by small windows at ceiling level and a concealed window near the altar. The plan of the building is elliptical; inside, the benches are splayed like a fan in three wedge-shaped sections. The stone altar-table stands on four cylindical columns; the stone ambo is a simple cylinder. The doors of the church are overlaid with attractive beaten copper panels. The windowless walls make the exterior a little forbidding, although the bunker-like appearance is relieved by bright white pebble-dash.

While the architect called by the Church to design a new building in the spirit of the Council has an interesting challenge, the architect called to adapt an old church, particularly a large one, to meet the new requirements, has a far greater demand on his ingenuity and skill. Larry McConvill won the competition for the adaptation of St Patrick's Cathedral, Armagh, but the design he exhibited has not yet been implemented. In many churches all that has

been done is to place an altar-table in front of the old altar, to allow the celebrant to stand behind it and face the people. Often these tables are graceless pieces of furniture, the thoughtlessness of the choice suggesting that the concession to change has been made grudgingly.

The adaptation of the Pugin cathedral of St Mary's, Killarney, Co. Kerry, is an outstanding success, although it has exercised, and shocked, some devoted Puginites. The architect of this magnificent restoration and adaptation was D. J. Kennedy of Tralee, and the consultant artist Ray Carroll of Glencullen, Co. Dublin. The cost was a staggering £278,500. Of this, £26,000 went on roof repairs, gutters, piping, trusses, etc.; £24,200 on the car park, paved areas, driveways and landscaping; £28,900 on removing the plaster from the interior stonework and replacing brickwork with stone; and £31,200 on a new floor structure and tiling. The new seating, confessionals, altar, bishop's chair, celebrant's chair, ambo, baptismal font, and crucifix over the sanctuary cost, with miscellaneous items, £40,500.

The work was guided by a committee of five lay residents elected at a public meeting at Killarney in December 1970, and nine priests nominated by the Bishop because of their special knowledge of ecclesiastical architecture or liturgy.

Ray Carroll, the artistic director retained for the work, approached the problem of changing Pugin's building with great sensitivity and understanding. While eschewing Pugin's nostalgia, he admitted that no one who worked on the restoration at Killarney could fail to be overshadowed by the stature of Pugin's genius. Regarding the approach to the more radical changes, Ray Carroll has written: 'In re-designing the necessary new positions of the liturgy's elements and the elements themselves, we loyally sought to follow Pugin's thought and feeling. Where the inevitable conflict arose between Pugin's medieval philosophy of liturgy and the now-for-next-300-years-established modern one, we deferred to Pugin in matters of mood (namely, his sense of the sacred and his sense of mystery); took into account the internal, inbuilt commands of his building; and simultaneously followed, as faithfully as we knew how, the new guide-lines set down by Rome.'[7]

The new sanctuary has been created in the crossing. Thus the mighty supporting arches of the central tower form a magnificent lofty canopy over the altar. The sanctuary also accommodates the bishop's and celebrant's chairs of Tasmanian oak, the ambo and, in accordance with the renewed liturgy, the baptismal font: a limestone bowl fitted at the base of one of the massive pillars of the crossing. The Blessed Sacrament is reserved in what was formerly a side-chapel.

The internal Victorian plasterwork had been damaged by damp, so it was removed and the natural stone exposed and cleaned by sandblasting. The result is a success, though it dismays some visitors. The walls and pillars now have a wonderful unity, and the strength of Pugin's soaring arches is revealed as never before (p. 159).

In parishes where the old church seemed too small or too dilapidated, and where the parish priest had the necessary enthusiasm, the necessity to make changes was transformed into an excuse to build a new church. They have gone up in all shapes and sizes, with varying degrees of success. The new one at Listry, Co. Kerry, is neat and plain with a detached belfry. The chapel of Our Lady of the Wayside between Leenaun and Clifden, Co. Galway, is like a pegged-down tent on the windswept Connemara plain.

The polygonal chapel beside the eighteenth-century farmhouse at Westcourt, Callan, Co. Kilkenny (where Father Edmund Ignatius Rice, the founder of the Christian Brothers, was born), and linked to it by a pergola, was built to commemorate the centenary of the Christian Brothers' school at

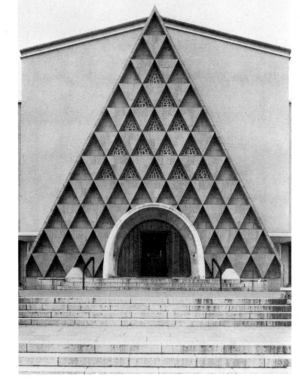

Catholic church at Raheeny, Co. Dublin.

Our Lady of the Wayside, near Leenaun, Co. Galway.

Father Edmund Ignatius Rice Memorial Chapel, Westcourt. Callan, Co. Kilkenny.

Callan. The Bishop of Ossory laid the foundation-stone on 8 September 1968. The chapel was designed by Guy Moloney and Associates of Dublin. The walls are of cut grey stone, as are the altar and ambo; the chapel is carpeted throughout with anthracite-grey carpeting. This same discreet grey theme was used in the church at Borris-in-Ossory in 1969. Both churches have non-figurative stained-glass windows by Helen Moloney, and here too is the fitted anthracite-grey carpet, grey-stone altar and ambo, and stone pergola which at Borris links the church to a free-standing belfry.

Our Lady Mother of Divine Grace, Raheeny, a suburb of Dublin, was built to replace the old church across the road, which was considered too small and shabby. Some of the parishioners find that the large new church lacks intimacy, and would have preferred a second, smaller church in another part of the parish to serve the increased population, keeping the old one in use. Some clergy and laymen are acutely aware of the danger of losing the feeling of a community in too-large parish churches. While the new church at Raheeny has a self-consciously modern air, the design of the frontispiece is based on the Romanesque door of Clonfert Cathedral. Some of the triangular niches are lights, and the effect from the inside is pleasing. There is an arcade on each side of the entrance, one of which links it with a free-standing bell-tower. Architecturally the interior has little to commend it: the long, lofty nave is separated from the lower flanking aisles by absurdly slender polygonal columns, banded with coloured mosaic, which support the roof.

The new church at Cong, Co. Mayo, was built mainly at the instigation of the owner of Ashford Castle Hotel, who promised a handsome sum towards the building. It was built at the gate of his hotel by his architect and the foundation-stone was blessed 8 December 1972. The site, beside the ruins of the Augustinian abbey, was not well chosen for the appearance of the building. The exterior is awkward and the interior disconcerting. Stiff, impractical red felt covers not only the floor but also the benches, engulfing all but the shiny black ends on the aisles. The brilliant stained-glass windows mounted as free-standing screens behind the sanctuary are the most attractive feature of the church. By J. Early of Dublin, they were removed from the previous church where they had been much admired.

St David's, Johnstown, near Arklow, Co. Wicklow, opened in 1972, replaces a pretty 'Gothick' church mentioned in Chapter 8. The best feature is the stained-glass designed by Lua Breen, then an art teacher in Dublin. The most striking is the cock of Peter's denial of Christ. Others depict the Stations of the Cross, the Crown of Thorns, the palms the Hebrews carried when they acclaimed Christ, and the chalice. The cost of each panel, including the Stations (to a donor whose name would be inscribed on a plaque), was £350. The subscription price of the altar was £350, of the crucifix for the sanctuary, £150. The sum of £60 provided for the baptismal font or a seat, and £20 for a sanctuary lamp, a credence table, an offertory table, or a candelabrum.[8]

St Catherine's Church, Oristown, Co. Meath, interior with baptismal font.

The very pleasing new church of St Catherine at Oristown, Co. Meath. was built in 1969 at a cost of £66,700,[9] a considerable sum for a rural parish with a population of only fourteen hundred. The work of Messrs Feehily and Associates, to a design chosen by the clergy and parishioners, it was consecrated 15 November 1970. The pine seats are splayed out in four wedge-shaped sections; the ceiling and doors are also of pine. Big glass panels ensure that the church is full of light, and link the natural surroundings with the interior. The green creepers growing behind the altar enhance this union. A number of visitors have written in the Visitors' Book lamenting the absence of Stations of the Cross, but a greater number have praised the uncluttered purity of the white walls and glass. The new parish church at Rathkenny, Co. Meath, a newer neighbour and rival of Oristown, built to accommodate five hundred persons at a cost of £80,000,[10] was dedicated in June 1974. The architect was David Duignan of Navan. The shape of the church is suited to the new liturgical requirements, but the exterior is unprepossessing.

A church can be defined simply as a structure which encloses space to be used for ecclesiastical activity. A successful church is one which is not only functional, but by its design and decoration both delights the beholder and induces a sense of reverence and tranquillity. In the race to build more and more impressive new churches, the opportunity to build a beautiful and successful church has often been lost through inattention to important decisions. Frequently parish priests, bishops and parochial committees have gone little further than to ensure that they have engaged an architect with the necessary technical capacity, without ascertaining whether he has the sensibility to select and then integrate the elements available to him in a harmonious and aesthetic expression which attempts, at least, to respond to the intellectual, emotional and spiritual requirements of the people. Nor have they considered whether the design related to the site and environment.

Press reports on new churches reflect a consumer-society interest in quantity, rather than in mood or quality. Typical is the headline 'Church for new parish to seat 960' in the *Irish Times* in 1974, above the report on the blessing of the foundation-stone for the new parochial church of St Matthew in the populous Dublin suburb of Ballyfermot Upper. The cost, £120,500, made this church, the newspaper reported, 'one of the most inexpensive in the diocese, but its design is in line with the archbishop's recent reminder that a church can be both beautiful and inexpensive'. No mention is made of the style or appearance of the church save of 'the large moveable

St Michael's Church, Creeslough, Co. Donegal, and below, the bell.

screen which, when moved into position reduces the church to an intimate chapel accommodating only 140'.[11] Intimacy in Ballyfermot might be considered a crowd elsewhere.

The most beautiful new churches in Ireland are those designed by Liam McCormick and Partners of Derry. These are not the *only* beautiful new churches in the country, but as the product of one architectural studio they are outstanding. Above all Liam McCormick and his partners have always carefully studied the site of each project, and taken the maximum advantage of it.

Their best-known church is St Aengus, Burt, Co. Donegal (pl. XIX, p. 191). Liam McCormick was the architect and Una Madden the designer. It was built by John Hegarty, and opened 27 June 1967; it serves about nine hundred persons. The circular building stands in a beautiful position on a slope below the circular stone ring-fort, Grianan of Aileach, and owes much of its inspiration to this ancient royal seat of the O'Neills. It overlooks Lough Swilly. The unusual design was approved by the clergy, and this exceptional church was built for only £50,000, exclusive of the contents. The curate in charge writes: 'At first the local people thought it strange as it was such a change from the old church. They have now come to like it and are very proud of it.'[12] He adds, 'liturgically the church is eminently suitable for all functions and especially the Mass'.[13] The circular altar, lit by a lantern in the roof above, stands on three concentric raised circular platforms. The benches are curved and deployed in sections which are segments of a full circle. Non-figurative coloured glass windows, high in the wall, provide colour-relief and light; there is a wooden crucifix on beaten silver on the wall behind the altar, and plain crosses denote the Stations; a lovely woven panel depicting the symbols of the Four Evangelists in brilliant reds, blues and purple hangs on the ambo. The landscaping is good, the outside stone decorations attractive and the entrance doors have fine nailed beaten-copper panels.

The contour of St Michael's Church, Creeslough, Co. Donegal, has been arranged to follow the line of the mountains behind it. The site, in the plain below Muckish and overlooking Sheephaven Bay, is superb, and the architects have taken full advantage of it. This church is also by Liam McCormick and Partners, with art-work by Helen Moloney, Veronica Rowe, John Behan and Ruth Brandt. The builder was John Hegarty. It was opened in August 1971. The brilliant white rough-cast exterior looks splendid against the muted colours of the Donegal landscape – gorse, rock, grass, distant slate-blue mountains and green-blue ocean. This unity with the

Maghera, Co. Derry, the Catholic church.

Church of Mary, Queen of Peace, Garrison, Co. Fermanagh.

land is enhanced by the judicious use of local materials in a modern form. The handsome simplicity of the scrubbed oak doors, small ornamental pool, stone paving of the courtyard and dramatic detached steel bell-tower with its huge bell all add to the beauty of the exterior. Much in the church is evocative of the traditional simplicity and frugality of rural life in Donegal; the stone stoops for instance, and the cauldron-like font with the Early Christian symbol of the fish.

The curvilinear building presents a solid face to the road, but through the glass wall of the Chapel of Our Lady, within the sweep of the curve, there is a view of the mountains. There are also chapel-areas for the Blessed Sacrament and the baptistery. (The parish priest and the people had wanted the Blessed Sacrament Chapel where the baptistery is; they deemed a formal baptistery unnecessary.) The altar, lit from a circular light in the roof, is on two raised circular platforms. The walls are of whitewashed rough-cast plaster; in order not to detract from the beauty of wood, stone and metal, the use of colour has been restricted. The brilliant woven altar frontal, designed by Helen Moloney, is extremely effective. The parishioners took some time to accustom themselves to the new church, but now they are happy with it. Only the fixed kneelers have been found impractical, making cleaning difficult.

Another successful church by McCormick and Partners is at Maghera, Co. Derry. In the vestibule is a modern interpretation of the early Crucifixion scene at the ruined church in the same town (see p. 22), and there is decorative stonework of early Irish Christian inspiration on the exterior. The belfry is a free-standing openwork steel tower with several bells. A solemn and dramatic effect has been achieved in the interior by skilful lighting.

The Church of Mary, Queen of Peace, at Garrison, Co. Fermanagh, on the trouble-racked border dividing Northern Ireland from the Republic, was opened in October 1972. This has the most exciting interior of all the churches from McCormick's studio. The architects responsible with him were J. J. Tracey of Derry and T. C. Mullarkey; the artistic direction was entrusted to Ray Carroll, whose excellent advice at Killarney has been mentioned. The seating capacity is five hundred, and the cost a modest £60,000. The plan is square with a pyramidal roof. The wall behind the altar is mostly glass, so beyond it the people see the landscape of Lough Melvin and the majestic mountains of Leitrim, a superb backdrop for the ceremonies. The colours of the natural surroundings are continued inside the church; the benches and confessionals in natural wood have been stained olive-green; the carpeting and synthetic floor-covering is fawn. The

XIX St Aengus, Burt, Co. Donegal (p. 189) >

Dunmanagher, Co. Derry, the Catholic church.

Garvagh First Presbyterian Church, Co. Derry.

Martyrs Memorial, Belfast, Dr Ian Paisley's Free Presbyterian Church.

lighting fixtures are hanging spheres of smoked brownish-green glass. A criss-crossed steel infrastructure supports the roof. To take advantage of the sloping site, the sacristy and offices have been placed underneath the church, communicating with it by a stair at the rear. The celebrant and assistants ascend, and cross the church in procession, to the altar. The mensa, flanked by the sedilia and ambo, is of red hardwood. On the Gospel side of the predella is the tabernacle, on the other side the font.

Despite the strife in Northern Ireland in recent years, new churches have been built by all denominations. The Catholic churches are undoubtedly the most interesting architecturally. Besides McCormick and Tracey, several other architects, such as Charles Hegarty, George White and Patrick Haughey have actively experimented with new forms. Haughey's church at Dunmanagher, Co. Derry, is reminiscent in shape of his earlier ones in Co. Tyrone. The lower part is stone, the upper part and roof, aluminium. Orange, red and white predominate inside – colours which Haughey found evocative of the Sperrin Mountains. The Stations of the Cross in red mosaic look like strip cartoons, and the whole church has a determinedly trendy atmosphere.

The foundation-stone of the new Garvagh First Presbyterian Church, Co. Derry, was laid by the Moderator of the General Assembly on 16 June 1970, and the church was opened for public worship in November 1971. Its design, while unadventurous, is far from effortless; but the functional planning is good, with a spacious, covered porch and vestibule, connected classrooms and recreation-rooms. Two palatial crystal chandeliers adorn the church; the main window has coloured glass with a design of autumn leaves.

The Reverend Dr Ian Paisley MP is enthusiastic about building new churches for his followers, members of the Free Presbyterian Church. In 1974 he led a procession over the border into Co. Monaghan to celebrate the building of a new church there. Dr Paisley's own church, The Martyrs' Memorial Church in Ravenhill Road, Belfast, is large and well equipped, but few would call it beautiful.

One of the newest Church of Ireland churches, St Peter's, Belmont, in a well-to-do suburb of Derry, is traditional, save for the surprising blue and yellow roof over the white rough-cast walls, and the curious spire. It has an oddly colonial air, something like an Anglican church in Kenya or Rhodesia. The foundation-stone was laid on 28 July 1965 by Sir Basil A. T. McFarland, Bart., CBE, ERD, HML, and the church was consecrated in 1966.

It was reported in the English press in August 1974 that the Church of Ireland cathedral of St Anne,

< *XX Christ surrounded by Jesuit saints, window in St Stanislaus' Retreat House, Tullabeg, Co. Offaly, by Evie Hone (p. 183).*

St Anne's Cathedral, Belfast, the north transept unfinished in 1974.

St Anthony's, Craigyhill, Larne, Co. Antrim, finished and opened 1974, maliciously burned 1975.

Belfast, was in financial difficulties. Major building work had been carried out on its transepts while the necessary funds fell short by no less than half a million pounds.[14] Appeals for money failed in Northern Ireland because industrialists deemed it unwise to finance a possible bomb target. Work on the south transept proceeded, nevertheless, aided by a bank overdraft of £200,000, and was completed in June 1974.

The decision to build the cathedral was made in 1896, when Belfast was part of the united diocese of Down, Connor and Dromore, which already had three cathedrals, Downpatrick, Lisburn and Dromore. Building another, even then, seems, to say the least, a luxury. A debt of half a million pounds, and a still-unfinished colossus eighty years later, certainly do not mitigate the folly. One reason for building advanced in 1896 was that the cathedral would 'exert a wholesome moral influence on a district whose present condition is by no means satisfactory'.[15]

The eighteenth-century church of St Anne was hastily levelled to clear the site. Sir Thomas Drew made the original plans, which were for an orthodox High Victorian Gothic building, then changed to Romanesque, but without discarding all the Gothic elements. Work was still in progress when Sir Thomas died in 1910, and W. H. Lynn (who had been asked from the outset to co-operate), carried on until he in turn died in 1915. Since then five successive architects have been in charge, each imposing his own ideas. The result is extraordinary. Sir John Betjeman described it in an appeal for funds, as 'Britain's finest cathedral'.[16] C. E. B. Brett, on the other hand, calls it 'an unsatisfactory edifice',[17] and adds, 'the problem of welding its disparate parts into a harmonious whole seems an insoluble one.'[18] At best, it could be considered a panoply of revival miscellanea, including practically every known architectural idiom (and a few hitherto unknown ones, born of determined cross-breeding), plus the curiosity of a front completed as a First World War Memorial in 1927. The north transept is not finished.

Some see in the monumental Belfast Cathedral a last paroxysm of Imperial pride; others, a symbol of stability and continuity.

In 1975 the Irish Bishops' Conference published the results of a survey made by their Research and Development Unit. Reporting this in *The Times* of 20 August 1975 the Religious Affairs Correspondent commented that the Irish must be 'the most church-oriented nation on earth', for the survey showed that more than nine out of ten of the adult population attended church at least once weekly and about one quarter more frequently.

Within a week of the publication of this survey the country was shocked by a revival of the ancient Irish practice whereby quarrelling factions burned their neighbours' churches. On the first anniversary of its completion, the Catholic church of St Anthony at Larne which had cost £120,000 and served 3,000 people, was destroyed by fire. Signs of forced entry and traces of petrol left little doubt that the church was a victim of the sectarian strife in Ulster.

As for the churches of Ireland of the years to come, the tradition of faith, generosity and beautiful work is there at hand. If the architects, the clergy, and, it is to be hoped, the people also, do not lack the necessary discernment, skill and inspiration to raise their future churches above the threshold of a commonplace expression of the consumer society, all will be well. If the new churches at Oristown, Creeslaugh and Burt in the Republic, and at Garrison in Northern Ireland are a sample of what is to come, it augurs well.

St Michael's Church, Creeslough, Co. Donegal >

Dunmanagher, Co. Derry, the Catholic church >

Notes on the Text

CHAPTER I

1 *Vita Tripartita Sancti Patricii* (ed. W. Stokes, London 1887).
2 *Annals of Loch Cé* (ed. W.M. Hennessy, London and Dublin 1871; reproduced Dublin 1939).
3 *The Book of Mulling* (ed. H.J. Lawlor, Edinburgh 1897).
4 *The Book of Armagh* (ed. J. Gwynn, London and Dublin 1913).
5 *Martyrology of Oengus* (ed. W. Stokes, London 1905).
6 *Acta Sanctorum*, begun by J. Bollandus, 1643.
7 *Leabhar Breach.*
8 *The Book of Mulling.*
9 *Annals of Clonmacnois* (ed. D. Murphy, Dublin 1896).
10 H.J. Lawlor, *The Monastery of Saint Mochaoi of Nendrum* (Belfast 1925).
11 M. Esposito, 'Conchubrani Vita Sanctae Monennae', *PRIA*, vol. XII (1910).
12 *St Bernard of Clairvaux's Life of St Malachy of Armagh* (ed. H.J. Lawlor, London 1920).
13 Bede, *Historia Ecclesiastica Gentis Anglorum* (ed. C. Plummer, Oxford 1896).
14 *Annals of Tigernach* (ed. W. Stokes, 1895).
15 *Annals of Ulster* (ed. W.M. Hennessy and B. MacCarthy, Dublin 1887–1901).
16 *The Book of Armagh.*
17 J. D'Alton, *The Memoirs of the Archbishops of Dublin* (Dublin 1838).
18 *Collectio Canonum Hibernensis* (ed. H. Wasserschleben, Leipzig 1885).
19 *Annals of Ulster.*
20 *Patrologia Latina* (ed. J.P. Migne, vol. LXXII, 1844–64).
21 Ibid.
22 *Vita Tripartita Sancti Patricii.*
23 *Patrologia Latina* (vol. LXXII).
24 *Vita Tripartita Sancti Patricii.*
25 Ibid.
26 *St Bernard of Clairvaux's Life of St Malachy of Armagh.*
27 J. Ryan, *Irish Monasticism, its origins and early development* (London 1931).
28 *Collectio Canonum Hibernensis.*
29 L. Bieler, *The Irish Penitentials* (Dublin 1963).
30 A.T. Lucas, *The Plundering and Burning of Churches in Ireland, 7th to 16th century*, North Munster Studies (Limerick 1967).
31 *Annals of Loch Cé.*
32 E.J. Gwynn and W.J. Purton, 'The Monastery of Tallaght', *PRIA*, vol. XXIX (1911).

CHAPTER 2

1 *Annals of Loch Cé* (ed. W.M. Hennessy, London 1871).

2 Ibid.
3 Ibid.
4 Ibid.
5 Ibid.
6 Ibid.
7 J.F. Kenney, *Sources for the Early History of Ireland*, vol. I, *Ecclesiastical* (New York 1929).
8 Ibid.
9 Dom H.J. de Varebeke, *Benedictine Bishops in Medieval Ireland*, North Munster Studies (Limerick 1967).
10 *Annals of Clonmacnois* (ed. D. Murphy, Dublin 1896).
11 *Annals of Loch Cé*, confirmed by other Annals.
12 C. Costantini, *Il Crocefisso nell'Arte* (Florence 1911).
13 P. Germano di S. Stanislao, *La Casa Celimontana dei SS. Martiri Giovanni e Paolo* (Rome 1894).
14 F. Henry, *La Sculpture Irlandaise pendant les douze premiers siècles de l'ère chrétienne* (Paris 1932).
15 F. Henry, *Irish Art*, vol. III (Cornell U.P., Ithaca, New York 1967).
16 M. Archdall, *Monasticon Hibernicum* (ed. Moran, Dublin 1873–76).
17 G. Petrie, *The Ecclesiastical Architecture of Ireland* (1845).
18 A.C. Champneys, *Irish Ecclesiastical Architecture* (London and Dublin 1910).
19 F. Henry, *La Sculpture Irlandaise* . . . .
20 H.G. Leask, *Irish Churches and Monastic Buildings*, vol. I (Dundalk 1955).
21 F. Henry, *Irish Art*, vol. II.
22 *Irish Litanies* (ed. Rev. C. Plummer, London 1925).
23 See description and illustrations of Ani in J. Strzygowski, *Die BauKunst der Armenier und Europa* (Vienna 1918); in M.F. Brosset, *Les Ruines d'Ani*, and in N. Okunew, *Ani, Capitale dell'Armenia.*
24 See A. Eadmer in *Historia Novorum*, vol. IV, p. 27.
25 A. Gwynn, 'St Anselm and the Irish Church', *Irish Ecclesiastical Record*, vol. LIX (Dublin 1942); Dom H.J. de Varebeke, 'The Benedictines in Medieval Ireland', *JRSAI*, vol. LXXX (1950); 'The Synod of Rathbreasail', *Archivium Hibernicum*, vol. III (1914).
26 *St Bernard of Clairvaux's Life of St Malachy of Armagh* (ed. H.J. Lawlor, London 1920).
27 Ibid.
28 *JRSAI*, vol. XLII, pp. 140–7 (1912).
29 P. Harbison, *Guide to the National Monuments of Ireland* (Dublin 1970).
30 M. and C. Cruise O'Brien, *A Concise History of Ireland* (London 1972).

31 *Acta Sanctorum*, begun by J. Bollandus, 1643.
32 *Cambrensis Eversus* (ed. Kelly, Dublin 1850).
33 W. Wattenbach, 'Die Kongregation der Schottenklöster in Deutschland', *Zeitschrift für Christliche Archäologie und Kunst* (Leipzig 1856).
34 *Cambrensis Eversus* (trans.).
35 A. Gwynn and D.F. Gleeson, *A History of the Diocese of Killaloe* (Dublin 1962).
36 J. Gatrio, *Die Abtei Murbach in Elsass* (Strasbourg 1895); also F.X. Kraus, *Kunst und Alterthum in Ober-Elsass* (Strasbourg 1884), and Winterer, *L'Abbaye de Murbach* (1867).
37 E.F.J. Dronke, *Codex Diplomaticus Fuldensis* (Cassel 1850).
38 L. de Paor, *Cormac's Chapel: The Beginnings of Irish Romanesque*, North Munster Studies (Limerick 1967).
39 Champneys, op. cit.
40 Leask, op. cit.
41 *Annals of Ulster* (ed. W.M. Hennessy and B. MacCarthy, Dublin 1887–1901).
42 *Annals of the Kingdom of Ireland by the Four Masters* (ed. J. O'Donovan, Dublin 1856).
43 L. de Paor, op. cit.
44 O. Davies, 'The Churches of Co. Cavan', *JRSAI*, vol. LXXVIII (1948).
45 *Annals of Clonmacnois.*
46 *The Annals of Innisfallen* (ed. S. Mac Airt, Dublin 1951).

CHAPTER 3

1 *St Bernard of Clairvaux's Life of St Malachy of Armagh* (ed. H.J. Lawlor, London 1920).
2 Ibid.
3 Ibid.
4 Ibid.
5 Ibid.
6 Ibid.
7 Father Colmcille, OCSO, *The Story of Mellifont* (1958).
8 *Annals of the Kingdom of Ireland by the Four Masters* (ed. J. O'Donovan, Dublin 1856).
9 *Annals of Loch Cé* (ed. W.M. Hennessy, Dublin 1939).
10 F. van der Meer, *Atlas de l'ordre Cistercien* (Amsterdam-Brussels 1965).
11 Ibid.
12 *Monasticon Anglicanum* (ed. Dodsworth and Dugdale, London 1673).
13 A. Gwynn and R.N. Hadcock, *Medieval Religious Houses: Ireland* (London 1970).
14 L. Janauschek, *Originum Cisterciensium* (1877).
15 R.A. Stalley, *Architecture and Sculpture in Ireland 1150–1350* (Dublin 1971).

16 F. van der Meer, op. cit.

17 *Annals of Loch Cé.*

18 *Annals of Connacht* (ed. A. M. Freeman, Dublin 1944).

19 *Annals of Loch Cé.*

20 *Annals of the Kingdom of Ireland by the Four Masters.*

21 *Annals of Loch Cé.*

22 Gwynn and Hadcock, op. cit.

23 Janauschek, op. cit.

24 F. van der Meer, op. cit.

25 J. Ware, *De Hibernia et Antiquitatibus ejus* (London 1654).

26 *Monasticon Anglicanum.*

27 Gwynn and Hadcock, op. cit.

28 *Annals of Loch Cé.*

29 Gwynn and Hadcock, op. cit.

30 Ware, op. cit.

31 P. Harbison, *Guide to the National Monuments of Ireland* (Dublin 1970).

32 H. G. Leask, *Irish Churches and Monastic Buildings*, vol. II (Dundalk 1958).

33 Gwynn and Hadcock, op. cit.

34 Leask, op. cit.

CHAPTER 4

1 A. Gwynn and D. F. Gleeson, *History of the Diocese of Killaloe* (Dublin 1961); L. Janauschek, *Originum Cisterciensium* (1877); J. Ware, *De Hibernia et Antiquitatibus ejus* (London 1654).

2 R. A. Stalley, *Architecture and Sculpture in Ireland 1150–1350* (Dublin 1971).

3 *Annals of the Kingdom of Ireland by the Four Masters* (ed. J. O'Donovan, Dublin 1856).

4 H. G. Leask, *Irish Churches and Monastic Buildings*, vol. II (Dundalk 1958).

5 H. S. Sweetman and G. F. Handcock (eds.), *Calendar of Documents relating to Ireland, 1171–1307* (London 1875–86).

6 Ibid.

7 A. Gwynn and R. N. Hadcock, *Medieval Religious Houses: Ireland* (London 1970).

8 Ibid.

9 Ibid.

10 Stalley, op. cit.

11 Leask, op. cit.

12 J. Ware, *De Hibernia et Antiquitatibus ejus* (London 1654).

13 *Black Book of Limerick* (ed. J. MacCaffrey, Dublin 1907).

14 *Annals of the Kingdom of Ireland by the Four Masters.*

15 J. Ware, *History of the Bishops of Ireland* (ed. W. Harris, Dublin 1739).

16 Ibid.

CHAPTER 5

1 R. A. Stalley, *Architecture and Sculpture In Ireland, 1150–1350* (Dublin 1971).

2 Earl and Countess of Dunraven, *Memorials of Adare* (Dublin 1865).

3 J. Begley, *The Diocese of Limerick*, vol. I (Limerick 1906).

4 W. Carrigan, *History and Antiquities of the Diocese of Ossory* (1905).

5 W. H. Bliss and J. A. Twemlow (eds.), *Calendar of Papal Letters, (1198–1484)* (London 1893–1961).

6 J. Ware, *De Hibernia et Antiquitatibus ejus* (London 1654).

7 *Annals of Ireland by Friar Clyn* (ed. R. Butler, Dublin 1849).

8 H. G. Leask, *Irish Churches and Monastic Buildings*, vol. II (Dundalk 1958).

9 Ibid.

10 *Annals of the Kingdom of Ireland by the Four Masters* (ed. J. O'Donovan, Dublin 1856). (*Annals of Dubhaltach Mac Firbisigh*).

11 E. C. Rae, 'The Rice Monument in Waterford Cathedral', *PRIA*, vol. LXIX, Section C, No. 1, 1970.

12 G. E. Cokayne (ed.), *The Complete Peerage* (London 1910–40).

13 This and other fonts are discussed at length in Roe, *The Medieval Fonts of Meath* (Dublin 1968).

14 H. G. Leask, op. cit., vol. III (Dundalk 1960).

15 H. G. Leask, 'Taghmon Church, Co. Meath', *JRSAI*, vol. LVIII (1928).

16 *Burke's Peerage*, 99th edition (London 1949).

17 *Calendar of Papal Registers* cited by A. Gwynn and R. N. Hadcock (eds.), in *Medieval Religious Houses: Ireland.*

18 *Annals of the Kingdom of Ireland by the Four Masters.*

19 E. B. Fitzmaurice and A. G. Little, *Materials for a History of the Franciscan Province of Ireland* (Dublin 1920).

20 Gwynn and Hadcock, op. cit.; H. G. Leask, *Irish Churches and Monastic Buildings*, vol. III.

21 Rev. B. Jennings, OFM, 'The Abbey of Muckross', *Journal of Cork Historical and Archaeological Society*, vol. XLV (1940).

22 *Annals of the Kingdom of Ireland by the Four Masters.*

23 C. Mooney, OFM, *Franciscan Donegal* (Wexford 1952).

24 Gwynn and Hadcock, op. cit.

25 Ibid.

26 Ibid.

27 *Annals of Ulster* (ed. W. M. Hennessy and B. MacCarthy, 4 vols, Dublin 1887–1901).

28 A. Coleman, OP, *The Ancient Dominican Foundations of Ireland* (1902).

29 Gwynn and Hadcock, op. cit.

30 Ibid.

31 Ibid.

CHAPTER 6

1 *Annals of Loch Cé* (ed. W. M. Hennessy, London 1871).

2 C. Maxwell, *Irish History from Contemporary Sources, 1509–1610* (London 1923).

3 Ibid.

4 Ibid.

5 Ibid.

6 Episcopal Visitation Books 1690–92, quoted by Reverend J. B. Leslie in *History of Kilsaran* (Dundalk 1908).

7 *Calendar of State Papers: Ireland* (ed. H. C. Hamilton and others, London 1867–1910).

8 M. Archdall, *Monasticon Hibernicum* (1786).

9 *Analecta Hibernica*, 6 November 1934.

CHAPTER 7

1 C. Brooking, *A Map of the City and Suburbs of Dublin* (London 1728).

2 S. Lewis, *Topographical Dictionary of Ireland* (London 1837).

3 W. P. Burke, *The Irish Priests in Penal Times* (Waterford 1914), quoting Co. Leitrim Sessions Records.

4 Ibid.

5 Ibid.

6 Letter from Stratford Eyre to Primate Boulter, formerly in Public Record Office, Dublin quoted by Burke, op. cit.

7 See quote from Lloyd, 'Citizen of London' in M. Craig, *Dublin 1660–1860* (Dublin 1969).

8 C. Smith, *The Antient and Present State of the County and City of Cork* (Dublin 1750).

9 M. Lenihan, *Limerick; its History and Antiquities* (Dublin 1866).

10 Ibid.

11 Ibid.

12 Ibid.

13 C. Smith, *The Antient and Present State of the County and City of Waterford* (Dublin 1746).

14 Craig, op. cit.

15 C. P. Curran, *Dublin Decorative Plasterwork of the 17th and 18th Centuries* (London 1967).

16 Ibid.

17 Very Reverend C. W. Wolfe, *Cashel – its Cathedrals and its Library* (Clonmel n.d.).

18 Illustrated in B. de Breffny and R. ffolliott, *The Houses of Ireland* (London 1975).

19 E. McParland, 'Emo Court, Co. Leix', *Country Life*, 23 May 1974.

20 R. Mant, *History of the Church of Ireland* (London 1840).

21 Ibid.

22 D. H. Akenson, *The Church of Ireland, Ecclesiastical Reform and Revolution* (Yale U.P. 1971).

23 P. Rankin, *Irish Building Ventures of the Earl Bishop of Derry* (Belfast 1972).

24 Ibid.

25 Ibid.

26 Ibid.

27 Lewis, op. cit.

28 Rankin, op. cit.

29 Ibid.

30 Ibid.

31 J. O'Laverty, *History of the Diocese of Down and Connor* (1880).

32 'Historic Buildings . . . in and near the City of Derry', prepared by W. S. Ferguson, A. J. Rowan and J. J. Tracey (*UAHS* 1969–70).

CHAPTER 8

1 S. Lewis, *A Topographical Dictionary of Ireland* (London 1837).

2 D. Dunlop, *Life of W. J. Barre* (1868).

3 C. E. B. Brett, *Buildings of Belfast 1700–1914* (London 1967).

4 D. H. Akenson, *The Church of Ireland, Ecclesiastical Reform and Revolution, 1800–1885* (Yale U.P. 1971).

5 Lewis, op. cit.

6 Ibid.

7 R. E. Parkinson, *The Cathedral Church of Down, Downpatrick* (n.p., n.d.).

8 Akenson, op. cit.

9 Ibid.

10 *The Dublin Builder*, 1 February 1868 and 1 July 1869.

11 Lewis, op. cit.

12 M. Craig, *Dublin 1660–1860* (Dublin 1969).

13 J. Britton, *The Architectural Antiquities of Great Britain*; J. Britton, *The Cathedral Antiquities of Great Britain*; T. Rickman, *An Attempt to Discriminate Styles of English Architecture* (London 1817).

14 E. Bolster, *A History of Mallow* (Cork 1971).

15 J.A. Gaughan, *Doneraile* (Dublin 1968; revised ed. 1970).
16 Craig, op. cit.
17 Lewis, op. cit.
18 P. Stanford, *Pugin* (London 1971).
19 Rev. J. McKenna, *St Mary's Cathedral Killarney; The Diocese of Kerry and Its Cathedral* (Tralee 1973).
20 *Tralee Chronicle*, 24 August 1855.
21 McKenna, op. cit.
22 Stanford, op. cit.
23 M. Lenihan, *Limerick; Its History and Antiquities* (Dublin 1866).
24 Ibid.
25 *The Dublin Builder*, 1 February 1859.
26 Ibid.
27 *The Dublin Builder*, 15 January, 1863; 1 February 1863.
28 Ibid.

CHAPTER 9
1 *The Dublin Builder*, 15 February 1863.
2 Ibid.
3 *The Dublin Builder*, 1 April 1863.

4 *The Dublin Builder*, 1 September 1863.
5 *The Irish Builder*, 15 June 1879.
6 C.E.B. Brett, *Buildings of Belfast 1700–1914* (London 1967).
7 *The Irish Builder and Engineer*, 20 January 1912.
8 St Patrick's Cathedral, Armagh (brochure, anon., Belfast n.d.).
9 'Historic Buildings . . . in and near the City of Derry', by W.S. Ferguson, A.J. Rowan and J.J. Tracey (*UAHS* 1969–70).
10 S. Lewis, *Topographical Dictionary of Ireland* (Dublin 1837).
11 Father B. Egan, *Franciscan Limerick* (Limerick 1971).

CHAPTER 10
1 S. Lewis, *Topographical Dictionary of Ireland* (London 1837).
2 *The Irish Press*, 18 March 1965.
3 *The Irish Times*, 18 March 1965.
4 See Abridged version of the sermon printed in a brochure, *Background to St Dominic's, Athy*.
5 Quoted in 'St Mary's and the New Liturgy' by Father T. Egan in *St Mary's Cathedral, Killarney* (Tralee 1973).
6 *Irish Independent*, 18 March 1965.
7 'Notes on the Re-construction of St Mary's', by R. Carroll, in *St Mary's Cathedral, Killarney* (Tralee 1973).
8 L. Breen, PP, *Parish of Arklow, Church of St David, Johnstown*, brochure (1972).
9 Letter to authors from parish priest, June 1974.
10 *Meath Chronicle*, 1 June 1974.
11 *Irish Times*, July 1974.
12 Letter of Father J. Farrell to authors, 18 June 1974.
13 Ibid.
14 *The Daily Telegraph*, 14 August 1974.
15 *A Cathedral for Belfast*, brochure (1896).
16 *The Daily Telegraph*, 14 August 1974.
17 C.E.B. Brett, *Buildings of Belfast 1700–1914* (London 1967).
18 Ibid.

Glossary

ABACUS The flat slab on top of a capital.

ANTAE Projections on the north and south corners of a church.

ARCHIVOLT The underside curve of an arch.

ARRIS A sharp edge at the junction of two surfaces.

BILLETING Decorative moulding consisting of bands of short, square or rectangular pieces raised at regular intervals.

BOLECTION MOULDING A moulding covering a joint between elements on different surface levels and projecting from both.

BOWTELL A form of convex roll moulding.

BRATTISHING Ornamental cresting on Late Gothic screens or cornices consisting of miniature battlements, flowers or leaves.

BUCRANIA Sculptured ox-skull, usually garlanded.

CASHEL A circular or oval stone-walled enclosure around a church or early monastic site.

CHAMFER Surface created when an arris is removed.

CORBEL A projecting stone used as a support.

CLERESTORY The upper storey of the nave, over the aisle roofs and pierced by windows.

CLOGHAUN (Irish) A bee-hive shaped hut of dry-stone corbelled construction.

CROCKET Carved decoration of leaves projecting from the edges of a spire, canopy, or pinnacle.

DAIMHLIAC (Irish) A stone church.

DUIRTEACH (Irish. Lit. 'house of oak') A wooden church.

LUCARNE A small opening in a sloping attic or spire, sometimes capped.

MISERICORD A bracket on the underside of a hinged choir-stall, serving as a support while the occupant stood through long services.

OCULUS A round window.

OGEE-ARCH A pointed arch compounded of convex and concave curves.

PATERA Small sculptured ornament, oval or circular, usually decorated with acanthus or rose leaves.

REREDOS A wooden or stone screen raised behind the altar and usually decorated.

SEDILIA A series of seats (usually three – for priest, deacon and sub-deacon) in the south wall of the chancel.

SLYPE Covered passage leading east from the cloister.

SOFFIT-ARCH The underside of the arch.

SPAWL A small stone used as a wedge in dry-stone masonry.

TRABEATED Of doorways, constructed on the post and lintel principle.

VOUSSOIR A wedge-shaped stone forming one of the units of an arch.

Map showing the main cities and towns of ecclesiastical importance

Appendices

I EARLY CHRISTIAN CHURCHES *(by counties)*

The list below of single chamber stone churches does not claim to be comprehensive, but indicates a number of the best examples.

I CHURCHES WITHOUT LATER ADDITIONS

Co. Armagh	Killevy
Co. Carlow	Killoughternane
Co. Cork	Labbamolaga
Co. Down	St John's Point
Co. Dublin	St Begnet's, Dalkey Island
Co. Galway	High Island
	St Caillin's, Chapel Island, Galway Bay
	St Kieran's, Inishmore, Aran Islands
	Temple Benen, Inishmore, Aran Islands
	Kilcanonagh, Inishmaan, Aran Islands
	Kilgobnet, Inisheer, Aran Islands
	St MacDara's on St MacDara's Island
Co. Kerry	Illauntannig, Maharee Islands
	Inishvickillane, Blasket Islands
	Skellig Michael
	Church Island, Valentia
	St Brendan's Oratory, Brandon Mountain
	Gallerus
Co. Limerick	Killulta
	Kilrush
	Mungret
Co. Longford	St Mel's, Ardagh
	St Diarmuid's, Inchleraun
Co. Mayo	St Brendan's Oratory, Inishglora
	St Columcille's, Inishkea North
Co. Sligo	Inishmurray

II CHURCHES WITH LATER ADDITIONS

At the following places stone churches of the Early Christian period exist with good examples of the plain flat-headed west doorway, but with later additions such as a chancel built on to the east end of the original nave.

Co. Clare	Tuamgraney
Co. Dublin	Kill of the Grange
Co. Galway	St Patrick's, Inchagoill
	Kiltiernan
Co. Kerry	Ratass
Co. Kilkenny	Clonamery
	Kilree
Co. Westmeath	St Feichin's, Fore
Co. Wicklow	St Mary's, Glendalough
	Reefert Church, Glendalough

II CISTERCIAN FOUNDATIONS *(by counties)*

Co. Clare	CORCOMROE founded 1175/95	See text (p. 58 et seq.).
Co. Cork	ABBEYMAHON founded 1172	Some church walls remain; the plain square tower was a later, 14th-century addition.
	ABBEYSTROWRY founded 1228	Some remains.
	AGHAMANISTER founded 1172	No remains; the community moved to Abbeymahon soon after its foundation.
	FERMOY founded 1170	No remains.
	MIDLETON founded 1180	No remains.
	TRACTON founded 1225	No remains.
Co. Derry	MACOSQUIN founded 1218	No remains.
Co. Donegal	ASSAROE founded 1178	A very modest foundation of which a cemetery and some traces remain, the rest being incorporated into a house: The Abbey.
	KILMONASTER founded 1194	No remains.
Co. Down	COMBER founded 1200/20	No remains of interest.

Co. Down (contd)	ERENAGH founded 1127	Destroyed in 1167. No remains.
	GREY ABBEY founded 1193	See text (pp. 60–1).
	INCH founded 1187	See text (pp. 48–9, 60).
	NEWRY founded 1153	No remains.
Co. Dublin	ST MARY'S ABBEY founded 1147	Originally Savignian, the monks colonized it from Chester. No remains of the church can be seen, but its floor tiles were discovered during excavations in 1886. The fine vaulted chapter-house, and a passage adjoining, date from the late 13th century.
Co. Galway	KNOCKMOY founded 1190	See text (pp. 52, 54, 57).
Co. Kerry	ABBEYDORNEY founded 1154	No remains of interest.
Co. Kildare	MONASTEREVIN founded 1189	No remains.
Co. Kilkenny	GLANDY founded 1185	No remains.
	GRAIGUENAMANAGH founded 1204	See text (pp. 48, 54, 63).
	JERPOINT founded 1180/88	See text (pp. 49–54, 82–3, 88–9).
Co. Leix	ABBEYLEIX founded 1184	No remains of interest.
	KILLENNY founded 1185	No remains. A small monastery used as a grange to Graiguenamanagh and possibly the same place as Glandy.
Co. Limerick	ABBEYFEALE founded 1188	Little remains except a wall and cemetery.
	ABINGTON founded 1205/6	No remains.
	MONASTERANENAGH founded 1148/51	See text (pp. 48, 59, 67).
Co. Longford	ABBEYLARA founded 1214	Part of the transept crossing built about 1214 and the 15th-century tower remain.
	ABBEYSHRULE founded 1200	There remain some 12th-century window details and, near the centre of the church, a pulpit-like structure with three compartments.
Co. Louth	MELLIFONT founded 1142	See text (pp. 47, 50, 52, 59).
Co. Mayo	CLARE ISLAND founded 1220 as a hermit cell of Knockmoy	The church, still standing, is of the 15th century and consists of a nave and chancel with a sacristy. Medieval frescoes in the chancel are among the very few in Ireland.

Co. Meath	BECTIVE founded 1147	One of the earliest Cistercian foundations, with some good remains incorporated into a private residence. There are remains of the 12th-century chapter-house and parts of the church and domestic buildings. The beautiful cloister is 15th century (p. 48).
	BEYBEG founded 1216 as a cell of Beaubec in France	No remains of interest.
Co. Roscommon	BOYLE founded 1148/61	See text (pp. 48, 52–4).
Co. Tipperary	HOLY CROSS founded 1180	Beautifully restored; there are many elements of interest in this foundation of the 13th and 15th centuries: the processional doorway, the exquisite vaulted chancel, the sedilia with arms of the English royal family and Earls of Ormond and the lovely cloister (pp. 93–4).
	HORE ABBEY founded 1272	Extensive ruins of the cruciform church with its adjoining cloister and chapter-house, all of the 13th century (p. 48).
	INISHLOUNAGHT (Marlfield) founded 1151	Only fragments of the original church remain in the modern church, i.e. the doorway of about 1200, now high in the west wall.
	KILSHANE founded 1198	No remains.
	KILCOOLY founded 1182/4	The original church was destroyed and the remains of the 14th- and 15th-century church include some very fine tomb sculpture of the Callan school, one being the formidable tomb of Piers Fitz Oge Butler (p. 88). The quality of the carved stonework in the church is very fine (p. 94). Near the church is the ruin of a two-storey building, probably the infirmary.
Co. Waterford	GLANAWYDAN founded 1200 as a cell of Inishlounaght	No remains.
Co. Westmeath	KILBEGGAN founded 1150	No remains.
Co. Wexford	DUNBRODY founded 1180/2	See text (pp. 49, 61–2).
	TINTERN founded 1200	See text (pp. 61, 63).
Co. Wicklow	BALTINGLASS founded 1148	See text (pp. 48, 50, 54).

Acknowledgments

We wish to acknowledge with thanks the help of Bord Failte Eireann in our travels in Ireland and especially Mr John Kennedy. Also the Northern Ireland Tourist Board for their assistance in our travels in Northern Ireland, and especially Mr T. L. H. Huston of their Photographic Department.

All but seven of the photographs in this book were taken by George Mott, the others were supplied as follows: Skellig Michael on p. 15, Bord Failte Eireann; Murbach Abbey on p. 29, Bildarchiv Foto Marburg; aerial view of Athassel Priory on p. 67, Aerofilms; St James's, Piccadilly, on p. 134, Thames and Hudson archives; eighteenth-century drawing of Coolbanagher Church on p. 135, *Country Life*; St George's, Belfast in happier days, on p. 147, Northern Ireland Tourist Board; and St Anthony's, Larne, after its destruction, on p. 194, Pacemaker Press, Belfast. The drawing on p. 9 and the plans and diagrams are by Peter Bridgewater and the map is by David Eccles.

Also for their help we wish to express our thanks to Miss Rosemary ffolliott and Mr Gordon Ledbetter of Dublin, Miss Willis, Librarian of The Representative Church Body of the Church of Ireland, Dublin, Mr Eagar, Librarian of the Royal Dublin Society, Mr Doherty of the Photographic Archives of the Office of Public Works, National Monuments Department, and the Hon. Guy Strutt who read the manuscript.

Lastly we must thank all those friends in Ireland and in Rome whose constant encouragement and prayers helped to make this book possible.

Further Reading

Akenson, D. H., *The Church of Ireland, Ecclesiastical Reform and Revolution*, Yale 1971.

Bieler, L., *Ireland, Harbinger of the Middle Ages*, London, New York 1963.

Brett, C. E. B., *Buildings of Belfast, 1700–1914*, London 1967.

Burke, W. P., *The Irish Priests in Penal Times*, Waterford 1914.

Champneys, A. C., *Irish Ecclesiastical Architecture*, London, Dublin 1910.

Craig, Maurice, *Dublin 1660–1860*, Dublin 1969.

Craig, Maurice, and the Knight of Glin, *Ireland Observed*, Cork 1970.

Evans, E. E., *Prehistoric and Early Christian Ireland – A Guide*, London, New York 1966.

Gwynn, A., and R. N. Hadcock, *Medieval Religious Houses; Ireland*, London 1970.

Harbison, P., *Guide to the National Monuments in the Republic of Ireland*, Dublin 1970.

Henry, F., *Irish Art in the Romanesque Period 1020–1170 AD*, New York 1969, London 1970.

Henry, F., *Irish High Crosses*, Dublin 1964.

Hughes, K., *The Church in Early Irish Society*, London 1966.

Leask, H. G., *Irish Churches and Monastic Buildings*, vols. I–III, Dundalk 1955–60.

Paor, Liam de, *Cormac's Chapel: The Beginnings of Irish Romanesque*, North Munster Studies, Limerick 1967.

Potterton, H., *Irish Church Monuments 1570–1850*, Belfast 1975.

Rankin, P., *Irish Building Ventures of the Earl Bishop of Derry*, Belfast 1972.

Ryan, J., *Irish Monasticism, its origins and early development*, London 1931, New York 1972.

Stalley, R. A., *Architecture and Sculpture in Ireland 1150–1350*, Dublin 1971.

Warren, F., *The Liturgy and Ritual of the Celtic Church*, Oxford 1881.

Index of Personal Names